Folklore of
WELSH BORDER

COUNTY BOUNDARIES PRE 1974

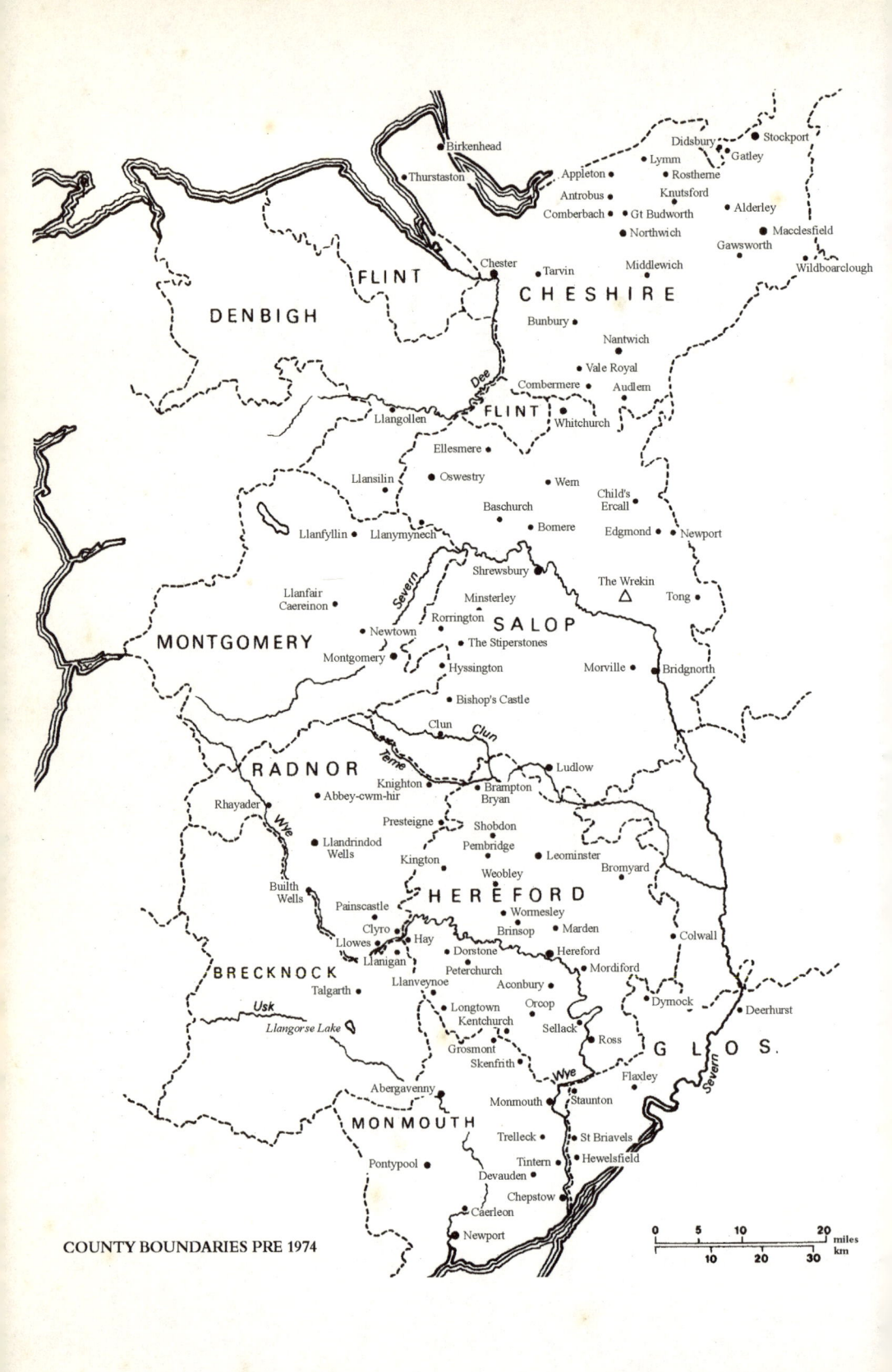

Folklore of the
Welsh Border

Jacqueline Simpson

TEMPUS

Originally published by B.T. Batsford, 1976
This revised edition published 2003

Tempus Publishing Limited
The Mill, Brimscombe Port,
Stroud, Gloucestershire, GL5 2QG

© Jacqueline Simpson, 2003

The right of Jacqueline Simpson to be identified as the Author
of this work has been asserted in accordance with the
Copyrights, Designs and Patents Act 1988.

All rights reserved. No part of this book may be reprinted
or reproduced or utilised in any form or by any electronic,
mechanical or other means, now known or hereafter invented,
including photocopying and recording, or in any information
storage or retrieval system, without the permission in writing
from the Publishers.

British Library Cataloguing in Publication Data.
A catalogue record for this book is available from the British Library.

ISBN 0 7524 2623 0

Typesetting and origination by Tempus Publishing Limited
Printed in Great Britain by Midway Colour Print, Wiltshire

CONTENTS

Map of the Welsh Border	2
Acknowledgements	6
Foreword	7
Introduction	11
1. The Landscape	17
2. Rumours of War	31
3. Local Heroes, Fools, Rogues and Villains	44
4. Wizards and Witches	59
5. Fairies	75
6. Ghosts	87
7. Holy Wells and Healing Charms	102
8. From the Cradle to the Grave	117
9. The Turning Year: January to May	139
10. The Turning Year: June to December	165
Notes	189
Select Bibliography	208
Index of Tale Types	211
Motif Index	212
General Index	218

ACKNOWLEDGEMENTS

The author and publishers wish to thank those who have given permission to quote from the following books (page references are to *Folklore of the Welsh Border*): Chris Barltrop in *Folklore* 113, 2002 (pp. 143-44); A.W. Boyd, *A Country Parish*, Collins, 1951 (pp. 91-92, 182-83); Cheshire, Federation of Women's Institutes, *Cheshire Village Memories*, 1952 and 1961 (p. 51); F.H. Crossley, *Cheshire*, Hale, 1949 (pp. 180-81, 186); R.T. Davies in *Folklore*, XLVIII, 1937 (p. 65); H.L.V. Fletcher, *Portrait of the Wye Valley*, Hale, 1968 (p. 13) and *Herefordshire*, Hale, 1948 (p. 151); C.M. Hole, *Traditions and Customs of Cheshire*, Wakefield, SR Publishers, 1937 (p. 158), W.H. Howse, *Radnorshire*, Hereford, Thurston, 1949 (pp. 47-48, 74); Ronald Hutton, *The Stations of the Sun*, Oxford University Press, 1996 (p. 183); F.R. Kilvert, *Diary* (ed. Plomer), Cape, 1960 (pp. 22, 27, 67, 75, 93, 94, 118, 140, 157, 173-74, 175), V. Newall, *An Egg at Easter*, Routledge, Kegan, Paul, 1971 (p. 153); Roy Palmer, *The Folklore of (Old) Monmouthshire*, Logaston Press, 1998 (p. 107); T.A. Ryder, *Portrait of Gloucestershire*, Hale, 1966 (p. 105); I. Waters, *Folklore and Dialect of the Wye Valley*, 1973, (p. 184).

FOREWORD

The Welsh Borders or, as they are often called, the Marches, recall, not entirely by coincidence, the name of Mercia. This was the kingdom which embraced the whole of central England, but took its title from the borderlands in which it arose. Gloucester, in one of the March counties, became its capital – in Roman times a civil metropolis facing the disturbed areas to the west, with the now lost Ariconium in the Forest of Dean.

From Ariconium, above the Severn estuary, to the Wrekin beside its northern reaches, there are scattered place-names suggesting a border region once known to the ancient Britons as Erchin. 'All friends around the Wrekin' is a traditional Shropshire toast, and it may unwittingly commemorate a unity older than that of the modern county. The Wrekin shares its root name with Wroxeter, the Viroconium of the Romans, capital of Britannia Secunda and a city which, during the 300 years of its existence, reached a peak of civilization unsurpassed in contemporary Britain.

Viroconium and Deva, the modern Chester, were linked by complementary interests. Both lay within the territory of the British Cornovii; one was an important cultural and commercial centre, the other a strongly fortified base upon which the good order of the district depended. When Deva, or Castra Legionum, was abandoned, Viroconium soon fell to barbarian invaders.

Wroxeter lies only a few miles from Shrewsbury, capital – with Ludlow – of the sixteenth- and seventeenth-century Council of the Marches. In its earliest days, through the final quarter of the fifteenth century and into the sixteenth, the council was closely linked to the See of Lichfield, the central and south-western portions of which it embraced. Also under its wing were the dioceses of Hereford and Worcester, as well as the borderlands in Wales itself. Even in Stuart times, a century after the Principality's administration had been aligned with that of England, it was usual to have one lord lieutenant for Wales and the Marches. Aside from the Prince's domains, this included Shropshire, Herefordshire, Gloucestershire and Worcestershire, and sometimes Warwickshire – not, in fact, a March county, but connected ecclesiastically with Worcester.

The Council of the Marches, an outgrowth of the suppressed independent Earldom of March, was historically successor to the Marcher Courts, superseded in the thirteenth century by the Council of the Prince of Wales. The unruly areas for which it was responsible had been slow to stabilize under feudalism, and the council in effect supervised the transition to modernity. It was only abolished in 1689. The dates at which different areas were removed from its jurisdiction are therefore instructive. This happened to Bristol, which had been promoted to a see at the time of the Reformation, twenty years later, in 1562. Worcester, regarded as the gateway to Wales since it became capital of the Hwicca kingdom in the seventh century, made a decisive bid for independence in 1574, though this was prevented, chiefly for bureaucratic reasons. Neither of these areas is the concern of this book.

Because of their separate cultural background, the Marches beyond the Border have not been covered in great detail. Cheshire, which still owes titular allegiance to the Prince of Wales, is a different matter. On technical grounds, the council's writ ceased to apply there in 1569 but, for everyday purposes, this made little difference. The Palatinate courts still functioned, and the county's Chief Justice was customarily deputy to the Lord President of the Marches. Around the time John Speed, the map-maker, was born on Cheshire's western border, the county recorded more violent deaths than the whole of Wales, yet his own idyllic description is very different: 'The champion grounds make glad the hearts of their tillers; the meadows imborderd with divers sweet-smelling flowers; and the pastures make the kines udders to strout to the paile, from whom and wherein the best cheese in all Europe is made.'

A well-ordered society is the prerequisite for successful pastoral economy, and much the same applies to cultural continuity. The necessary progress took place in Speed's lifetime and, despite the later horrors of Civil War, Ralph Vaughan Williams was able to record a carol – 'Awake, awake, sweet England' – which must have been known in Herefordshire before its onset. He did collecting work in the Marches, the region of his birth, five or six years after beginning the study of English folk songs and fifteen years before he became mentor of the English Folk Dance and Song Society. So he remained, closely linked to the world of folklore studies, until his death. Shortly before this occurred, he and A.L. Lloyd prepared *The Penguin Book of English Folk Songs*, and in their introduction they quote Virginia Woolf: 'Masterpieces are not single and solitary births, they are the outcome of many years of thinking in common, of thinking by the body of the people, so that the experience of the mass is behind the single voice.' In one sense, then, masterpieces are a product of social stability and this is true, par excellence, of the heights of folk genius. Change, no doubt, enriches experience, but even intellectual revolution, and the artistic achievements which it can inspire, grows out of a firmly based cultural identity.

Vaughan Williams himself belonged to a group of notable Anglo-Welsh families, all of them related, who played an important role in modern British cultural life. His paternal great-grandfather came to England from south-west Wales in the eighteenth century, the identical origin of his maternal great-grandmother. His mother, Margaret Wedgwood, was both a niece and a niece-by-marriage of Charles Darwin, which underlines the close kinship between the three families. Distinguished members of each – the Darwins, Vaughan Williamses and Wedgwoods – were closely linked to the March counties, and Darwin spent all his early years at Shrewsbury. Here he 'read and re-read' the *Personal Narrative* of Alexander von Humboldt – a close friend of the Grimms – the book which was to set the whole course of his life. An early nineteenth-century description by a visitor to the Wedgwood home portrays the unusual intellectual atmosphere into which he was born, and the actual household in which his wife grew up: '(There is) freedom of speech upon every subject (and) no difference in politics or principle that makes it treason to speak one's mind openly, and they all do it.'

Though he was only in his tenth year when Darwin died, Vaughan Williams spent seven of his first nine years at Leith Hill Place, a Wedgwood property within twenty-five miles of Down House, where Darwin lived. Hugh Foss, the composer's biographer, hears traces of Darwinism in Toward the Unknown Region, a notion which is, considering the undefinable quality of musical expression, truer perhaps of the intellectual background than of the composition itself. More obviously apposite would seem to be the same author's comparison between Hardy and Vaughan Williams. In him Frank Howes, for many years musical critic of *The Times*, saw the first British composer to take England out of the German musical province, and certainly the desire to preserve and build upon what is best in national popular tradition is common to both author and musician. Apart from his interest in folk song, Vaughan Williams had a life-long association with the Three Choirs Festival, established in the Marches only a few years after the Council was abolished, and long a cultural focus for the region.

Jacqueline Simpson's study straddles the whole area adjacent to Wales, and has had an excellent reception since it was first published in 1976. She has ably tackled an area with which folklorists have been little concerned, and her book will therefore be especially welcome to scholars. The countryside in which her material flourished is beautiful and little spoiled, and those who love the area will be stimulated by discovering its folklore. While man adapts his environment, he is also influenced by it, and it is interesting to note how he reacts, in his everyday philosophy, within a given background.

Venetia Newall
London University December 1975

INTRODUCTION

That the counties along both sides of the Welsh Border are rich in folklore is almost a truism; most people, if asked whereabouts in this island one could most readily find traditional tales, beliefs and customs, would point first to the northern and western fringes, to Scotland, Wales, Cornwall, and the West Country. The material has indeed been recorded in these regions, and in abundance, though it would be a mistake to assume that it is specifically limited to them; on the contrary, the great majority of beliefs and tales can be matched elsewhere, and even customs, which are often more limited in their distribution, do not wholly follow regional boundaries. As regards seasonal customs, it is particularly enlightening to set the material presented in this book in the nation-wide historical and geographical context provided by Ronald Hutton's thorough study, *The Stations of the Sun: A History of the Ritual Year in Britain* (1996).

Nevertheless, many travellers coming to the Welsh Border have been impressed by the abundance of its folklore; Shelley, for instance, when staying at Nantgwillt in the Elan Valley in 1812, noted appreciatively, if somewhat flippantly:

> A ghost haunts this house, which has been frequently seen by the servants. We have several witches in our neighbourhood, and are quite overstocked with fairies and hobgoblins of every description.

Two of the counties on the English side attracted the attention of outstanding folklore collectors, Miss Charlotte Burne and Mrs Ella Leather; the former's *Shropshire Folklore* (partly based on unpublished collections by Miss Georgina Jackson) appeared in 1883-86, and the latter's *The Folklore of Herefordshire*, the fruit of seven years of fieldwork, appeared in 1912. Both are masterly works, so impressive in their scope and thoroughness that they unwittingly exerted a rather daunting effect upon further collecting and publishing within their areas, authoritatively fixing the 'correct' form of local tales, beliefs and customs, which have been constantly repeated by subsequent writers. Fresh fieldwork here would present much interest. The third English county has also been studied by a professional folklorist, Miss Christina Hole, whose *Traditions and Customs of Cheshire* appeared in 1937; this, however, seems to have stimulated rather than inhibited other local writers, for many additional items appear in A.W. Boyd's *A Country Parish* (1951), F.H. Crossley's *Cheshire* (1949), J.H. Ingram's *Companion Into Cheshire* (1947), and the two volumes of *Cheshire Village Memories* compiled by the Cheshire Women's Institutes in 1952 and 1961.

On the Welsh side, two counties have received detailed attention in Roy Palmer's *The Folklore of (Old) Monmouthshire* (1998) and *The Folklore of Radnorshire* (2001); Wales as a whole has of course been frequently studied, a seminal work being Sir John Rhys's *Celtic Folklore*, 1901. There have, however, been several articles and pamphlets on aspects of folklore in Monmouthshire (Gwent) and the Wye Valley, for which see the entries in the Bibliography under R.T. Davies, E.J. Dunhill, H.C. Ellis, L.M. Eyre, I. Waters and B.A. Wherry. W.H. Howse's *Radnorshire*, 1949, also contains much that is relevant. Finally, special mention must be made of the *Diaries* which the Revd F.R. Kilvert kept from 1870 to 1879, but which were only published in 1938-40; he was keenly interested in folklore, and recorded many items from the Clyro area and from Herefordshire, either from personal observation or from named informants. His comments thus have an immediacy that is particularly pleasing and valuable. It was his intention eventually to publish a book on local folklore. Unfortunately he never did so, and his manuscript disappeared after his death. Some of the material, however, was used by his wife's niece Essex Hope for an article in *The Occult Review* in 1921.

Readers should be warned against accepting at face value a work variously known as *The Journal of Anne Hughes* or as *The Diary of a Farmer's Wife, 1796-1797*, which purports to be an autobiographical account of life on a Herefordshire farm. It first appeared in serial form in *Farmers' Weekly* from October 1937 to June 1938; it was published as a book in 1964 and again in 1981. A TV play based upon it was shown on Christmas Day 1978. Mrs Jeanne Preston, who had sent the script to *Farmers' Weekly*, claimed it was copied from a manuscript belonging to her nanny, a daughter of 'Anne Hughes' who had herself copied it out as a child in the 1890s. This original document is now lost, and there seems to be no evidence of it having been seen by anyone else. Jeanne Preston died in 1952, and in 1977 her daughter Mollie declared the book was a work of fiction of which her mother was the sole author, and claimed compensation from *Farmers' Weekly* for infringement of copyright. Though the 'diary' may well contain some real items of tradition, such as old household recipes, its overall authenticity is extremely dubious, and it should not be regarded as a genuine eighteenth-century source.

The present work, covering as it does a large geographical area within limited space, cannot aim at all-inclusive thoroughness. Instead, it seeks, by concentrating on particular topics, to reveal the unity of tradition which the arbitrary lines of county boundaries obscure — a unity which, one suspects, would often have come as an unpleasant surprise to the tradition-bearers themselves. For a curious paradox lurks at the heart of local folklore. It is precisely because some site or object (e.g. a mound, a standing stone, a church effigy, an odd grave, a never-failing spring) seems to those living nearby to be a unique feature, that it inspires speculations about its origin and qualities which find expression in a story built around it; and yet the story itself is hardly ever a unique one, but follows well-established patterns. Individual story-tellers, however, were unlikely to realize this; to them, not only the site or object but also the legend surrounding it formed a unique focus for local pride. To this day, there is a strong tendency in any community to maintain that its own tradition about a ghost, a treasure or a tunnel must have something in it; how could it be otherwise, when reputable people in past generations have vouched for it? H.L.V. Fletcher caught this aspect well, in a snatch of pub talk:

'There's graves on our farm, soldiers' graves.'
'There's monks' graves in one of our fields.'
'There's a tunnel going from our place to the Abbey.'
'That's four miles. Don't talk dull! Have you seen it?'
'My grandsir said there was.'

Another aspect of this wish to annex for one's own home all the glamour of history and mystery is a preoccupation with origins, place-names, and topographical details. Thus it is said in Cheshire that Wildboarclough and Wulvarn Brook are so called because there the last wild boar and the last wolf in England were respectively killed; that tree stumps below the tide-line at Meol Stocks are remnants of a forest that stretched all the way to Ireland; and that another forest covered the whole Wirral:

> *The squirrels ran from tree to tree*
> *From Formby Point to Hilbree.*

Many oral local tales are far more elaborate than these simple assertions of belief, but behind them lie the same impulses of curiosity and pride which a community feels about its surroundings, and about its past. Often, they embody the simplified version of national and local history which has become embedded in the communal memory; it is natural that a region which has seen so much turbulent history should reflect this in traditions about battles and warrior-heroes. Other tales concern outlaws, highwaymen, robbers, murderers and poachers; others again concern past members of prominent local families, especially medieval figures (such as Sir Ralph de Staveley, Sir William Brereton, Sir Thomas Venables, or Sir Thomas Vaughan) about whom sensational or romantic tales were told.

At their best, these local tales can be small-scale works of art – for oral story-telling is an art, as anyone who makes a practice of telling anecdotes knows well enough. Tales like those of the Child's Ercall Mermaid, the avenging ravens, or the laying of the Gatley Shouter (pp. 26, 55, 96) have undeniable qualities of drama or humour. It is a pity that folklore collectors have so often paraphrased what their informants told them; in particular, one regrets that Miss Burne did not reproduce more of the verbatim tales from Miss Jackson's manuscripts. One can agree with her point that 'strongly-marked dialect makes a book tiresome' if this involves laboriously fiddling with the spelling in a hopeless attempt to convey shades of pronunciation, as she clearly assumed it must. However, when one compares her two versions of the Child's Ercall Mermaid legend, the first in full dialect and the second in standard English, one sees that the second has been stripped of many vivid touches of rural idiom in word-order, grammar or choice of tenses, which could perfectly well have been left undisturbed. For this reason, the version I have given here is a compromise between the two, restoring the wording of the dialect rendering, but without the elaborate phonetic spelling.

The first three chapters having been given to legends that centre on topography and history, the next three explore various aspects of beliefs and tales about supernatural beings, or human beings with supernatural powers: wizards, witches, fairies and ghosts. Here the emphasis has changed since Shelley's day; the fairies and hobgoblins with which he was 'overstocked' have vanished from living belief, and the malevolent witches and devil-raising wizards have probably gone the same way, though 'charmers', i.e. those who claim to heal by supernatural means, still have a following – it is only a few decades since a wart charmer at Whaley Bridge in Cheshire wrote to the *Observer* about her powers. Only the belief in ghosts remains strong today, though with the difference that modern apparitions are more likely to be dignified and elusive 'psychic phenomena,' not the macabre or grotesque animal-ghosts, skulls and skeletons, and ghosts that leap on horseback, which fired the robust imaginations of earlier generations. The stories chosen for this chapter display this typical rural blend of horror and humour, and also the recurrent theme of ghost-laying, which is finely developed in this region.

The next two chapters turn to a different category of folklore, the great mass of traditional beliefs about luck and ill-luck, omens, the human life-cycle, non-rational healing methods, and other magical procedures. Those selected for discussion concern healing (including Holy Wells, which are numerous in this area), and the lore surrounding marriage, birth and death. Finally comes the extensive category of seasonal observances – an assortment of varied customs, festivals, games, rituals and beliefs linked to particular dates. These are often sharply localized (some, indeed, are exclusive to a particular town or village), but there are also some that were known over a wide area with only slight variations. The majority of them belonged to the nineteenth century and the first few years of the twentieth, the period that ended when the First World War and the modernization of agriculture and transport broke the old patterns of rural life. Some, however, have survived, or been revived, and are extant today;

wherever this is so, I have tried to obtain up-to-date information on the point.

It would, indeed, be an error to see folklore solely in terms of the past. Pure oral tradition can still sometimes be encountered; I myself was taught the tune of the ballad 'Lord Randal' in 1950 by a fellow student from the Wirral, who had learnt it from her grandmother, a working-class woman who was certainly untouched by the folk-song revival movement — nor did my friend and I realize at the time that we were doing anything particularly momentous in passing on a tune that must be several hundred years old. Then, books of folklore studies themselves ensure the survival and spreading of the lore to fresh generations; the massive works of Miss Burne and Mrs Leather have been quarried by more recent writers such as Maxwell Fraser, H.L.V. Fletcher, and Jean Hughes. Of course, as has been said already, they tend to fix the legends into a 'correct' form, but even a story as well known as that of the Giant of the Wrekin can still sprout new variants; in 1974 I was told by an informant from Acton Burnell that the hill was formed from a huge pile of shoes which a cobbler dropped in fright on meeting a giant, or the Devil. No one could claim this version is as dramatic or amusing as the 'correct' one, but it does show how elements of an old story can be reshuffled into a new pattern (possibly because of uncertainty of memory), and so long as this still occurs the legend must be classed as a living one, not a mere fossil. It is heartening, too, to notice that two of the most recent books I have used as sources, the volumes compiled by the Cheshire Federation of Women's Institutes, are also two of the most fruitful; between them, they contain no fewer than sixty-four items drawn directly from local tradition, of which some are memories of past tales and customs, but others relate to the present time.

Finally, I wish to express my thanks to Mr F.W. Gledhill, senior librarian of the Cheshire County Library; to Mr A.M. Carr, local history librarian of Shrewsbury Public Library; to Mr F.A. Milligan, assistant county librarian of the Hereford and Worcester County Libraries; to Mrs Winifred Leeds of Ross-on-Wye; to Mr C.T.O. Prosser, hon. secretary of the Kilvert Society; to the Revd L.J. Forster of Great Budworth; to the Revd A.J. Birch of Lymm; to the Revd R.A. Alden of Appleton Thorn; and to Mrs E.E. Butcher of Hereford. All have been most kind in replying to my requests for information.

ONE

THE LANDSCAPE

Landscape and folklore are closely linked; it is around famous landmarks that legends cluster thickest, each tale reflecting both the physical features of the spot and the feelings it has aroused in the story-tellers. Sometimes, though rarely, these are awe and admiration; thus the Skirrid is regarded as a holy mountain, and the great cleft in its side is said to have split open in the earthquake at Christ's death. 'More than one Monmouthshire church,' wrote J.H. Matthews in 1904, 'was built on a mound formed of earth brought from this mountain, and it was the custom at the burial of Catholics, right down to the early nineteenth century, to sprinkle on the coffin earth brought from the chapel of St Michael, which stood on the slope near the landslip.' Other writers add that its soil was said to be so holy that no snail or worm could live in it; that part of it had moved to America; that pilgrims climbed it on St Michael's Eve; and that even in recent times its earth was scattered on local farms for luck.

More often, however, startling features such as rocky outcrops, isolated hills, boulders or mounds seem to have been regarded as blots on the landscape, things which cannot have been part of the Creator's plan, and so must be due to some stupid or mischievous being – the devil, a giant, or a local superman. These tales are almost always humorous, as in the two famous accounts of the making of the Wrekin. The first tells of two giants who quarrelled as they built a hill to live in; one split the hillside with a blow of his spade, creating the cleft called the Needle's Eye, but then was attacked by the other's raven which pecked at his eyes – and the tear he shed formed a pool called the Raven's Bowl. Eventually the victor took possession of the Wrekin, and imprisoned his rival under Ercall Hill.

The second Wrekin legend is possibly the best-known story in all this region. It tells of a Welsh giant who hated Shrewsbury, and set out carrying a huge spadeful of earth with which to dam the Severn and flood the town, or, some say, bury the town itself. On the way he met a cobbler who was carrying a sackful of old boots and shoes:

> And the giant called out to him. 'I say,' he said, 'how far is it to Shrewsbury?' 'Shrewsbury?' said the cobbler, 'What do you want at Shrewsbury?' ... 'Eh!' he said, 'You'll never get to Shrewsbury, not today, nor tomorrow. Why, look at me! I'm just come from Shrewsbury, and I've had time to wear out all these old boots and shoes on the road since I started.' And he showed him his sack. 'Oh!' said the giant, with a great groan, 'Then it's no use! I'm fair tired out already, and I can't carry this load of mine any further. I shall just drop it here and go back home.' So he dropped the earth on the ground just where he stood, and scraped his boots on the spade, and off he went back home to Wales, and nobody ever heard anything of him in Shropshire after. But where he put down his load there stands the Wrekin to this day, and even the earth he scraped off his boots was such a pile that it made the Little Ercall by the Wrekin's side.

This lively tale has parallels in Herefordshire. Two hills called Robin Hood's Butts at Canon Pyon and King's Pyon were said to have been formed when Robin Hood (or the Devil) dropped a couple of bags of earth with which he meant to smother the monks at Wormesley (or, in the Devil's case, to bury Hereford). Robin was tricked by a cobbler in just the same way as the Wrekin giant; the Devil, however, was either scared off by a crowing cock or dissuaded by a holy man disguised as a cobbler, who convinced him that Hereford people were too wicked to be worth killing. At Shobdon, on the other hand, the Devil was caught by yet another lying cobbler's tale, and the tumulus called the Devil's Shovelful can be seen there to this day. In noting this legend in 1911, Mrs Leather added that 'from time immemorial a cobbler has lived in the house immediately opposite the mound'; one may perhaps surmise that shoemakers, conscious of their quiet and sedentary craft, liked to cast themselves as quick-witted heroes in the tales they told.

Outcrops of rock, standing stones and scattered boulders also cry out for 'explanations', especially since they are, from the farmer's point of view, an unmitigated nuisance and a waste of good land. No wonder the Devil is so often held responsible for them! The huge mass of quartzite called the Stiperstones is his 'chair', surrounded by a scattering of boulders that fell from his leather apron one day when its strings broke; it is said that he often sits there, hoping that his weight will sink the chair into the ground, for if it ever does, England will be ruined. If anyone else sits in it, a thunderstorm at once breaks out; furthermore, 'if you go up there in hot weather, you may smell the brimstone still, as strong as possible!' In Gloucestershire, there are two Devil's Pulpits, one an outcrop of rock overlooking Tintern Abbey, the other at a disused ancient iron mine near Bream in the Forest of Dean (known also as the Devil's Kitchen, or the Devil's Chapel). Back in Shropshire, there is a Giant's Chair on Titterstone Clee, a hill with a sharp basalt summit; the scattered rocks around it are said to be the weapons with which two giants fought.

Many single natural boulders and prehistoric standing stones have similar tales to account for them. The Lea Stone, a big boulder near the castle ruins at Bishop's Castle, is a mere pebble which the Devil picked out of his shoe one day that he was sitting on the Stiperstones, and tossed to its present site, some five miles away. Two giants, one living at Stockport and the other in a castle where Arden Hall now stands, hurled rocks at each other till the latter won. A rock in a field at Bluestone in Cheshire was aimed by the Devil at Acton church, but fell short by half a mile; another that once lay in a meadow at Bartestree was similarly aimed at the spire of Hereford Cathedral by a giant who lived in a cave at Adam's Rocks. The fallen megalith on Brown Clee in Shropshire must have been the subject of a similar tale, as it was called the Giant's Shaft. Other stones are said to have been dropped by the Devil flying overhead with rocks in his apron – those at Beeston Castle, for instance, and those in the Oakwood at Trelleck.

Again, there is 'Moll Walbee's Stone' at Llowes in Radnorshire, a large boulder on which a cross has been carved. It used to stand in the churchyard, but has now been moved inside the church to protect it from weathering; it may originally have served as a prehistoric standing stone. The story goes that Moll, a giantess, built Hay Castle in a single night; either the stone fell from her apron as she passed Llowes, or else she felt it in her shoe and hurled it angrily across the border from Hay. Curiously, this giantess can be identified; her name is a distortion of that of the redoubtable Maud de St Valery, wife of Baron William de Braose, in the times of King John. Her husband too figures in local legend as a giant, though not a stone-thrower; his stronghold was at Painscastle, and he is said to have carried off local girls there until the lover of one of them, aided by forty giants from another castle, each seven foot tall, stormed Painscastle and slew him. Even Robin Hood can be transformed into a giant; in Cheshire it is said that he stood on the barrow called Werneth Low and hurled a rock into the Tame at Arden Mill, on which his finger-marks can still be seen.

Some features of the landscape of the southern Border counties are said to be due to the superhuman activities of a curious local hero, Jack O' Kent or Jackie Kent, a wizard whose chief joy in life was to make the Devil look a fool. For instance, the cleft in the Skirrid, usually ascribed to the earthquake at the Crucifixion, was accounted for in a different way by a Kentchurch woman in 1903:

> Jack did some wonderful things in his time. Why, one day he jumped off the Sugar Loaf Mountain onto the Skirrid, and there's his heel mark in the Skirrid to this day. An' when he got there he began playing quoits; he pecked [i.e. threw] three stones as far as Trelleck, great big ones, as tall as three men (and there they still stand to this day), and he threw another, but that didn't go far enough, and it lay on the Trelleck road just behind the five trees until a little while ago, when it was moved so that the field might be ploughed; and this stone, in memory of Jack, was always called the Pecked Stone.

Others account for the three standing stones at Trelleck by saying that Jack and the Devil met and quarrelled on Trelleck Beacon, and the Devil challenged Jack to a throwing match; Jack threw first, then the Devil threw a bit further, then Jack threw further still, and the Devil ran off. Similarly with two stones at Stroat and Thornbury in Gloucestershire; they are said to have been tossed from Tidenham Chase, one by the Devil and one by Jack. Again, the Robin Hood's Butts already mentioned above are sometimes said to be spadefuls of earth flung by Jack and the Devil from Burton Hill; stones near Grosmont Bridge were dropped either by Jack or by the Devil (working under Jack's orders) when building that bridge, and so were the White Rocks on Garway Hill. In short, as was said in the Wye Valley in 1905, 'he were always a-flinging stones', and the stones he flung or dropped could never be shifted again.

In contrast to these frivolous tales, one strikes a grimly moralizing note: the four pillar-like stones called the Devil's Rocks at Dawnton Castle, near Ludlow, were said to be four women who were turned to stone after dancing with the Devil. Legends of this type are descended from the pious and alarming anecdotes with which medieval preachers adorned their sermons.

Landscape legends do not always involve supernatural beings and marvellous events. Hills or tumuli named after historical personages may simply be said to be the spots from which they watched some battle (or, in the case of Robin Hood, shot an arrow). The Trelleck stones are sometimes said to commemorate a victory of Harold Godwinson against the Welsh. A stone at Willaston in Cheshire is locally believed to mark the site of an Anglo-Saxon moot, and another on Irby Heath, near Thurstaston, to be an altar on which Vikings offered sacrifices to Thor. Such traditions might in some cases contain a grain of truth; in any case, they reveal an interest in historical realities, not merely an exercise in fantasy and humour.

Prehistoric chamber-graves are sometimes still thought of as burial-places in traditional tales, even when their earth mounds have vanished and only the stones remain. Not surprisingly, however, they are assigned to dates that are far too recent. Thus it is said that at the Bridestones on Cloud Hill in Cheshire a Viking was buried beside his bride, a Saxon girl from Biddulph. At Dorstone in Herefordshire is another chamber-grave with a fine capstone, and a large boulder lying nearby; the monument as a whole is known as Arthur's Stone, and some say it marks King Arthur's own grave, while others say he killed and buried some king or giant there. There was once a curious belief that the stones were gradually sinking and shrinking; when the Revd Francis Kilvert visited the spot in 1878, he noted in his diary:

> Joseph Gwynne told me that when he was a boy the great stone called Arthur's Stone was much longer than it is now. A hundred sheep could lie under the shadow of it. Also the stone stood much higher on its supporting pillars than it does at present, so high indeed that an ordinary sized man could walk under it. Across the green lane and opposite the stone was a rock lying flat on the ground on which were imprinted the marks of a man's knees and fingers. These marks were believed to have been made by King Arthur when he heaved the stone up on his back and set it on the pillars.

That standing stones are eerie things is a notion which lingered long. Writing in 1948, W.H. Howse remarked that in Radnorshire many farmers still felt awe of them, and left the hay unmown around them, while some people avoided going near them after dark. There is a common type of tale which, at first glance, seems to express these attitudes, for it apparently alleges that a stone acts like a living being. Thus the Four Stones at Walton, which are said to mark the graves of four kings killed in battle, are alleged to go down to Hindwell Pool to drink when they hear the sound of Old Radnor bells; the Whetstone on Hergest Ridge goes down to the Wye to drink as soon as it hears a cock crow each morning; the Long Stone near Staunton in the Forest of Dean will bleed if you prick it with a pin at midnight; another stone in the same forest, said to commemorate a murder, will bleed whenever you stick a pin in it; the Lea Stone at Bishop's Castle turns round when the clock strikes thirteen; and the Colwall Stone turns round nine times when it hears the clock strike midnight. It is tempting to see in such tales the survival of an archaic belief in living stones, or a memory of pagan rituals; usually, however, they were simply passed on as poker-faced jokes, so phrased as to catch the gullible. The catch, of course, lies in 'if you prick...' and 'when it hears...', for how can a stone feel pinpricks or hear clocks?

Lakes have legends too, some telling of their origins, others of what lies hidden in their depths. Such tales are widespread in Wales, one famous example being the legend, current since the sixteenth century, of Llangorse Lake (Llyn Syfaddon) in Breconshire. The story goes that a young man who loved a proud heiress killed and robbed someone so as to be rich enough to marry her, and when he told her of his crime she merely sent him to the victim's grave to find out if the murder would ever be avenged. At the grave, a voice cried out: 'Not till the ninth generation!' Thus reassured, the callous young couple married, but when in extreme old age they held a feast at which all their descendants gathered, an earthquake engulfed them and a sheet of water covered the spot, forming Llangorse Lake. There is a similar tale about Llyndys Lake near Oswestry; according to a sixteenth-century version, it covers the palace of a heretical king who would not listen to orthodox preachers, but another version, current among Welsh-speaking people of the area in 1862, tells how the Llyndys family were warned by an unearthly voice that their riotous and wicked lives would be punished in the sixth generation. One night, when the sixth heir was giving a feast, the harper left the house, leaving his harp behind; when he turned to go back, the building had suddenly vanished under a newly-formed lake, and on its waters his harp alone was floating.

A further variant concerns the marshes, now drained, which lay near Shobdon in Herefordshire, and which were believed to have swallowed up Old Pembridge. Here too the sole survivor was a musician, in this case a fiddler who had been playing at a dance, and went back for his gloves, only to find a swamp where the village had stood. It was still being said in 1911 that if one dropped a pebble down a certain well at Shobdon, one would hear it strike the steeple of a sunken church far below. A pool near Dorstone and another in Trelleck were similarly said to conceal in their depths the steeples of long-lost churches.

Several of the Shropshire lakes have legends featuring sunken churches whose bells can be heard ringing, as at Colemere, Croesmere, and Bomere. At Bomere, indeed, a whole village is said to have been swallowed up one Christmas Eve at midnight, because its people would not go to church in honour of the festival. Alternatively, some said doom came on them because a farmer cut his grain on a Sunday. Be that as it may, Miss Burne noted that 'it is said that at intervals glimpses of houses and buildings have been seen in the waters, and that children have been heard crying below, and especially that the church bells have been heard ringing on Sunday mornings.'

At Ellesmere, the wickedness which called down punishment was greed and selfishness. Where the lake now stretches, there was once a fine meadow with a well of such pure water that people used to come from miles around to draw their water from it. At length the owner — some say it was a churlish farmer, others a miserly old woman called Mrs Ellis — took to charging a fee to those who wanted water, however poor they were, or even forbade anyone to take it at all. So one night the well overflowed, and by morning the whole area had become a lake. Some add that the wicked Mrs Ellis drowned, and that the mere takes its name from her.

Several lakes were thought once to be bottomless, either in the sense that they were linked to the sea by underground channels, or that they went down to unfathomable depths. Rostherne Mere is an example of the former, Bomere of the latter:

> Many have tried to fathom Bomere, but in vain, Though waggon ropes were tied together and let down into it, no bottom could be found — and how should there be? When everyone knows that it has none! Nor can it be drained; the attempt was made once and found useless; for whatever the workmen did in the day was undone by some mysterious power in the night.

With no feeling of inconsistency, tradition also alleges that 'bottomless' pools have something at the bottom of them, whether this be a church or a village, as at Bomere, or merely a treasure or a single bell. The numerous bell legends all follow the same pattern: Once upon a time, the bell of a local church or chapel was flung into the lake, whether by Puritans at the Reformation, or by Oliver Cromwell, or by thieves, or by a demonic force; alternatively, the bell fell in by accident while being transported or repaired. In every case an attempt was made to recover it, and in every case it failed, and for the same reason — that somebody swore. At the sound of the oath, the bell rolled back into the water, sometimes crushing the blasphemer and dragging him down too. In Cheshire, this tale is told of Rostherne Mere and Combermere; in Shropshire, of Colemere,

Shomere, and Berth Pool at Baschurch, and at all three oxen were used in the attempt to drag out the bell. In Herefordshire the scene is Marden, and the details are particularly picturesque:

> In former times Marden stood close to the river, and by some mischance one of the bells was allowed to fall into it. It was immediately seized by a mermaid, who carried it to the bottom and held it there so fast that any number of horses could not move it. The people of the parish were told how to recover it, by wise men, according to some; others say the bell itself gave instructions from the bottom of the river. A team of white freemartins, i.e. heifers, was to be obtained and attached to the bell with yokes of the sacred yew tree and bands of 'wittern', i.e. mountain ash; or, in some versions, the drivers' goads were to be of witty or wittern. The bell itself was to be drawn out in perfect silence; it was successfully raised to the edge of the river with the mermaid inside fast asleep. In his excitement a driver, forgetting that silence was all-important, called out:
>
> *In spite of all the devils in hell,*
> *Now we'll land Marden's great bell.*
>
> This woke the mermaid, who darted back into the river, taking the bell with her, singing:
>
> *If it had not been*
> *For your wittern bands*
> *And your yew-tree pin,*
> *I'd have had your twelve freemartins in.*
>
> So Marden folks have never had their bell back from the bottom of the river to this day, and sometimes it may still be heard ringing, echoing the bells of the church. It lies in a deep clear pool.

Mermaids figure more than once in the stories told of these inland waters; it is said that one swims into Rostherne Mere from the sea by underground channels, to ring its sunken bell each Easter Day, while another was believed to live in a pool at Child's Ercall in Shropshire. Those who told the latter tale in 1879 were vague as to the mermaid's appearance ('Well, I canna say just exactly what it were like – I wanna there, you know – but it were a mermaid, same as you read on in the papers'), but they were positive that two men had seen her once early one morning, about a hundred years before:

Her voice was so sweet and so pleasant, they fell in love with her there and then, the both on 'em. Well, and her told 'em as how there was a treasure hid at the bottom of the pit, lumps of gold, and dear knows what. And her 'ud give 'em all as ever they liked, if so be as they'd come to her in the water and take it out of her hands. So they wenten in – nearly up to their chests it were – and her ducked down in the water and brought up a lump of gold, big as a man's head, very near. And the chaps were just a-going to take it off her, and the one on 'em says 'Eh!' says he (and swore, you know), 'if this isna a bit of luck!' And my word! If the mermaid didna take it off 'em again, and give a kind of a shriek, and ducked down again into the pit, and they never seed no more on her, not after, nor got none of her gold; nor nobody's never seed nothing on her, not since.

There are tales of other strange marvels in the waters. In the depths of Bomere there swims a huge fish with a sword belted round its body; it has only once been caught, in a net forged of iron links, and even so it drew the sword and cut itself free. The weapon once belonged to Wild Edric (see below, p. 33), who entrusted it to the fish before he vanished; when his true heir appears, the fish will willingly give up the treasure. A recent writer, Miss Ruth Tongue, whose family came from Whitchurch, recalls several traditions current in the early years of this century about the Shropshire and Cheshire meres. It was said that gentle female water-fairies called Asrais lived in their depths, rising to the surface once in a hundred years to see the moon; a fisherman once caught an Asrai and tried to bring her home with him, but as soon as the sun's rays touched her, she melted into foam. Another fisherman made a more terrible catch on Ellesmere; when foolishly and defiantly fishing on a Sunday, he caught the Devil himself, who dragged him overboard.

At Peterchurch in Herefordshire there is a tablet in the church showing a trout with a golden chain around its neck, of which many tales are told. Some merely say that a fisherman caught it nearby in the Golden Well; others, that some poor monks caught it in the river Dore when they were almost starving; others, that St Peter himself baptized converts in the Golden Well, blessed the well, and threw into it a trout with a gold hair round its neck, which was to live there for ever. In 1876, Kilvert heard yet another version from an old man at Peterchurch, who spoke of a great hunt to slay the fish:

> They do say the Fish was first seen at Dorstone and speared there, but he got away, and they hunted him down to Peterchurch and killed him close by the church. He was so big as a salmon, and had a gold chain round his neck. They do say you can see the blood now upon the stones at Dorstone where the Fish was speared first.

All this water lore has strong affinities with Celtic tales and beliefs. The magic trout or salmon in a sacred well, beasts wearing gold chains, the epic hunt for a supernatural beast, waters that overflow to punish crime, female water-spirits, a hero's sword hidden in deep waters – all can be paralleled in medieval Irish, Welsh and Arthurian literature, and in the folktales of Celtic areas. The frequency of these motifs along the Welsh Border clearly reflects the Welsh influence in this region in earlier centuries.

The mysteries that allegedly lurk under the ground are of a more universal type. Here, as in all parts of Britain, there are tales of buried treasures, often associated with castle ruins, though not necessarily with any particular incident in the castle's history. There is said to be gold in Stokesay Castle, Bronsil Castle, Peynard Castle and Longtown Castle. The first of these belonged to giants, who locked it away in a chest but then lost the key in the castle moat; some say a raven is perched on the chest to guard it. The treasure at Bronsil is also guarded by a demonic raven; that at Peynard lies in a vault with iron doors, watched over by a jackdaw. It is said that a farmer once forced the doors open, but broke silence, and so lost the prize. Certainly it is not unreasonable to hope to find gold hidden in old castles, and in the sixteenth and seventeenth centuries many treasure seekers resorted to magic and clairvoyance when trying to locate hidden hoards and exorcise their guardian demons; it is recorded that in 1589 a prisoner in the Tower of London told Lord Burleigh that there was a treasure in Skenfrith Castle, watched over by the Devil himself, and his wife. What, if anything, Lord Burleigh did about it is not known.

Other types of site are also mentioned, and these too may have supernatural guardians. Wormelowe Barrow, in Shropshire, contains a treasure guarded by a dragon; at Bury Ditches, a hill-fort near Clun, fairies have hidden a pot of gold, but have left a slender gold wire visible to guide the seekers; at St Weonard's Tump in Herefordshire the saint is said to lie in a golden coffin, on top of a chest of gold with the riddling inscription:

Where this stood
Is another twice as good,
But where that is, no man knows.

Even where there is no guardian, treasure hunting seems doomed to frustration. Miss Burne's book records:

'The Giant's Grave' is the name given to a mound on the Shropshire side of Llanymynech Hill, where once was a cromlech, now destroyed. The story goes that a giant buried his wife there, with a golden circlet round her neck, and many a vain attempt has been made by covetous persons to find it, undeterred by the fate which tradition says overtook three brothers, who overturned the capstone of the cromlech, and were visited by sudden death immediately afterwards.

The Border counties have, like the rest of England, innumerable traditions of tunnels criss-crossing the countryside, linking up abbeys, churches, castles, old mansions, inns, wells, follies, and archaeological remains. It would be impossible to list them all. Some have factual basis, for castles certainly did have secret exits, abbeys had sewers, and disused mine-workings and smugglers' hiding places are also real enough. But many of the alleged tunnels are purely imaginary, appealing to the widespread fondness for romantic mystery; those who pass on such traditions, however, are usually pretty firm in asserting that the particular tunnel they are concerned with is a fact.

The interest of tunnel traditions is increased if they also involve buried treasure, as at the Hermitage cave near Bridgnorth, where popular belief in an underground passage leading under the Severn and containing a chest of gold led to much digging in 1878. It is also interesting, but unusual, to hear some reason given why the tunnel was made; at Trelleck, for instance, there was a tale that nuns used to come all the way from Tintern Abbey through a three-mile underground passage, in order to bathe there in a medicinal pool. The fact that the abbey never did contain nuns apparently did not matter to those who evolved this tradition.

Again, the mere belief in an underground passage is sometimes enriched by a story that it was once explored, with remarkable results. Near Orleton Hall in Herefordshire there is a cleft between some rocks called Palmer's Churn, and about four miles away is a place called 'Gauset' at Woofferton; the story goes that a goose once entered Palmer's Churn, waddled right through a four-mile tunnel, and emerged at the other end crying 'Goose Out!' – hence the name. A sadder tale tells of an old blind fiddler of Llanymynech; he wandered into Ogo Hole, a disused copper mine on the hillside which was said to be the entrance to fairyland, and lost his way in its passages. He was never seen again, but from the cellar of the village pub people dimly heard his fiddle still playing far below. There were similar legends near Trelleck early in the twentieth century; one concerned a cave, and the other a meadow, where music could be heard coming up from underground. When people dug the meadow, it is said that they found:

> ...an underground cave in which were two old men, hermit-like, one playing a violin, the other a harp. They had been there many years, and used to take it in turns to go out at night and fetch food. Very old and decrepit they were, and soon after they were taken out they died.

There are also the legends of sleeping warriors waiting in caves till their hour comes, but since such tales are as much concerned with history as with landscape, they will be given in the next chapter.

The legends considered so far concern the natural features of the landscape, but a word must be said too of those which purport to explain why man-made buildings come to be on the sites where they are, by saying that they have shifted in some mysterious way. Occasionally a whole town is involved, as when Shropshire folk believed that Oswestry had quite literally moved from the hill fort known as Old Oswestry, or when it was said that Ross was called 'Rose Town' because it very gradually rose up the hill on which it stands.

But by far the commonest of such tales concern churches, usually those which are inconveniently sited in relation to the village they serve. Sometimes the explanation given is that a heavenly sign dictated the choice of site; at Clodock the oxen drawing St Clydawg's bier stopped beside the ford, and when the builders refused to accept this sign and tried to build at Llanwinog instead, everything they built fell down, so that they had to return to the site by the ford. Kilgwrrwg church in Monmouthshire also owes its site on a remote and inaccessible tump to the inspired choice of two white heifers which lay down on it.

More frequently, odd church sites are said to be due to the intervention of hostile supernatural forces which interfered with the builders' first choice of site by pulling down by night whatever they had built by day, and shifting the stones to a new site. In Cheshire this tale is told of Bebington, Ince, Over and Stock; the first, it is said, was 'mysteriously' shifted, the second the fairies moved, the third was flown away with by the Devil, and then dropped, and the fourth was moved either by the Devil or by fairies. In Shropshire too, four churches are said to have had their sites shifted, namely Worfield, Broughton, Baschurch and Stoke-upon-Tern; Miss Burne notes that in each case the existing site is low and marshy, whereas that allegedly first chosen is a hill top. In the first two cases, tradition blames the Devil; in the other two, simply a mysterious 'something'. Building materials for the church of Much Cowarne in Herefordshire are also said to have been removed from a hill to the present site by 'an invisible agent'; in the same county, too, the site of Kingsland church was determined by the Devil's interference, while at Pencombe, old people in 1908 still told how it had once been proposed to rebuild their inconveniently-placed church on a better site, but the spirits of the dead in the old churchyard would not allow the work to proceed.

TWO

RUMOURS OF WAR

It is not surprising that an area that has seen as much warfare as the Welsh Border has preserved traditions about battles in almost every century of its troubled history. There are also tales which do not refer to any specified period, yet powerfully express a generalized awareness of bloodshed and tragedy. Thus we hear that at Dorstone there was once a battle so grim that the brook ran red with blood for three days; the same is said of a brook at Dulas, near Hay, and a huge burial mound nearby is said to hold the bodies of the slain; at Trelleck there is a stretch of gorse-covered land called Bloody Field, of which it was said in 1905: 'Eh, it have been ploughed again and again but 'tis no use, because of the blood spilt there, 'tis no use.' Even traditions about events clearly pinpointed in time can evoke the same note of apocalyptic horror; at Barber's Bridge station in Gloucestershire is a memorial to 500 Royalist Welshmen killed there in 1643, and local story-tellers still describe how the very soil was stained red, how the Leadon River ran red, and how cranesbill blossoms wherever a Royalist fell.

Fancy plays grimly too round place-names, claiming that a spot called the Slaughter near Symonds Yat was where Caractacus was defeated; that Scotland Bank near Dorstone is so called because the last few Highlanders left alive after the Battle of Worcester were massacred there by Welshmen who loosed their dogs on them; that Beachley, near Chepstow, gets its name from an English war-cry 'Beat-and-slay!'; and that Hewelsfield in Gloucestershire means 'Hew-and-slay-Field'.

The implied point of view is often that of sympathy for the defeated; slain leaders attract marvels to almost the same extent as martyred saints – sometimes, indeed, they are both at once, as were St Oswald and St Ethelbert. An interesting instance is that of Llewellyn ap Gruffydd, the last Welsh Prince of Wales, who was killed and then decapitated at Builth in 1282; according to Adam of Usk in the early fifteenth century, the head was washed in a nearby spring which 'through the livelong day did flow in an unmixed stream of blood', while modern tradition adds that a hawthorn grew in the ruins of Abbey-cwm-hir above the exact site of his grave, so that this should never be forgotten. The ideas involved here are ancient; the association between severed heads and springs or wells, and the magical properties of both, were common beliefs of the pagan Celts, and were transmitted to medieval times through various channels, notably the lives of Celtic saints, which abound in such marvels. That a tree, especially a holy tree like the hawthorn, should grow where some great man died or was buried is an idea with a similar history.

One remarkable pattern of belief and tale springs from the persistent loyalty with which a dead leader's followers may reject the bitter truth of his death, and cling to a hope that he has only mysteriously vanished. As time passes and the hero is still absent, explanations are devised; the usual one in pious ages was that he had renounced earthly glory and the use of arms, and was living obscurely as a monk or hermit. Hence the legend, found in many medieval sources, that Harold Godwinson survived the Battle of Hastings. According to the *Vita Haroldi*, he went abroad on pilgrimage, returned to live as a hermit near Dover, and then, after wandering through the Welsh Marches in disguise, ended his days as a hermit at Chester, where he revealed his identity in a deathbed confession. Later texts credit him with a fantastic life-span; some allege he was still alive in the reign of Henry II, by which time he would be over 150 years old. Often these survival legends take on a new twist as the centuries pass, and claim that the lost hero will one day supernaturally return. Sure enough, two nineteenth-century folklorists came upon versions which asserted that Harold will even yet return, to lead his countrymen against the Normans.

Alternatively, the hero may be transformed into a wholly supernatural figure. This has happened to Wild Edric, a Shropshire leader in Harold's time, who fought the Normans from 1067 till 1070, then made peace with William, but apparently rebelled again later. The real circumstances of his death are not known. In the late nineteenth century, many people believed that Edric was still alive, somewhere deep in the mines under the West Shropshire Hills. As Miss Burne tells us:

> He cannot die, they say, till all the wrong has been made right, and England has returned to the same state in which it was before the troubles of his days. Meanwhile he is condemned to inhabit the lead mines as a punishment for having allowed himself to be deceived by the Conqueror's fair words into submitting to him. So there he dwells, with his wife and his whole train. The miners call them 'the Old Men', and sometimes hear them knocking, and wherever they knock the best lodes are to be found. Now and then they are permitted to show themselves. Whenever war is going to break out, they ride over the hills in the direction of the enemy's country, and if they appear, it is a sign that the war will be serious.

One Shropshire woman from Rorrington, daughter of a miner, told a circumstantial tale of how she and her father had seen Wild Edric, his wife Lady Godda, and their companions riding northwards at Minsterley in 1853 or 1854, shortly before the outbreak of the Crimean War. She described them as dressed in medieval clothes, all green and white, with gold ornaments; Edric was dark-haired, carried a sword and a hunting horn, and rode a white horse; Godda had wavy golden hair reaching to the waist. The girl said her father had seen them once before, riding southwards, 'and then Napoleon Bonaparte came'. The visual details in the girl's account are suspiciously romantic, but the story certainly is based on authentic folk-belief, as can be seen from the detail that the girl's father 'bade her cover her face, all but her eyes, and on no account speak, lest she should go mad'. Wild Edric has taken on some of the terrifying attributes of the ghostly leader of the Wild Hunt, a figure in the folklore of many lands, to see whom brings death or madness; at the same time he and the other 'Old Men' of the lead mines resemble the friendly 'knockers' of the Cornish mines, while as a hero who returns when his country is in peril he belongs in the same category as King Arthur or Frederick Barbarossa.

Though much of Miss Burne's information about Wild Edric rests on the statements of this one young woman, the wide influence of her book has ensured that the legend lives on, and indeed tends to develop new variants – for instance, the scene of Edric's imprisonment underground and of his apparitions is now often said to be the Stiperstones, that famous landmark which attracts so many tales. The apparitions get updated, too; Miss L.M. Hayward, writing in 1938, said he had been seen before the Napoleonic and Crimean wars, but not in 1914, whereas Miss Jean Hughes, writing recently, had heard of sightings before the Boer War and in 1914, but not in 1939. The rule would seem to be 'not last time, but the time before'.

Of all hidden heroes whose return is awaited, the most famous is of course King Arthur. A recurrent legend localized in several different parts of Britain (e.g. in a cave near Caerleon-upon-Usk) tells how a man is led by a wizard into an underground cavern, where he sees Arthur and his men sleeping, awaiting the hour of peril when they will return. A fine and well-developed version of this tale has been current in Cheshire since the middle of the eighteenth century, and is probably far older; it used to be told by the Revd Shrigley, the curate of Alderley in 1753, who declared that the events had actually happened some eighty years before his time.

The scene of the tale is Alderley Edge, a dramatic outcrop of rocks rising from the plain, honeycombed with the tunnels of disused mines, and scarred with old quarries. A farmer, so the story goes, was once on his way to sell a fine white mare at Macclesfield Fair, when he was stopped here by a wizard (or, some say, an old man in a monk's robe), who wanted to buy the mare. He refused, so the wizard declared that he would find no other buyer. Sure enough, that evening the farmer had to return, with his mare still unsold. Again the wizard met him, and made him follow him through huge iron gates into the rock itself, where he saw many warriors and horses, all asleep; they would emerge on the day that England's fate hung in the balance:

Thrice England shall be lost, thrice won,
Twixt dawn of day and setting sun...
Then dabbled wings shall ravens toss,
Croaking o'er bloodstained Headless Cross.

The wizard explained that the warrior band needed one more white horse to complete their numbers; he paid the farmer well, and led him out of the cave, whose iron doors shut, and were never seen again. In some versions of the story, but not all, it is explained that the sleepers are Arthur and his knights, and the wizard is Merlin.

The story is in no danger of being forgotten. Not only is there a pub called the Wizard's Inn on the road to Macclesfield, and a wishing well at Alderley called the Wizard's Well (the customary offering is a bent pin), but the legend has been vividly rehandled by Alan Garner in his children's novel *The Weirdstone of Brisingamen*. It has long been, and still is, an amusement for local children to search the rocks and quarries of Alderley Edge for traces of the secret gates, and to tell each other that the place is haunted.

Such stories are not necessarily always linked with Arthur. The poem quoted above, from a nineteenth-century guide to Alderley, does not identify the sleepers as Arthur and his men, nor give the wizard any name; its phrasing shows influence of the vague prophecies of war which in Cheshire are ascribed to Nixon (see below, pp. 38-43). A story located at a cave at Penlascarn in Monmouthshire tells of sleeping warriors who are 'King George's men' and are awaiting a trumpet call. In Scotland, where the versions closest to the Alderley legend may be found, the wizard who seeks horses is Thomas of Erceldoun, and he himself will lead the sleeping army. The ever-growing fame of Arthur tends to infiltrate into what were originally independent legends; fortunately, the Wizard of Alderley Edge has so far preserved his individuality, and refuses to merge wholly into Merlin.

At the other end of the Border, not far from Symond's Yat, is a 'King Arthur's Cave' where Merlin is said to have hidden all the king's treasure. As we have seen in the previous chapter, many tales of buried treasure are unconnected to any specific historical event, but those that do claim a historical background are, reasonably enough, set in the context of some defeat or act of destruction. Thus it is said that Richard II flung a vast quantity of gold down the deep well of Beeston Castle rather than let Bolingbroke lay hands on it, while others say it was the Royalist owners of the castle who hid it there before Cromwell sacked the place. In either case, it is guarded by demons, and all who have tried to reach it have gone mad, or been stricken dumb with horrors. A more realistic tradition concerns the disappearance of the church silver at Guilden Sutton; it is said to have been buried under an oak tree for safety in the Civil War, and never found again, as no one could remember which tree it was.

The destruction of abbeys and expulsion of monks at the Reformation also gave rise to tales of treasure; it is said that when Birkenhead Priory was closed, several monks fled with the prior's gold down an underground passage, but its roof caved in, and they were never seen again. The last three monks of Abbey-cwm-hir are said to have buried their wealth somewhere on the hills between the Ithon and the Morteg, and even nowadays some local people claim to know where it lies:

> Some said that if you stamped on the ground there was a hollow sound. One night... some young men decided to dig and see if they could find anything. They actually started, but there came such a terrifying thunderstorm, with such awful hullabaloo, that the treasure seekers ran away.

In the 1930s, people at Easthope thought the treasure of Wenlock Abbey lay under two old gravestones in their churchyard, but anyone who tried to get it would be struck dead; it was said that the rector had wanted to open the tombs, but the Home Offce had forbidden it.

There was also a strong and widespread belief that the monks laid a curse on those who took over their vast estates, and on all their descendants too; sometimes the curse was thought to take the form of financial disasters, since 'ill-gotten gains never prosper', or sometimes sudden deaths and other personal misfortunes in the families concerned were attributed to it. Such ideas probably existed, though unexpressed, at the Reformation period itself; in the seventeenth and eighteenth centuries they were discussed openly and widely, not only orally but in books and pamphlets, and have continued to this day. Thus in 1895 Fletcher Moss vigorously expressed his conviction that the financial bad luck which pursued descendants of the Cotton family who received Combermere Abbey was due to the power of the dead monks, that the place could not be let or sold, and that local people

> ...may tell you, with bated breath, that the curse of the monks is on it, that ill-luck comes to all who meddle with it, that rest and sleep flee away, for the monks 'come again' even to the bedside. There is a deeply rooted tradition in the neighbourhood that the Cottons only hold Combermere so long as they dispense hospitality to all comers, and although they have been hospitable in the past, it is not right to shut up the house and leave it.

Another Cheshire property, Abbey Grange at Ince, was also believed to carry a monks' curse with it; while in Radnorshire the trout in Llyn Gwyn, near Nantmel, which was once a monastic fishpond, are never eaten by the local people, for it is said that when they are caught they croak aloud, 'to testify their abhorrence of the wrong that had been done'. In Herefordshire, according to a modern author, some people say that the Scudamores of Holm Lacy were punished by a curse that the direct heirs to the estate would always die before their fathers – a misfortune which did indeed happen, though only twice.

The upheavals of history naturally leave many traces in local ghost lore; it would be tedious to attempt to list all the named historical personages who are said to haunt castles, bridges, or notable houses where they once lived or died, especially since this class of ghost is constantly referred to in guide-books. A more curious example on the interaction of history and folklore at a purely local level is the story of the Headless Woman of Duddon in Cheshire. There is in the village a pub of this name, which originally had as its sign a hanging painting of a woman holding her head in her arms. In more recent years this was replaced by a yet more dramatic emblem: a life-size ship's figurehead, gorily painted, with its head sawn off and balanced on its right arm, though this figure too has now been removed. Normally, pubs that display this sign are named 'The Silent Woman' (the only silent woman in the world being one whose head has been chopped off), and this joke may perhaps have been the original point of the pub-sign at Duddon too. Local involvement in the Civil War, however, has inspired a very different explanation for it. The woman, so the story goes, was a servant at Hockenhull Hall at Tarvin; some say her name was Grace Trigg. Cromwell's soldiers broke into the Hall after the Royalist owners had fled, and found her hiding in the cellar; they tried to torture her into revealing where the family treasures were hidden, but she would not speak, so they killed her on the back staircase. It is said that her headless ghost now walks the road between Duddon and Tarvin: some people add that an undergound passage links the pub to Hockenhull Hall.

After such ghoulishness, it is agreeable to find that a few local traditions about past wars are cheerful. There is appreciation for cleverness and courage, as in the tale of how a little drummer boy saved Hereford Castle in a siege by noticing how his drum vibrated, and correctly deducing that the walls were being undermined. And there are gleeful tales of how the enemy were routed by simple tricks, as when it is said that Roundheads fled from bees at Llansilin and from women armed with knives at Acton, or that the citizens of Wem drove off a whole Royalist army in 1643 though they had only forty troopers to defend them – 'the story goes that they posted old women in red cloaks at well-chosen spots, and thus scared the enemy, who took them for soldiers.'

The interaction of history and folklore is not a one-way process; there are occasions, rare but fascinating, when one can observe propagandists consciously manipulating traditions and beliefs in order to influence the outcome of a political crisis. A case in point is the appearance of pamphlets about Robert Nixon 'the Cheshire Prophet' in 1714 and 1719, when tension between Jacobites and Hanoverians was running high. Those that were printed represent only one side in the controversy, the Hanoverian, but it is clear from reading between the lines that vigorous attempts were also being made in Cheshire to enlist Nixon's reputation for the Jacobite cause.

But first, who was Robert Nixon? According to the pamphleteers, he was an ugly, greedy, ill-tempered imbecile who worked as a ploughman on the estates of the Cholmondeleys of Vale Royal in the reign of James I (or, alternatively, of Richard III and Henry VII). He used to fall into trances and utter prophecies, and eventually died in London at the King's court, to which he had been taken as a result of his local fame, through being accidentally locked into a room and starved to death. It is almost certain that the 'prophecies' attributed to him, though genuine late medieval sayings, are in no way peculiar to Cheshire. They come from a very widespread body of floating 'prophecies' about terrible battles and the downfall of kings, which can be found in Wales as early as the twelfth century, in Scotland in the fourteenth, and in England in Tudor and Elizabethan times. It was very common for the same prophecy to be attributed to different prophets, and to be interpreted differently at different periods. Those that are said to be by Nixon consist of eight or nine pages of doggerel verse foretelling wars, famines, social upheavals and calamities; they begin:

When a raven shall build in a stone lion's mouth
On a church top beside the Grey Forest
Then shall a King of England be drove from his crown
And return no more.

When an eagle shall sit on the top of Vale Royal house,
Then shall an heir be born who shall live to see great troubles in England.

There shall be a miller named Peter,
With two heels on one foot,
Who shall distinguish himself bravely
And be knighted by the victor;
For foreign nations shall invade England,
But the invader shall be killed,
And laid across a horse's back,
And led in triumph.

A boy shall be born with three thumbs on one hand,
Who shall hold three king's horses,
Whilst England is three times lost and won in one day.

The verses ramble repetitively on, with millstreams running blood, crows drinking blood, symbolic beasts fighting, and so forth. At one point,

> *Foreign nations shall invade England with snow on their helmets,*
> *And shall bring plague, famine and murder in the skirts of their garments.*

Finally, peace will return:

> *Then rise up, Richard son of Richard,*
> *And bless the happy reign,*
> *Thrice happy he who sees this time to come*
> *When England shall know rest and peace again.*

The whole thing is a medley of material from various medieval and Tudor sources; the influence of sayings attributed to the Scottish Thomas of Erceldoune is particularly strong. It may have been circulating orally in Cheshire throughout the sixteenth and seventeenth centuries; by about 1700 handwritten versions certainly existed at Vale Royal and elsewhere. Then, in the second decade of the century, Nixon's prophecies suddenly became notorious, and knowledge of them spread far beyond the county boundaries. The political situation of 1714 (date of the first pamphlet about him, John Oldmixon's *Nixon's Cheshire Prophecy*) provides the clue to this surprising development.

On 1 August that year, Queen Anne, last of the Stuart monarchs, died; George I was at once proclaimed King and arrived in England from Germany at the end of September, but at the same time there remained a strong possibility that the exiled Stuart pretender might come over from France to claim the throne. In such a situation, the prophecies attributed to Nixon were potential political dynamite. The third and fourth lines of the opening would seem clearly to refer back to James II's abdication in 1688, and it would be only natural to assume that this was one of the 'great troubles' foretold for England. And who were the foreign invaders whose leader would be killed – the newly-arrived Hanoverians, or the pretender's French allies, whose troops might land at any moment? The most straightforward interpretation would be to take the exile of the Stuart dynasty as a calamity, and to cast George as the foreign villain – a pro-Jacobite interpretation. From contemptuous asides in the pamphlets of 1714 and 1719 we learn that there were indeed 'some silly people, almost as stupid as Nixon'; who thought the prophecies favoured the pretender; since many leading Cheshire families showed Jacobite sympathies in the rising of 1715, we may suspect that these 'silly people' constituted quite a worrying threat to the Government party.

Faced with this problem, the Hanoverian hack-writer and propagandist John Oldmixon cleverly set out to enlist Nixon's reputation in support of his own party, while at the same time adopting an ironic tone to indicate his own superior detachment from the whole affair. He is very careful not to quote any of the prophecies verbatim (they were only printed much later, after the furore had died down), yet he boldly claims that they are indeed coming true, and are giving great joy to 'bold Britons and subjects of King George'. The two-heeled miller, for instance, is alleged to be alive, and hoping to receive his knighthood from King George very soon! Oldmixon concedes that the prophecy about a king's exile does refer to James II, but adds, quite unjustifiably, that 'it was foretold he would endeavour to subvert the laws and religion of the country'.

Five years later a second pamphlet appeared, written by one 'W.E.', which elaborates the anti-Jacobite theme with sneers at the collapse of the risings in 1715; according to this work, the foreigners with snow on their helmets are quite obviously the French, 'for none but French Papists would bring such destruction among Protestants'. Further editions of Oldmixon's pamphlet later appeared which manipulate the material even more blatantly; for instance, the allusion to 'Richard son of Richard' is altered into 'George son of George', in compliment to George II who became king in 1727. Both pamphlets were frequently reprinted throughout the first half of the eighteenth century, which may mean that there was a recurrent need to scotch pro-Jacobite rumours; the Cheshire historian Ormerod notes that Nixon's sayings 'were a subject of general curiosity about the time of the Rebellion of 1745'.

Towards 1800, when all political danger was safely over, the actual prophecies themselves were at last printed. So too was an anonymous *Life of Robert Nixon of Bridge House*, which adds new material, a group of anecdotes and prophecies presumably drawn from oral sources and relating mainly to Cheshire affairs, such as the fate of Vale Royal Abbey at the Dissolution, or changes that affected local estates:

> *Through Weaver Hall shall be a lane, Ridley Park shall be sown and mown,*
> *And Darnell Park shall be hacked and hewn.*

Long after the echoes of political controversy died away, local belief in Nixon continued strong; to this day some sayings attributed to him are remembered, if no longer taken very seriously. Thus a modern writer mentions his prophecy that Northwich will be destroyed by water, and speculates whether the subsidence of old salt-mines might yet make this come true; he also quotes a saying that when the ivy on Lower Bebbington church reaches the top of the spire the end of the world will be at hand, and says that local people regularly clip it back to postpone the coming of Doomsday.

Thanks to the pamphlets, Nixon's name was also at one time widely known outside his own region; indeed, he was sometimes regarded as almost on a par with the famous Mother Shipton. As late as 1875 the Revd Francis Kilvert was told by a countryman in Wiltshire that 'there was once a prophet named Saxon who was born a peasant boy and used to drive plough oxen', and died of starvation, as he had himself foretold, locked up in a gentleman's house. This and other details given by the Wiltshire man make it certain that he was thinking of Nixon of Cheshire, though Kilvert does not seem to have realized the fact.

The pamphlets were also circulating in cities, where Nixon became so famous that Dickens can allude to him with casual brevity, taking it for granted that the reference will be understood:

> 'Vell now,' said Sam, 'You've been a-prophecyin' away, very fine, like a red-faced Nixon as the sixpenny books gives picters on.'
> 'Who wos he, Sammy?' inquired Mr Weller.
> 'Never you mind who he wos,' retorted Sam; 'he warn't a coachman, that's enough for you.'

Few Cockneys would now know Nixon's name – but in the First World War they, and others, still gossiped about the coming of mysterious foreigners, though by that time they were Russians, and the snow was on their boots. For in all ages 'there shall be wars and rumours of wars...'.

Three
LOCAL HEROES, FOOLS, ROGUES AND VILLAINS

The previous chapter has shown how large-scale events are reflected in local traditions; equally frequently, persons and events of purely local importance become subjects of legends, of varying degrees of historical value. At one end of the scale one finds sober, factual accounts of, say, the exploits of smugglers and poachers three or four generations ago; at the other, extravagantly romantic, eerie or humorous tales which, though much relished, are not taken too seriously.

Paradoxically, the wildest flights of fancy usually have some concrete object as their starting-point, preferably one to which the story-teller can triumphantly point as 'proof' of the tale. In Berrington church in Shropshire there is a wooden effigy of some unknown knight, with his face damaged, and a battered lion at his feet; he is locally nicknamed 'Owd Scriven', and it is said that as he was on his way to visit his lady-love he met a lion by a stile at Banky Piece, and cut it in two, though his face was badly mauled. In Cheshire, there is the tomb of Sir Hugh Calverly at Bunbury, adorned with a lion and a lamb; these are miscalled a calf and lamb, and legend claims that Sir Hugh ate one of each every day of his life. The fact that the marble effigy of Constancia Pauncefoote formerly in the church of Much Cowarne in Herefordshire lacked one hand has given rise to a legend that she let her hand be chopped off to ransom her husband from the Saracens.

The most elaborate of these tales concerns Sir Ralph de Staveley, whose effigy lies in Mottram church, with his wife at his side and a dog at his feet. They are locally called 'Old Roe and his dog', and the story about them follows pattern well known in fairy tales. Sir Ralph, it is said, was a Crusader who was imprisoned with Richard Lionheart for so long that when at last he came home he learnt that his wife, believing herself to be a widow, was about to be married the next day. Sir Ralph, who was in disguise, happened to meet his old dog and one of his servants near the hamlet called Roe's Cross; the man did not recognise him, but the dog did. Next day, Sir Ralph went to the wedding feast, disguised as a beggar, and contrived to drop into a glass of wine one half of a broken ring which his wife had given him at parting, and to send it to her as a token of who he was. In order to be certain, she then asked the beggar to describe a mole on her body which only her husband knew of; the reply was correct, and so husband, wife and dog were happily reunited, while the new suitor hastily withdrew.

Other legends undertake to 'explain' the coat-of-arms of some prominent local family. Why do the Vaughans have on their arms three boys' heads with snakes round their necks? Some say, because the ancestor of the Vaughans of Hergest Court was actually born with a snake round his neck; others, because a nurse in the household of the Vaughans of Courtfield once left the baby in her charge on a lawn, and returned to find a snake coiled round him, which she cleverly lured away with a saucer of milk. Why do the Venables have as their crest a dragon holding a child in its jaws? Because the founder of the family once shot an arrow at a poisonous dragon in the swamps by Bache Pool, near Moston, and so saved a child which the monster was on the point of swallowing – a deed which won him much land as his reward. And why is a muzzled bear the emblem of the Breretons? Because a Sir William Brereton once murdered his valet in a fit of rage, simply for interrupting him at dinner, and when he then went to London to seek the King's pardon, the King would only grant him his life on one condition: within three days he must invent a muzzle that could control a bear. If he failed, the bear itself would be his executioner. So for three days Sir William was shut in the Tower of London, and then taken to confront an unchained bear; he threw the muzzle he had devised over its head, it held, and Sir William survived unharmed.

A local hero or heroine may also be remembered (or invented) in connection with some charitable custom he or she is said to have founded. The most striking instance in this area is the variant of the Godiva story which is told at St Briavels, to explain how it came about that the people of this parish had a right to cut as much wood as they pleased from a large coppice called Hudnolls. 'This privilege,' wrote Samuel Rudder in 1779, 'was obtained from some Earl of Hereford, then Lord of the Forest of Dean, at the instance of his lady, upon the same hard terms that Lady Godiva obtained the privileges for the citizens of Coventry.' A recent writer elaborates on this, saying that the Countess had to repeat her naked ride every year, and furthermore that King John 'was so charmed by this pleasant custom that he ordered that all the girls of St Briavels should do the same'. The wood-cutting custom is also said to be confirmed by the annual distribution of bread and cheese from the village church (see below, p. 164), an occasion which helps to keep the story alive.

Less implausible is the story told of the sixteenth-century William Jones who founded almshouses and schools in Monmouth, though it too is more likely to be legend than fact. He is said to have been born in poverty at Newland in the Forest of Dean, and to have worked as a potboy in Monmouth till he ran away to London, where he grew rich. Later he returned, pretending to be a mere beggar, and since he was roughly turned away at Newland but charitably helped at Monmouth, he spent all his money on good works for the latter town. Another tale connected with charities is one explaining why some benefactor has left funds to pay for the ringing of a nightly curfew; it is told at several places, for instance at Tong, at St Mary's church in Shrewsbury, at Chepstow, and at Aymestrey in Herefordshire. In each case it is said that a man lost his way dangerously in darkness or in fog (further misled, at Aymestrey, by a will-o'-the-wisp), and vowed that if he got safe home he would make sure that other travellers would have the sound of a bell to guide them. In the case of the Chepstow man, it is said that when dawn came he found he had strayed to the very edge of the Black Rock. Such tales are not intrinsically impossible; it is their constant recurrence at different towns in many parts of England that marks them out as legends rather than history.

One of the noblest exploits for a hero is to kill a dragon, so it is no surprise to find the Border regions well-stocked with dragon-slayers. Besides Sir Thomas Venables of Moston, the founder of another Cheshire family, that of Grimesditch, is said to have killed a dragon in a ditch by the Grimesditch Brook. Herefordshire can boast of the presence of St George himself, whose famous adventure is firmly localized at Brinsop; the dragon, they say there, lived in a well in Duck's Pool Meadow just south of the church, and the saint fought him in a field called Lower Stanks. The reason for the legend is obvious to all – the church at Brinsop is dedicated to St George, and has a fine medieval tympanum showing the saint in the act of spearing the monster.

But dragon-slayers are not necessarily saints or aristocrats; on the contrary, several are quite plebeian heroes, and used various odd and ingenious methods to dispose of their quarry. At Deerhurst in Gloucestershire, according to an eighteenth-century account, a dragon which was poisoning men and livestock was lured to its death by 'one John Smith, a labourer', who enticed it with a huge trough of milk and then crept up on it while it 'lay in the sun with its scales ruffled up...and, striking between the scales with his axe, took off its head'. A monster's head carved above a door in Deerhurst church serves as focus for this legend.

On the Welsh side of the Border, at Llandeilo Graban in the Wye Valley, the last dragon of Radnorshire met its dramatic end. This creature, which terrorised the district by day, was in the habit of sleeping on top of the church tower by night; a story current in the early years of the twentieth century tells how a ploughboy managed to kill it without any risk to himself:

> He made a dummy man out of a large log of oak, and, aided by the local blacksmith, armed it with numerous iron hooks, powerful, keen and barbed. Then he dressed the dummy in red and fixed it firmly on top of the tower. At dawn the following day the dragon first saw his

daring bedfellow, and dealt him a violent blow with his tail, which was badly torn by the hooks. Infuriated by the pain, he attacked the dummy with tooth, claw, wing and tail, and finally wound himself round his wooden foe, and bled to death.

Herefordshire can boast of the story of the famous Mordiford Dragon. This legend has a long, well-documented history, and like several of the others was at first linked to a visible object – in this case, a large picture of a green two-legged dragon, with red gullet, forked tongue, and curling tail, which was painted on the outside of the west wall of Mordiford church. It is first mentioned in 1670, and was periodically repainted until, most regrettably, it was deliberately erased during church repairs in 1810-12. Possibly it originally represented the arms of the Priory of St Guthlac at Hereford, which included a wyvern (i.e. a two-legged dragon), since this priory held the living of Mordiford.

Also recorded in 1670 are some verses which seem to refer to the picture on the church:

> *This is the true Effigy of that strange*
> *Prodigious monster which our woods did range.*
> *In Eastwood it by Garston's hand was slaine,*
> *A truth which old mythologists maintain.*

Presumably the slayer was some early member of a local family, the Garstones, who are occasionally mentioned in the parish records of the sixteenth and seventeenth centuries for their charitable bequests; how he slew the dragon, however, has been long forgotten.

Instead, a vigorous local tradition, first recorded in 1802 and persisting to this day, declares that the hero was some anonymous criminal under sentence of death, who volunteered to tackle the dragon in exchange for a pardon. The dragon, it is said, used to live in the high wooded ridge called Haugh Wood, but when it needed food or drink it would come crawling down a sunken path, which is still called Serpent Lane (and where, some say, no grass will grow), till it reached the junction of the Wye and the Lugg. There it would first drink, and then set out to take whatever it could catch – poultry, ducks, sheep, cows, or human beings. One old man in the early nineteenth century used to explain that it had not always been so fierce; when it was first found by a little girl in the woods it was no bigger than a cucumber, so she took it home and fed it on milk, in spite of the warnings of her parents, till it grew to its full size and developed different tastes.

Various tales were current in the 1840s about how the fearsome monster met his doom. One was that all the people of Mordiford surrounded him while he slept, having gorged himself on a whole ox, and hacked him into pieces. But most versions concerned the brave criminal; some said he tracked the dragon to its lair, slew it as it slept, and brought back its tongue as proof, but the most popular version, then as now, is that of the 'Battle of the Barrel'. This tells how the hero borrowed a cider barrel and hid inside it on the river bank, where he waited till the serpent came down to drink. Some say the barrel was studded with knife-blades and spikes, so that when the dragon attacked it he wounded himself fatally; others say the man stuck the muzzle of a gun through the bunghole, and shot the dragon at close range. But he did not live to enjoy his triumph; the poison of the creature's dying breath penetrated into the barrel, and so the man and monster died together.

The tale, like that from Llandeilo Graban, has a pleasing touch of humour; the cider barrel, in particular, makes a strong appeal to Herefordshire hearts. But some people apparently once took it more seriously, for it is remembered that a Rector of Mordiford in the 1870s once came upon some old women in his church trying to drown two newts in the font because, so they said, these creatures were dragon spawn, and would grow into a pair of monsters if they were not dealt with straight away.

This is of course a joke about foolishness, it being obvious that newts cannot drown. There are many standard jokes about fools in English tradition, several of which can be found in this region. It is said, for instance, that the people of Madeley-on-Severn wished to keep the cuckoo with them all the year round, so they went into a field where a cuckoo was and made a ring round it, holding hands, thinking this would easily imprison it. They were amazed and disappointed that the bird flew away over their heads. After that they were known as the Wise Men of Madeley. A rather similar joke was told about an old clergyman of Edgmond (who died in 1864), who was alleged to have raised his garden wall by a foot all the way round, to keep sparrows out. He had noticed that when they came into the garden they just skimmed low over the wall, so he reasoned that if the wall was a bit higher they wouldn't be able to get in at all.

Another recurrent old joke about fools is that they notice some harmless animal or object which happens to be unfamiliar to them, are horrified, and try to kill it, believing it to be the Devil. In the seventeenth century, John Aubrey tells an anecdote which he takes for granted is true, but in which we can recognise a variation on this traditional joke. The fools are servant girls at Holm Lacy in Herefordshire; the object of suspicion is a watch, belonging to a celebrated Cambridge mathematician who died in 1632, Thomas Allen. The story implies that he, like so many learned men, was suspected by the ignorant of being a wizard with a demon as his familiar:

> One time being at Hom Lacy in Herefordshire, at Mr John Scudamore's (grandfather to the Lord Scudamore), he happened to leave his Watch in the Chamber windowe (Watches were then rarities). The maydes came in to make the Bed, and hearing a thing in a case cry Tick, Tick, Tick, presently concluded that it was his Devill, and took it by the String with the tongs, and threw it out of the windowe into the Moat (to drowne the Devill). It so happened that the string hung on a branch of elder that grew out of the Moat, and this confirmed them 'twas the Devill. So the good old Gentleman gott his Watch again.

So far, the hero-tales in this chapter have belonged to the world of fantasy, being products of the perennial storyteller's wish to astonish or amuse. Other types of local tradition are more solidly based on real events; memories of notable crimes, or of the lawless deeds of smugglers, poachers and highwaymen, can survive orally in a district for many generations, especially if some landmark such as a grave, a gibbet or a notorious inn remains there to help keep the story vivid. No one was likely to forget the fact that James Price was hanged in 1790 for robbing the Warrington mailcoach, while his skeleton hung in chains for thirty years on a gibbet on Trafford Green, and robins nested in his empty skull.

Many traditions about highwaymen are sober and factual, and can safely be regarded as accurate. For instance, there were inns on or near the road from Macclesfield to Buxton which are said to have been regular haunts of theirs – 'The Setter Dog', so called, it is said, from the slang term for a robber's decoy, and 'The Puss in Boots', said to be named after a highwayman whose nickname this was. Memories of Higgins, the gentleman-highwayman of Knutsford who was hanged for murder in 1767, were still vivid in his home town when Mrs Gaskell wrote about him (in 'The Squire's Story') almost a hundred years later. And when, in our own times, the last of a family of blacksmiths from Mollington talked of a family tradition that highwaymen used to call at the forge by night to get their horses shod, there is every likelihood that this was in fact the case.

Yet there is always a tendency for tales to grow in the telling. For one thing, a nationally famous figure like Dick Turpin may oust some more obscure local robber from his rightful place in tradition. It is presumably as a result of this that we hear of Dick in so many parts of Cheshire – playing bowls at the inn on Hoo Green to establish an alibi, holding up coaches on the Ashley to Knutsford road, patronising The Swan with Two Nicks at Bollington, hiding in an old thatched cottage in Lostock Gralam. There is also much pleasure in describing cunning tricks to outwit the law (smuggled salt carried in coffins, stolen goods hidden in graves, robbers' horses with muffled hooves or with their hooves shod backwards), some of which may be true, but others not. Another good trick was that of a horse-thief from Lindow who lay flat in the road as a rider drew near because, so he said, he could hear 'ground-fairies' singing; the rider dismounted and lay down – and when he got up, the thief was galloping off on his horse! One very hoary old anecdote has been transferred to a comparatively recent character, of whom it is told as truth:

> On one occasion the Foresters of Tatton Park searched in vain for a stolen buck in the house of old Isaac Lowndes of Mobberley; his good wife sat quietly spinning, and gently rocking the old wooden cradle, in which lay the buck – covered over like a sleeping baby.

This is a joke which has been doing the rounds at least since the fifteenth century, when it figured in the Wakefield 'Shepherds' Play' as the story of Mak the Sheep-Stealer.

The local robber or highwayman can also become inflated in popular imagination to almost supernatural stature. Naturally, the process usually takes time, as can be seen in the case of Wild Humphrey Kynaston, a Shropshire gentleman who was outlawed in 1491 (possibly for political reasons), and pardoned two years later. Tradition has focused particularly on his wonderful horse and its amazing leaps; an early account, in 1700, only mentions a reasonably plausible leap across a broken bridge, but by the time Miss Burne was collecting Shropshire lore in the 1880s, the horse was credited with wholly supernatural strength – it was said to have bounded from the top of Nesscliff Hill to Ellesmere or to Loton Park, nine miles and five miles respectively. Indeed, one informant told her this horse had been the Devil himself, while there were several tales of its hoofprint being stamped into solid rock. A vaguer Shropshire bandit, Ippikin, has been wholly supernaturalized into an ogrish ghost lurking in a cave to guard his gold treasures. Sometimes panic can accelerate the process, and even a contemporary bandit takes on the features of an ogre. In 1834 the daughter of a Rector of Tattonhall kept a diary in which she entered many anecdotes about the doings of burglars and highwaymen who were active in the district; some, she had heard, were hiding in 'Bloody Bones Cave' on 'Raw Head, Hart Hill' – names which seem to come straight out of nursery tales of man-eating giants.

Of all crimes, murder arouses the most potent mixture of fascination and horror. The commonest way in which these emotions find expression in oral traditions is through the idea of haunting. The chapter on ghosts will supply several examples of such tales, with the stress on the haunting rather than on the crime that originally caused it. The emphasis is reversed in the grim story told about Plaish Hall at Cardington, a fine mansion whose tall, twisted chimneys of patterned brick are an unusual feature for a Shropshire house. At the beginning of the seventeenth century it belonged to William Leighton, Chief Justice for North Wales, who had it enlarged and beautified. The story goes that a criminal who happened to be a master-builder was on trial before Judge Leighton, and he offered that if the Judge would spare his life he would build him such fine chimneys 'as no man ever saw before, or could build the like of after'. The Judge accepted; the chimneys were duly built; and as soon as the work was done the Judge had the man hanged – some say, from the very chimneys he had made – to make sure that no other house could ever equal his. The victim of this heartless double-cross can still be heard, some say, moaning high up on the roof.

Murder combined with injustice may also give rise to a legend of a curse. In the late nineteenth century, Condover Hall was commonly thought to be an unlucky place; it was said that in Henry VIII's time the owner, Lord Knevett, was murdered by his own son, who contrived to pin the blame on the butler. At the foot of the gallows, the butler prayed that no son of any owner of the house should ever succeed peacefully to his father's estates, and it was believed that this curse had come true. There was also said to be an indelible bloodstain in the chapel, where Lord Knevett died. Indeed, as late as 1885 Miss Burne found that 'wild and painful stories are current of a recent apparition of the wronged man at a scene of festivity, to renew his curse', and she took pains to point out that there is no historical basis at all for the story of the murder.

Near Capel-y-ffin there used to be a house called Ty Dial, 'Revenge House'; its name was explained by a legend rather similar to the ones told about certain lakes (above, p. 23):

> The spot, in a dingle on the mountainside, lay under a curse because of some crime committed there. Workmen starting to build the house heard a disembodied voice telling them to move because the curse had nine generations to run. Nevertheless, they persisted, but only at the third attempt did they succeed in building a house which stood. One winter's night a young man went to court his sweetheart there, but despite every effort at persuasion, his greyhound would not go inside. The man took this as a bad omen, and went back home. Later that night a landslide swept away the whole house, killing everyone in it.

Another reflection of the horror felt at murder is a belief that no grass will grow on the spot where it has occurred. At Nass in Monmouthshire a girl was killed in a meadow; at Black Hill in Cheshire a certain William Wood was murdered in 1823; a murder victim is said to have been buried in the garden of a farm near Godley; in each case, it is said that no grass has grown there since. The same thing is said of the grave of John Davies, a robber who was hanged for murder in 1821 and lies buried in the churchyard at Montgomery; in this case, however, the sign is held to show that Davies was falsely accused and unjustly executed, and it is said that he himself foretold the marvel, to prove his innocence. A bare patch can in fact be seen, shaped roughly like a cross, and a white rosebush also grows on the grave.

Supernatural powers might sometimes intervene to frustrate murder. W.E.T. Morgan, who collected folklore in south Radnorshire in the first quarter of the twentieth century, was told how a girl's life was saved because the curate of Glasbury took heed of a telepathic warning. The girl, it is said, was the rather feeble-minded daughter of wealthy parents, who was secretly courted by a farmer's son whose wild ways had led him into debt. He persuaded her to meet him at the church one midnight, alone, wearing her best jewels and bringing as much cash as she could, and said they would be married then and there. She believed him. That night, the curate woke suddenly, convinced that someone was calling to him, 'Come at once to the church'. Ignoring his wife's protests, he dressed and went out. As he passed through the churchyard he heard the noise of a pickaxe, and at the same time the girl, assuming he had arrived to perform the ceremony, called to him from the porch, 'Why are you so late, sir? I've been waiting for you here a long time.' – 'But why are you here?' he asked, 'What's the matter?' – 'Oh, we're going to be married,' says she. – 'You can't be married at this time of night!' – 'Oh yes, I'm going to be married to Tom,' she said. But Tom never appeared, and the curate at length persuaded her to let him take her back home. As they passed the part of the churchyard where he had earlier heard someone digging, they saw an open grave. Tom had meant to rob and kill his foolish sweetheart, but ran off when the curate arrived and was never seen in the district again.

The notion that guilt and innocence will always be revealed, by supernatural means if need be, makes a strong appeal to storytellers. One Shropshire tale concerns a man named Thomas Elks who lived at Knockin in 1590; he drowned his young nephew and fled to Herefordshire, only to be betrayed by the persistent calls of two ravens that followed him everywhere, and circled round him as he hid in a haystack. He was brought home, and hanged on Knockin Heath. Mrs

Leather was told a similar story in Herefordshire in 1903 by a very old shepherd:

> Years ago, on the Black Mountain above Longtown, there lived a hired shepherd who managed a little farm for his master. There were on either side of this farm two brothers, farming for their father. I can remember, in my time, there was terrible jealousy and animosity between the shepherds on the mountain, where the sheep all run together... Well, it was worse nor ever for this man, because the brothers were together, and they hated him. He stuck to his master, and they to their father. At last, one day, they got him alone on the mountain, and caught him, and said they would murder him. They said there was no one about, and it would never been known. 'If you kill me,' he said, 'the very crows will cry out and speak it.' Yet they murdered and buried him. The body was found after some time, but there was no evidence to show who the murderers were. Well, not long afterwards the crows took to come whirling round the heads of those two brothers, 'crawk, crawk, crawk', there they were, all day long – when they were together, when they were apart. At last they could scarcely bear it, and one said to the other, 'Brother, do you remember when we killed the poor shepherd on the mountain top there, he said the very crows would cry out against us?' These words were overheard by a man in the next field, and the matter was looked into, so that in the end the brothers were both hanged for the murder.

Public opinion, however, is not always on the side of the law. There is often sympathy and admiration for smugglers and poachers, and even for highwaymen too, if they are not also murderers; a bandit of the distant past, like Humphrey Kynaston, may be thought to have 'robbed the rich to give to the poor', in the true spirit of Robin Hood. When a law is generally resented, those who break or evade it are admired; hence some Cheshire stories about Quakers who found clever ways to avoid paying the church tithes to which they had conscientious objections. One, it is said, picked the apples from his orchard at the rate of ten a day, so that the vicar's servant had to come every day in order to collect just one apple; another brought a hiveful of bees to the vicarage, but insisted on taking back the hive itself, thus filling the vicar's study with infuriated bees.

The more widespread and serious outbreaks of popular unrest during the Industrial Revolution and the early struggles of the trade unions show an interesting connection with folk customs in the disguises and pseudonyms adopted by some secret societies engaged in illegal activities. The need for secrecy often led to oaths and rituals imitated from Freemasonry, sometimes blended with traditions from the old guilds, as when the newly-formed Nantwich Shoemaker's Union 'purchased a full set of secret order regalia, surplices, trimmed aprons, etcetera, and a crown and robe for King Crispin' – this of course being St Crispin, patron of the shoemakers since medieval times. Other groups seem to have turned for their models to the ritual disguises worn by actors in the traditional folk-dramas common in many parts of England, such as the Christmas Mummers' Plays and the Cheshire Soulers' Play (see below, pp. 180-183, 188). These often involved male actors dressed as ludicrous 'women', or men masquerading as animals, wearing skulls and skins of horses or cattle; the Cheshire Hodening Horses belong to this tradition, which was then far more widespread than its present-day survivals. Blacking one's face, too, is a simple but effective disguise that is found in many forms of mumming. All three forms of concealment can be paralleled in the descriptions of certain groups who, in protest against social conditions, turned to illegal actions in the first part of the nineteenth century.

Thus, in Monmouthshire in the 1830s, there was much resentment of conditions in the iron and coal industries, and some groups of unionists, calling themselves 'Scotch Cattle' and organized into 'herds' led by a 'bull', set out to remedy their grievances by direct action. Members were dressed in animal skins and had their faces blacked; they met by night in isolated spots, and threatened to 'scotch' anyone who opposed their interests. They were particularly active in Nantyglo in 1832, and in 1834 round Pontypool and Blackwood, where they destroyed the shop of a man who opposed the formation of the union.

Female disguise was occasionally used by the Luddites; those who attacked steam looms at Stockport in 1812 were led by two men dressed as women, who called themselves 'General Ludd's Wives'. Female clothes were the invariable hallmark of the Welsh 'Rebeccas', who in the 1830s and 1840s rose up in protest against the highly unpopular tolls levied on traffic on the turnpike roads, which were a great burden on farmers. The movement was strongest in Carmarthenshire, where hundreds of people besieged the city in 1843, driving out all gatekeepers, and virtually controlling the countryside for almost two years. There were also outbreaks in the Border area round Rhayader and Kington; the rioters set out to smash and burn the toll-gates, disguising themselves in women's clothes, with blackened faces and grotesque horsehair wigs. They probably took their name from the Bible, from the passage (Genesis XXIV 60) which says that the descendants of Rebecca 'will possess the gates of them that hate them'; however, there is also a tradition that they were so called because their first leader, a Pembrokeshire man, borrowed his outfit from a particularly big woman called Great Rebecca of Llangollen. The question is largely irrelevant, since anarchic disguise, especially grotesque transvestism, was a deep-rooted popular symbol of role reversal and clown-like 'misrule', frequently adopted to serve the aims of popular justice, protest and rebellion.

Public opinion supported the Rebeccas; when travelling in Wales in 1854, George Borrow asked a man from Llangollen who Rebecca had been, and was told:

'I cannot say, sir; I never saw her, nor anyone who had seen her. Some say there were a hundred Rebeccas, and all of them men dressed in women's clothes, who went about at night at the head of bands to break the gates. Ah, sir, something of the kind was almost necessary at the time. I am a friend of peace, sir, no head-breaker, house-breaker, nor gate-breaker, but I can hardly blame what was done at that time, under the name of Rebecca. You can have no idea how the poor Welsh people were oppressed by those gates, aye, and the rich too. The little people and the farmers could not carry their produce to market, owing to the exactions at the gates... Complaints were made to the Government, which not being attended to, Rebecca and her byddinion made their appearance at night and broke the gates to pieces with sledge-hammers, and everyone said it was gallant work ... Aye, and I have heard that many a fine young gentleman had a hand in the work, and went about at night dressed as Rebecca. Well, sir, those breakings were acts of violence, I won't deny, but they did good, for the system is altered; such impositions are no longer practised at the gates as were before the time of Rebecca.'

The name was not forgotten, even when the grievance was past; it was taken up again in the 1850s by gangs of salmon-poachers who went out by night along the Wye and the Ithon, using spears and torches, and often fought bloody battles against police and water-bailiffs. An account in the *Hereford Times* of 6 December 1856 describes eighty of them marching into Rhayader four abreast, with blackened faces; the leader, who called himself Old Rebecca, had a gun, and the rest had swords, fish-spears, poles, and pitchforks. The clashes were particularly fierce in the years round 1880, when the gangs sometimes numbered as many as 100, and used the same disguise as the earlier Rebeccas. There were more big raids in 1904 and 1909. The wild doings and cunning tricks of these poachers have now themselves passed into folk tradition and become a topic for nostalgic reminiscences; Radnorshire people will not easily forget how, thanks to Rebecca and her daughters, salmon was selling for threepence a pound in Rhayader in 1907. And when there is cause for bitter anger in the farming community, as there was in the autumn of 1974, memories stir again of the earlier and fiercer Rebeccas who broke and burnt the toll-gates.

FOUR
WIZARDS AND WITCHES

Until recent times, it has been a tenacious belief in many parts of Britain that certain people possessed supernatural powers, whether for good or ill, by which they could heal or harm, bless or curse, or could control devils, ghosts and spirits. The most famous master-magician of the Border region, the hero of a well-known cycle of anecdotes, is the legendary Jack o' Kent or Jacky Kent (whose role as a rock-hurling superman was mentioned in Chapter I); he is said to have lived on the borders of Herefordshire and Monmouthshire at some vaguely medieval period, and was already famous by 1595, when he figures as an aged hermit with 'rare knowledge of the deepest arts in Antony Monday's play *John a Kent and John a Cumber*. Scholars do not agree as to who, if anyone, was the real Jack; there are at least six possible candidates, of whom the likeliest are a Welsh Franciscan friar named Dr John Gwent who died in 1348, and the learned astrologer Dr John Kent Caerleon, who lived in the fifteenth century and wrote a treatise on witchcraft.

Whoever he really was, and whether he lived in Kentchurch or in Grosmont, Jack is now a famous magician-hero. He is said to have sold his soul to the Devil as a boy, in exchange for the power to do whatever he set his hand to, and to command the Devil as his servant. Sometimes he used his power for the public good, as when he got the Devil to build a bridge across the Monnow at Grosmont in a single night. There was, of course, a price to pay: the first passenger to cross the bridge. But Jack threw a bone across, a hungry dog dashed across after it, and that dog was all Satan got for his pains.

On other occasions Jack made the Devil work on his lands, for instance by making a fishpool for him on Orcop Hill, or filling the farm dung-cart for him – which the Devil agreed to do, but only on condition that he could carry Jack off if he was not out of the sheepfold by the time the cart was full. At once Jack threw down his pitchfork and ran, but Satan was such a quick worker that he had finished the job and was already clutching Jack's coat as he leaped over the gate, and if the cloth had not ripped Jack would never have got away safe.

The two of them were constantly trying to do one another down, either in contests of strength (see above, pp. 20-21) or in trick bargains. One favourite tale tells how, as they were passing a freshly-sown field, Jack offered Old Nick the choice of taking either the tops or the bottoms of the crop when harvest time came round. 'Tops', said the Devil – but it was a field of turnips. At the next field the Devil chose bottoms, but as this time it was wheat, Jack won again. Another day, they competed in mowing hay; Jack won easily, having got up during the night and stuck harrow tines all over his rival's half of the meadow, so that his scythe was repeatedly blunted by what the stupid fiend thought were tough burdocks. Then one day they both went to Chepstow Market to buy pigs, and agreed that the one whose pigs had their tails straight next morning would have to pay for both lots. The Devil sat up all night with curling tongs, titivating the tails of his luckless beasts, which by dawn were so tired and fretful that their tails hung hopelessly limp; Jack, however, had given his lot a good feed of beans and plenty of straw to bed down in, so they came out all lively and curly-tailed.

Jack could do strange things by his own magic. Once he threshed a whole barnful of corn in one day – or rather, he played the fiddle all day, while his boot kicked the sheaves down from the stack all by itself, and his flail threshed them of its own accord. The Weobley man who told this tale in 1908 explained:

When Jack was doing anything like that, he always took out his little black stick as he carried, hollow at one end. In the hollow was a thing like a fly; one of the Devil's imps, it was. He would lay the stick down near him, and then he could do anything, like.

He had magic horses, which galloped through the air at fantastic speed, and which he stabled in the cellars of Kentchurch Court. People at Grosmont told how he once set out from there at daybreak to take a mince pie to the King in London, and got there in time for breakfast, with the pie still hot – though he lost a garter on the way, by getting it hooked up on a church weathercock as he rode overhead. He could also command animals, as we see from a well-known anecdote about his boyhood:

> Once he was engaged by a farmer to scare crows; but there was a fair going on in the town, and Jack didn't mean to miss it, so he called all the crows together from all the fields around, and when they were all collected, he sent them into an old barn, with no roof to it. But Jack put the crows in there and said something to them, and they couldn't get out, try as they might. So Jack, he went to the fair, but when he had been enjoying himself there a bit, he met his master. So the farmer said, 'Hullo, Jack, what art doin' here? Didn't I tell thee to look after th' crows?' But Jack says, 'T' crows be all right, master.' An' he took his master to the old barn, and sure enough there was the crows, and they couldn't get out, although that barn had no roof, until Jack told them to.

All these powers, as has been said, stemmed from the original compact made between Jack and the Devil, the precise terms of which were that the Devil was to take him, body and soul, when he died, whether he was buried outside a church or inside. But Jack had the last laugh, for he cheated his enemy in the end; he had himself buried in the thickness of the wall at Grosmont church (or, some say, the church at Skenfrith or Kentchurch), and as he was neither 'inside' nor 'outside' the Devil could not touch him. Despite this trick, it is said that on his deathbed Jack was anxious over the fate of his soul, and wanted to leave some public sign of the final outcome. He therefore directed that the liver and lights should be cut out of his body after death, and impaled on three iron spikes on the tower of Grosmont church (or, say others, on the beams of the roofless barn); he prophesied that a raven and a dove would fight over these remains, and that if the dove drove the raven away it would mean that his soul was saved. Presumably that was indeed what happened, for the legends about Jack are consistently sympathetic to him, even though occasionally mothers might scold their naughty children with the threat 'You be careful, or Jackie Kent will get you!'

Jack was not the only hero of this sort; in Radnorshire in the 1930s there were stories current of a wizard called Davies Sirevan whose exploits were often the same as Jack's – he too, for instance, imprisoned crows in a roofless barn, and left orders that his liver should be set up for the birds of good and evil to fight over. He is said to be buried at Llanfair Waterdine – either, like Jack, in the thickness of a wall, or under a tombstone which used to stand in the graveyard near the church porch, and was decorated with a carving of two birds, possibly a raven and dove. Like Jack, Davies is presented as a remote figure of timeless legend, and his deeds are regarded with amused appreciation, not fear or disapproval.

Tales about how the Devil was outwitted were always popular. One concerns a monk in Vale Royal Abbey whom the Devil tempted by offering to grant him any three wishes, in exchange for his soul. The monk's first wish was always to have as much ale as he could drink; his second, always to have as much venison as he could eat; and his third, to have six hay bands woven from grass growing on Merton Sands. The first two wishes were granted at once, but since no grass had ever grown on Merton Sands the Devil could not fulfil the last part of the bargain, and the monk's soul was safe. Just to make sure, the men of Over used to plough the sands once a year to prevent anything taking root there.

Another story explains why a stretch of road between Meldonra Castle and Brough is called 'The Doctor's Road'. There was once a doctor who had sold his soul to the devil in return for wealth and wisdom. When his time was up, he went on horseback to meet the devil on this road; the devil was also on horseback. The doctor challenged the Devil to a race, with his soul at stake. The Devil agreed, and was so sure he would win that he gave the doctor a start. He soon caught up with him, and as a joke caught hold of the tail of the doctor's horse and began twisting it and tearing it out by the roots, causing the poor beast such agony that it left the road and leaped across a stream. Since the Devil cannot cross running water, he had to abandon the race, and the doctor escaped.

In real life, too, there were people whose magic power was wholeheartedly believed in, and who were regarded with deeper awe and dread: those known as 'conjurers', 'cunning men', or 'charmers'. These men, whose reputations sometimes spread for many miles, were chiefly consulted for their powers of healing specified diseases, discovering thieves, and counteracting witches' spells; a few were also said to be able to raise the Devil. For instance, at Devauden in about 1880 there lived a 'quiet, harmless man' called Nicholas Johnson, who would cure toothache or stop bleeding by reading certain Bible texts, or writing them on paper. One day, it is said, Johnson boasted in a pub at Wentwood that he could raise the Devil, and took some men into the woods, where he drew a circle on the ground and read backwards from a book till Satan appeared, with hoofs, horns, tail and clinking chains. The men were terrified, but Johnson read on, and dismissed the Devil.

A similar character was old Jenkyns of Trelleck. He was famous for miles around for his ability to charm away rheumatism, toothache, and other pains; he simply asked his clients if they believed, and when they said they did, the pain was gone at once. People who cheeked him quickly regretted it, judging by a story told in 1903 by a woman from Trelleck who had often consulted him. Years before, as a child, she had visited him with her brothers, one of whom had toothache:

> When the toothache was gone, Jenkyns went out o' the kitchen to fetch a drop o' cider, and me brother seed a big, big book on the corner o' the table, and began to look at it. Jenkyns hollers out from the other side o' the house, 'Don't you touch that book, or it'll be the worse for you!' When 'e comes back, me brother says 'You must ha' got the Old Man 'imself about 'ere to have such-like goings-on,' says he. Just then there came a great noise in the room above, bowling about the floor, like as if a great ball were rollin' about. 'All right,' says Jenkyns, 'if you don't look out you'll have him a bit closer.'
>
> With that 'e takes a candle an' blows into it, puts it on the table, an' draws a circle round it. Then the light all burnt dim and blue, an'

the whole room got cloudy an' misty. Presently, we seed a little old man sittin' in a chair next to Jenkyns; 'e was rockin' 'imself to and fro, and squeaking: 'Jenky, Jenky, Jenky!', an' again 'Jenky, Jenky, Jenky!' Now 'e 'adn't come through the door, cos that was locked; an' 'e 'adn't come through the window, cos that was shut an' barred; an' yet there 'e was, sittin' in the chair, an' calling: 'Jenky, Jenky, Jenky!' an' 'Jenky, Jenky, Jenky!' Then Jenkyns blew into the candle again, an' the dim blue light went away, an' the candle burned clear, an' lo and behold! That little grey old man was vanished.

The story leads one to suspect that Jenkyns used hypnotism to impress people; so too do accounts of how Nicholas Johnson 'could make a small oak tree grow suddenly in his kitchen, and when the acorns fell would produce a sow and her litter to come in and eat the acorns, much to the annoyance of his wife', or of how a conjurer in Ross had only to bring out his little black stick and a hen and chickens would jump onto the table. Hypnotism could also be used to punish offenders. It is said, for example, that Jenkyns once put a spell on four people who had stolen some cider, so that they danced for two whole hours on the village green till they were ready to drop, while hundreds of people looked on – 'old Jenkyns, 'e was watching, quite pleased like, for some time; then 'e got tired, took the spell off, an' went home'.

Again, there is a tale of how Jenkyns revenged himself when the landlady at the Cock and Feather at Grosmont charged him the excessive sum of tenpence for bread and cheese and beer. He paid quietly, and left, but soon the woman started running round and round the table where he had been sitting, calling out again and again: 'Six and four's ten, here's off again!' After an hour and a half of this, her son came home from work and saw her, and realized at once that it must be a spell. He went off to find Jenkyns, who said it served her right for overcharging, but that if the son were to remove a piece of paper from under the candlestick at home and burn it without looking at it, the spell would be broken. Oddly enough this story, which Miss Wherry collected in 1903 from a farmer's wife near Kentchurch, was also told to Mrs Leather in Weobly the following year, this time about a 'wise man' who had lived between Hereford and Bromyard about 1860; in his case, the scene was laid at the Buck

Inn, Woonton, the spell affected not only the landlady but an ostler and a maid too, and it was broken when, on the wizard's instructions, someone picked up the coins with a pair of tongs. Such an episode (if it ever really did occur) could be readily explained as hypnotism.

Some conjurers were reputed to own books of spells, which were greatly feared. One long-ago vicar of Beguildy in Radnorshire was said to have had one, which he once used to help a boxer from Llanbadarn Fynydd to defeat a much better man from Newtown. By his magic he nearly prevented the latter from reaching Llanbadarn Fynydd at all; at one place his road was almost blocked by a host of hares, while further on his carriage overturned while fording a brook. In the end he did reach Llanbadarn Fynedd, only to find himself almost helpless against the local fighter. The spectators were astonished, until someone spotted the vicar hiding in a hollow yew tree, with a huge book of spells open in front of him, directing evil spirits to attack the Newtown champion and assist his own client.

Anyone handling magic books without permission had to be quick witted to deal with the consequences; for instance, a servant of a wizard in Abergavenny was once carrying a book from his master to a fellow-conjurer when he yielded to curiosity, finding himself on a lonely hill-top, and opened it:

> Immediately an evil spirit appeared and asked what he should do for him. The man, though frightened, had the sense to tell him to level the hill for him. The evil spirit proceeded to do so, and as the earth began to move vigorously, the man, still more upset, accidentally turned over another page, when another spirit appeared and asked the same question. 'Ah well,' said the man, 'stop that evil spirit who is levelling the hill, and replace the soil as it was.' The second evil spirit proceeded to tackle his fellow-spirit, and after a severe struggle carried him off and replaced the soil. The countryman was now more than satisfied; he shut the book, replaced it, and carried it carefully to the conjurer to whom it had been sent.

Books of sorcery, however, were probably more often talked about than seen. The first-hand reminiscences of clients who consulted conjurers mention very little apparatus, if any. Often, for instance, when the client's purpose was to recover stolen goods, the conjurer simply told him to go back home, and that the thief would soon replace the goods of his own accord; this duly happened, presumably because everyone soon got to know that the wizard had been consulted, and the thief was too frightened to keep what he had taken. For there were plenty of tales of how a wizard could punish a thief; he might, for instance, hold him motionless in a cabbage field all through a cold winter night, or make the stolen goods too heavy for him to lift, or set a mark on his face, or give him no peace by night or day till he returned them.

Sometimes a conjurer might appease an angry client's curiosity by a display of scrying, as in the following anecdote from Herefordshire:

> George L. of Longtown, when in service as a farmer's boy, was sent from Longtown to Llandovery to consult a celebrated conjurer who had at one time a great reputation. George's master had lost a ram, and he desired to know who had stolen it. George paid half-a-crown, and was told that for another half-crown he could be shown the face of the thief. So he paid again, and waited in fear while the wizard, an old man in black, showed him in a large mirror a man whom he recognised as a neighbour of his master. He was told to go back and be at a certain place at the foot of the mountain at nine o'clock on the evening of the third day, when he would meet the man who had stolen the ram. He would say, 'Here's your master's ram, I found him astray.' Old George assured me that he met the man exactly at the time and place mentioned by the conjurer. The ram was returned, 'and them very words did he say!'

Scrying procedures may serve simply to give a focus to the client's own subconscious suspicions. This process can be seen from a story told by a woman at Prees Heath in 1915, though she herself would certainly have indignantly rejected such a rationalistic interpretation. It seems that in about 1830 a Farmer Booth of Twemlose had his wheat ricks burned one night, and went at once to Whitchurch to consult John Thorne, a famous 'cunning man'. Thorne made him swear not to bring his name into the matter if he took the case to law, and then he raised a vision of Booth's own stack-yard, with two men moving about in it, and a spark of light. 'Do you know them men?' said Thorne. 'I know enough', said Farmer Booth. He went straight home, and next day took out a summons against two young men, swearing that he had actually seen them start the blaze going. They were hanged, and are said to have confessed on the scaffold.

Some procedures were much nastier. In the Revd Francis Kilvert's parish of Clyro lived an old man called James Jones the Jockey who practised various forms of magic. In January 1871 this man's wife had some linen stolen:

> and her suspicions fell on some of the neighbours. She and her husband consulted the ordeal of the Key and the Bible. The key said 'Bella Whitney.' Then Jones the Jockey went to the brickyard and got some clay which he made into a ball. Inside the ball he put a live toad. The clay ball was either boiled or put into the fire, and during the process of boiling or baking the toad was expected to scratch the name of the thief upon a piece of paper put into the clay ball along with him. Some other horrible charm was used to discover the thief, the figure of a person being pricked out upon a piece of day. It is almost incredible.

It is good to learn from another entry in Kilvert's diary some five years later that this particular wizard, whose procedures involved such cruel and malicious magic, had at last 'emerged from the atmosphere of charms, incantations, astrology and witchcraft' by the time he died.

To understand the deep-rooted dread of witchcraft throughout the countryside, one must remember that witches were regarded as essentially destructive and malevolent, and that few people doubted the reality of their powers – did not the Bible itself mention witches? There were also, of course, some women who, like the male conjurers, acted as healers and thief-catchers for their communities; in the Border regions, however, they do not seem to have been as numerous or as famous as their male counterparts, and in any case they were not called 'witches' but 'wise' or 'cunning' women. As for the romantic notion cherished by modern occultists and novelists that the witches were really simply practising benevolent fertility rites in honour of some pre-Christian god or goddess, this would have totally amazed those to whom belief in witchcraft was a living part of their everyday outlook. To them, witches caused painful and lingering diseases and even death to human beings and farm animals, brought blight to crops, stole milk, spoilt butter, and ill-wished their victims. As late as 1905, a woman in the Wye Valley exclaimed to Mrs. L.M. Eyre, 'They make children spoonies, they do, or clubfoot, or bleed to death, and make poor animals holler and bawl, and oh, my dear, what should be done to they old women?'

Any solemn curse, whether uttered by a witch or an ordinary person, was regarded with deep fear, and doubly so if it was thought to be deserved. From an examination of complaints brought before the Diocesan Church Court of Hereford in the seventeenth century, Keith Thomas has shown that in this area at least it was fairly common for someone who believed himself to have been deeply wronged to utter a public ritualized curse, kneeling on bare knees in the open air, in the presence of friends and neighbours. Among examples he cites are how in 1614 Catherine Mason cursed a man who, she said, had killed her husband, and 'prayed to God that his house, children, and all that he had were one wild fire'; how John Smyth cursed William Walton of Yarpole in 1598, 'kneeling on his knees in the churchyard there, and praying unto God that a heavy vengeance and a heavy plague might light on him and all his cattle'; and how in 1703 Jane Smyth cursed Mrs Rod of Hereford, 'wishing that before she died she might crawl upon the ground like a toad on all fours'.

From public curses to private malevolent magic is a small step. In 1892 a square lead tablet, believed to date from the seventeenth century, was found behind a wall cupboard at Wilton Place, near Dymock, on the border of Gloucestershire and Herefordshire. It is now in Gloucester Folk Museum. On it are inscribed the name 'Sarah Ellis', written backwards, symbols of sun and moon, the number '369', and the words 'Hasmodat Acteus Magalesius Armenus Licus Nicon Mimon Zeper make this person to banish away from this place and country Amen to be desier Amen'. And in Hereford City Library Museum is a roughly made doll, believed to be of the eighteenth century, which was found in 1960 hidden in the cellar of a house in Hereford; with it was a paper which reads:

> Mary Ann Ward. I act this spell upon you from my whole heart wishing you to never rest nor eat nor sleep the restern part of your life. I hope your flesh will waste away. And I hope you will never spend another penny I ought to have. Wishing this from my whole heart.

Hereford Museum also displays a small wooden coffin containing a crude human figure, well nailed down; it is thought to be from the nineteenth century and was discovered in 1987 at a house in Woolhope.

Another possible, but less certain, example of cursing magic concerns a small cottage by the high road near Bunbury in Cheshire, which is locally known as the Image House because of the roughly carved stone heads and figures which decorate its walls and gateposts and stand in its garden. Local tradition declares that these were set up some time in the eighteenth century by a poacher who had returned to live there after serving an eight-year sentence for killing a gamekeeper in a fight. He is said to have carved each figure to represent the judge, sheriff's officers and witnesses at his trial, and to have cursed each one as he put it in its place.

It was generally assumed that witches too ill-wished their victims, and that they did so because they had been offended or meanly treated. Thus the Revd T.A. Davies was told in Monmouthshire in 1937 that a certain farmer had once scolded Mother Locke of Devauden for picking nuts from his hedge, to which she had replied, 'Ah well, this hedge will not trouble you for long' – and that very winter the hedge died. He was also told of a farmer whose pigs had all died after he had refused to sell them to a suspected witch. W.H. Howse quotes from a letter written in 1825 to the Chairman of Talgarth Petty Sessions complaining about a similar incident; the five signatories alleged that a certain Thomas Ralph was suspected of 'having dominion over the evil spirit', and in particular that once, having failed to buy twenty wethers and a pig, he had 'witched the animals, so that all the wethers had died and the pig went quite distracted and was a terror to the neighbourhood'. As late as 1895, Mrs Murray-Aynsley records, an old woman came in great distress to the wife of a clergyman in the Golden Valley because her neighbours were accusing her of having bewitched two people who had recently died of flu – 'Indeed, indeed, I did no sich thing. I never ill-wished them, nor nothin', and I never said as they was marked for death, nor nothin'.'

Besides causing illness and death, witches were often said to be able to immobilize horses. Miss Burne gives an anecdote about an old witch called Priss Morris who lived at Cleobury North, and who had a grudge against a farmer for having prevented her from gleaning in his fields. One day, this man's wagoner was driving past the old woman's cottage when the horses stopped dead, and no amount of whipping could make them move. The farmer himself came by, and when he too could not get the team to start he went and hammered on the cottage door:

> 'Whad'n yo' bin doin'' at my 'orses?' says he. 'I anna bin doin' nothing at your horses,' says she. 'Yes, you han,' says he, 'here's a good road and a level, and they canna get by your house, let me thrash 'em as much as I like. You bin doin' summat at 'em,' he says, 'and if yo' dunna take it off 'em again, I'll flog you till you canna stir from the spot.' 'I anna done nothin' at 'em,' she says again. 'Yes, you han,' he says; 'now, you say "Pray God bless you and your horses," or I'll flog you till you canna stand.' 'No, no.' she says, 'I canna say it.' 'You just say it,' he says, 'or I'll serve you the same as them poor horses.' ' "My God bless you and your horses!" I'll say that,' she says. 'No, no, that wunna do,' he says; 'I'll have nothing to do with your God,' he says. 'I worship the true God, and I'll have nothing to do with none other. You say "May God bless you and your horses".' 'May God bless you and your horses!' says she. And the horses started off again this very minute, and took the load back home.

This story, together with another Shropshire one in which a witch is forced to say 'God bless the calves' rather then 'My God bless the calves', is unusual and interesting in its implication that witches worshipped the Devil. This idea, so constantly recurring in the witch-trials of the sixteenth and seventeenth centuries, is much more rarely found in oral tales and traditions; presumably the ordinary country people, unlike judges and heresy-hunters, were more concerned about the practical damage they thought a witch could do than about theological theories as to how she got her powers. No doubt they would have agreed that her wickedness (like all human wickedness) was due to her yielding to Satan's temptations, and they might well have also thought that she had pledged her soul to him in exchange for the right to call on him for aid. But what is unusual about the dialogue which this storyteller put in the mouths of old Priss Morris and the farmer is that it formalizes this relationship into that between a worshipper and her god. It may be that some recollection of the printed accounts of witch-trials was still remaining in nineteenth-century Shropshire, or it may be that the Scriptural account of Christ's encounter with Satan in the wilderness had familiarized the storyteller with the idea that Satan would demand to be worshipped before he would bestow power. In any case, it is necessary to stress (in view of the unhistorical but popular modern theories about secret fertility cults, Horned Gods, Moon Goddesses and so forth) that the 'god' implied in this anecdote is no more and no less than the Biblical Devil – as Miss Burne, who collected and published it, clearly recognised.

Other beliefs about witches found in oral traditions were that they kept toads or other animals as familiars, and that they could transform themselves into animals. The most widespread tale about a witch's transformation tells how huntsmen used to chase a hare which always escaped and disappeared near some old woman's cottage, till one day a hound managed to bite it, after which the old woman was seen to be limping. Other forms a witch could adopt were those of a cat, a rat, or a bat-like creature that vanished if caught. An old woman living in the Vale of Ewias (near Llanthony) was a fortune-teller and, reputedly, a witch who could transform herself into a crow. She was nicknamed 'Old Hag'. Once, some children who shouted insults at her were pursued by a crow which swooped round them until they reached Llanthony Priory. On another occasion, she stared silently at a shepherd who had chased her off his path, and from then on his sheep and his dogs were harried by a huge crow whenever he took that path.

Witches were also said to ride about on various weird objects, not simply on broomsticks; at Trelleck, so Miss Wherry was told in 1904, a man once saw three witches riding down the Buckle – one on a hurdle, 'another old hag leppin' an' gallopin' on a ladder, an' behind her came another, as I'm alive, trundlin' on a common grindstone!' Around St Briavels, at the same period, it was thought that they would ride on scythes, and so one must always sharpen one's scythe and lay it edge upwards before leaving it. At Trelleck again, in 1937, the Revd T.A. Davies was told how a man once spied on a witch as she took out her stick, murmuring 'Out I go!', and flew away; he took another stick, copied her, and followed her to the cellars of a nearby mansion, where they both got drunk. They were caught and condemned to death for robbery, but at the foot of the gallows they both took out their sticks, crying 'Up we go!', and soared away over the prison wall.

These tales about magic riding are fairly lighthearted – indeed, the last one among them has a parallel from Herefordshire about a boy who followed not witches but fairies, which was clearly told simply as entertainment. More serious was the fear that witches could get into stables at night, and torment the horses by tangling their manes and tails and riding them till they sweated. Sometimes it was thought that the witch took the form of a piece of straw to do this. Davies was told of a carter who saw a straw on a horse's back, tossed it out of the stable, and then saw a second one which he happened to double over before tossing it away; he then heard two voices: 'Come along, Hannah, we must be going.' – 'I'm afraid I can't, as I'm nearly doubled up.'

There were, of course, numerous charms to defend homes and farm buildings from these dangers. The commonest was to put up birch and mountain ash (wittan, rowan) over the doors, sometimes in the form of a cross; often this was done on May Eve (see below, pp. 157-58), and the twigs were left in place till the same date next year. Mrs Eyre and the Revd T.A. Davies both mention hawthorn (whitethorn) being used in the same way, at St Briavels and in Monmouthshire respectively, while the former also mentions twigs of yew. For Herefordshire, Mrs Leather lists as protective charms, besides the birch and wittan twigs, horseshoes, a stick of elder with nine notches on it, and a pattern of nine crosses chalked on the doorstep. In Cheshire, it was thought that a holly growing near the house afforded protection; in the same county in the early nineteenth century, according to Fletcher Moss, a parson's wig hung up in the fireplace was sure to stop any witch from coming down the chimney. Such charms were still in use in living memory; as recently as 1952, J.H. Massingham writes of seeing a dead ash sapling clamped to a barn door near Cusop to keep witches away.

It was also held that attack is the best form of defence. One way was to drive a knife or a large nail into the witch's footprint in order to break her power; this method is frequently mentioned all over the Border region, with slight variations – for instance the conjurer at Trelleck, Jenkyns, used to insist that one must get right close up to her and stab the third heel-mark from where she was standing. Another universally-known way of breaking a witch's power forever was to draw her blood 'above the breath', i.e. by scratching or stabbing her face. This could lead to tragic violence, as in the murder of Nanny Morgan of Westwood Common, in Shropshire, in 1857. She was an unpleasant old woman who in her younger days had been a thief and had later learned fortune-telling from gypsies; many consulted her, but she was feared rather than respected, and was said to have the evil eye – 'and no one durst refuse her nothing, for fear she should do something at them'. There was a much younger man living with her for whom she had a 'violent affection', and who feared her temper and her spells too deeply to leave her. One day, after a violent quarrel, he stabbed her repeatedly in the face, neck and arms; his defence was that he had not meant to kill, simply to break her power. He was condemned to death, but later reprieved and imprisoned.

To break one particular spell, or rather to induce the witch herself to remove it, the usual method was to employ a counter-charm of a type which generally involved either pins or burning. Mrs Leather gives instances of people burning the heart of a bullock, sheep or other animal, all stuck with pins, or burning a sprig of broom, or a lock of hair of the person bewitched; the idea was to cause such agony to the witch that she would be forced to come to the house of her victim, confess, and remove her spell. Similar procedures are reported from Monmouthshire in the late nineteenth century, such as cutting out the heart of a mare whose death was said to have been caused by witchcraft, sticking pins in, and sewing it back; or boiling the heart of a bewitched pig for a day and a night so that the rest of the herd might be saved. Writing in 1898, Fletcher Moss tells of a case he knew of in Cheshire, where a witch's power had been broken 'by having her image with nine pins stuck through it, and the nail out of a horseshoe, also a toad, all put in a bottle and burned by John, the Wizard of Hale Barns'.

The 'conjurers' and 'wise men' were often consulted in such matters; so too were various wandering rogues, for example a quack who was charged at Presteigne Assizes in 1867 for obtaining money by false pretences. He had sold to a sick man at Rhayader, for £4, a charm to be worn round the neck to break a spell; it was a piece of paper with geometrical designs and the following words, which seem to be part of a list of protective angels:

> The fourth is Maynons, one of the powers who hath the ability of superficient administration and protection, that is at one and the same time to be present with many. His presents [i.e. presence] must be sought by humility and prayer. The fifth good genius is Gaounum, an angel of celestial brightness who hath the peculiar ability of rendering his pupil invisible to any evil spirit whatsoever.

A charm like this is a late echo of the writings of learned Renaissance occultists; that a sick man should pay a quack £4 for it is a pathetic instance of how the discarded learning of one period may be exploited long afterwards by those who prey on human fears and credulity.

FIVE

FAIRIES

On 8 December 1870, Kilvert noted in his diary that he had been talking about fairies with a certain David Price who lived near Capel-y-ffin, who told him:

> We don't see them now because we have more faith in the Lord Jesus and don't think of them. But I believe the fairies travel yet. My sister's son, who works at the collieries in Monmouthshire, once told me he saw the fairies dancing to beautiful music, sweet music, in a Monmouthshire field. Then they all came over a stile close by him. They were very yellow in the face, between yellow and red, and dressed almost all in red. He did not like to see them. He fully believes in them, and so do I. 'They were about the size of that girl,' he said, calling to a child of eleven who was blowing the fire to stand up.

Kilvert's other countrymen, however, spoke of such beliefs as things long past. Old Hannah Whitney was his best informant on the topic; she was ninety years old in 1870, when she told him how as a child of eight or nine she used to listen to her grandfather and his friends telling tales about the fairies, in which they fully believed. She told Kilvert how 'Hob with his lantern' was to be seen by one particular pool (though she had never seen him herself), and how people used to warn one another to come home early from market 'lest they should be led astray by the goblin lantern, and boys would wear their hats the wrong way lest they should be enticed into fairy rings and made to dance'. She knew a story about a girl from Llan Pica who had been led astray in this way and at last killed by fairies, and another about an old man 'who used to sleep in the mill trough at the Rhos Goch Mill, and used to hear the fairies come in at night and dance to sweet fiddles on the mill floor'. Although Kilvert clearly enjoyed collecting such traditions, his other gleanings on this topic were meagre; in November 1871 Mrs Meredith of White Ash told him 'the old story of how the fairies used to feed the ploughmen at Penyshaplwyd till the wicked boy stole the silver knife'; and in February 1872 Hannah Jones told him that the Blue Rocks of Blaen Cwm, above Llanbedr, were one of the last places where fairies were ever seen.

Similar ideas could still be met with in Monmouthshire in 1903, when a schoolgirl collector, Miss Beatrix Wherry, recorded some traditions from a cottage woman living near Trelleck whom she calls 'Mrs Pryce'. She too thought of fairies as fairly small, and with queer complexions; she said their homes were underground, where they 'lived fine', and that they were about the size of a six-year-old child, barefoot, dressed in white, with lovely white skins, but also with white hair and white eyes. There had once been a little old fairy woman who came to Monmouth market; people knew her for what she was because 'she had white hair done in an old-fashioned way, and white eyes'. Fairies would carry off anyone who joined in their dance. There was a tale about two young men who saw fairies dancing round an oak, one of whom joined them and vanished at once; his companion was accused of murdering him, but the lost youth reappeared next night and explained what had happened, though later he went back to the fairies and stayed with them for ever. Mrs Pryce also believed that fairies had often stolen children in the old days, because 'they liked the babies of we country folk, as being fine and solid-like, and they used to rear them up with their own'. Once a child was stolen, she thought, there was no way one could get it back.

The dread of being carried off by the fairies was one of the most persistent elements in the tradition. Miss Burne said that the only belief about fairies still held in Shropshire in her time was the fear of what would happen if one stepped inside their rings. Mrs Leather met a Herefordshire woman who firmly believed that one of her own relatives had suffered this experience. As the woman's family came from Radnorshire, Mrs Leather considered it an obviously Celtic story; however, such tales are to be found in non-Celtic areas too. The narrator localized it at Kington:

> Mrs W., aged 75, one of the oldest inhabitants of Wigmore in 1909, told me a fairy story of her mother's. She said it happened to her mother's first cousin, and her mother remembered it well. The cousin, a girl of about eighteen, was very fond of dancing; she insisted on going to all the balls for miles around; wherever there was dancing going on, there was she. Her people told her something would happen to her one day, and one night when she was coming home just by the 'Dancing Gates' near Kington, she heard beautiful music. It was the music of the fairies, and she was caught into the ring. Search was made for her, and she appeared to her friends from time to time, but when they spoke to her she immediately disappeared. Her mother was told (probably by the wise man or woman) that if seen again she must be very quickly seized, without speaking, or she would never come back. So one day, a year after her disappearance, her mother saw her, and took hold of her dress before she could escape. 'Why mother,' she said, 'where have you been since yesterday?' The time must have gone very merrily with her, for the year had seemed but one day.
>
> The girl was none the worse, however, and they sent her to serve at a small shop in Kington. Before long the fairies came there, and used to steal little things off the counter. Afraid she herself might be accused when the things were missed, the girl told her employer. 'How can you see the fairies?' he said. 'They are invisible.' She told him that when she lived with them they used a kind of ointment, and she rubbed a little of it on one day, to try the effect. She could always see the little people with that eye since. She afterwards warned the fairies that their thefts were discovered; they were very much puzzled to find themselves visible to her. She was careful not to explain, lest they might try to damage the eye with which she could see them.

Herefordshire around 1900 was still fairly rich in such traditions and tales, particularly, Mrs Leather found, in the areas where Welsh influence was strongest. In Shropshire, in contrast, Miss Burne found no tales and only slight remnants of belief – a fear of stepping inside the rings, and a vague notion of one informant that the fairies dance. In Cheshire, fairy-belief seems to have died out even more thoroughly, almost its only appearance being in the joke about the horse-thief quoted in an earlier chapter (see p. 51). In Herefordshire, however, most of the traditional tales and ideas can be found represented in Mrs Leather's collection – including the dialect word for 'fairies,' which to all the old people was 'fareeses' (pronounced almost like 'Pharisees'), a form found also in the dialects of Sussex and Suffolk. They were thought of as small, and often invisible, beings who could dance, fly, steal from human homes, lead people astray in wild places, reward those who treat them well, but punish others with illness. They were often feared, chiefly for their powers of abducting adults and stealing babies, for whom they would substitute changelings. A woman at Kington named Jean Probert had a story about this, which she said had been told her by 'a woman who knew that it was true'; in fact, like the tale of the girl carried into fairyland, it is only a localized version of a legend known in very many parts of Great Britain and Europe:

> A woman had a baby that never grew; it was always hungry, and never satisfied, but it lay in its cradle year after year, never walking, and nothing seemed to do it good. Its face was hairy and strange-looking. One day the woman's elder son, a soldier, came home from the war, and was surprised to see his brother still in the cradle. But when he looked in he said, 'That's not my brother, mother.' 'It is indeed,' said the mother. 'We'll see about that,' he said. So he obtained first a fresh egg, and blew out the contents, filling the shell with malt and hops. Then he began to brew over the fire. At this a laugh came from the cradle. 'I am old, old, ever so old,' said the changeling, 'but I never saw a soldier brewing beer in an egg shell before!' Then he gave a terrible shriek, for the soldier went for him with a whip, chasing him round and round the room what had never left his cradle! At last he vanished through the door, and when the soldier went out after him he met on the threshold his long-lost brother. He was a man twenty-

four years of age, fine and healthy. The fairies had kept him in a beautiful palace under the rocks, and fed him on the best of everything. He should never be as well off again, he said, but when his mother called he had to come home.

Another type of fairy attested in Herefordshire is the Brownie, who is said to work helpfully in homes and farms, and for whom, in some houses, the iron bar over the hearth would serve as a seat. But Brownies could also be mischievous and troublesome creatures, in which case they readily merged into the bogies, buggans and boggarts who were thought to play tricks like poltergeists indoors, and to waylay and terrify travellers in the lanes. There are several tales about these in Shropshire and Cheshire, where the creatures in question are generally defined by the storytellers as 'spirits' or 'ghosts'; an example will be given in a later chapter (pp. 91–2).

In Shropshire in the 1840s a nursemaid used to amuse the children she was looking after by telling them about a pair of 'bogeys', which in this tale meant household goblins who were just mischievous, not frightening. The story was written down in dialect spelling by the folklore collector Georgina Jackson, and passed from her notebooks into Charlotte Burne's classic work on Shropshire folklore. Her spelling is here slightly modified for clarity:

> Behappen yo never 'eard the tale about the salt-box? Well, yo see, there wuz wunst some folks o' the name o' Runnells [Reynolds] as lived at the Gorsey Bank, an' they'd a rare good farm, and the house wuz a good 'un, only it wuz an ancient owd place as 'ad bin a fine mansion, or summat o' that, in some king's reign. But the worst on it wuz as it wuz 'aunted wi' sperrits, or boogies, or whadever yo callen 'em, an' they weren like a lickle owd mon an' 'ooman, and the Runnelses weren plagued to death wi' 'em, for they weren allays prancin' about the 'ouse an' the fold an' the fields an everyweer, an' nuthin cudna stand nor rest for 'em, an' they went on an' on for iverlastin, they weren that unlucky and naughty! An' they couldna get shot o' 'em, no road.
>
> They fetched the passon to 'em wunst, but they didna mind 'im, an' maden all manner o' game on 'im, an' I think as 'e wuz frittened on 'em.

So at last they wuz gotten so bad as the Runnellses coulna put up wi' 'em no longer; so they maden up their minds to go an' live at a bytack [smallholding] a good way off, an' try an' get away from the boogies.

So they gotten their things away a few at a time, as they could, unknowns to the owd mon an' 'ooman, till at last one night they gotten right clear off, an' left the boogies in the empty 'ouse. So atter they wuz come to the new place, they wuz feelin' fine an' glad as they wuz got out on 'em so well, an' begunnen to unload an' fettle [tidy] up a bit. An' everythin' wuz comen a'right, all but an owd salt-box as they weren uncommon fond on, and by gum if they hadna left 'im behind! An' they weren desp'rate vexed, an' told the cowman to go an' fetch 'im, but 'e wuz to be mighty careful as the boogies didna see 'im, or goodnis knows whad!

So 'e set out, an' 'e didna like the job at all, but they senten young Yeddart [Edward] wi' 'im, an' if yo'll believe me they 'adna gone no great way when by gum who should they see, comin' along right jimmy [sprightly], but the owd mon an' 'ooman; an' they seed the cowman an' Yeddert in a minute, so it wunna no use tryin' to turn back agen, and they sayen, "We'n brought yore salt-box, we'n brought yore salt-box!"

So then they all wenten to the 'ouse, an' the Runnellses weren in a most desp'rate way when they seen the boogies comin', but they acted as if they though nothing of it, an' maden out as they weren right glad to see 'em agen, an' axed 'em to come in an' 'ave some meat an' drink. So they wenten i' the best parlour, an' while they weren there the Runnellses gotten a lot o' logs from the 'ood pile an' maden a rousin' big fire i' the brew'ouse, an' then they gotten a boutin [truss] o' straw an' put it i' front o' the fire, an' maden the cowman lie down theer an' covered 'im all o'er wi' the straw, an' then they axed the boogies to come in an' warm 'em for it wuz a cold time o' year, an' put 'em to sit on the boutin. So they gied 'em some beef an' a can o' beer, an' comen an' talked to 'em an' told 'em the raps [news], an' all on a sudden up jumps th' cowman an' chucks 'em right smack into the fire, straw an' all, an' then they setten about 'em an' poked 'em wi' pikels [pitchforks] an' besoms, an' kept 'em in the blaze till they weren all snirped [shrivelled] up an' burnt to ash. An' they never seed no more on 'em atter that, but wenten back to the Gorsey Bank an' 'ad some peace an' quietness.

A persistent belief in supernatural beings and their activities usually requires both psychological function and some tangible 'evidence' to support it, especially if, as in the case of fairies, it has never been endorsed by the official teachings of religion. To some extent, belief in fairies satisfied the psychological need to account for unexplained illness, especially in the case of the ailing or mentally defective infants which were diagnosed as being changelings; in this field, however, it had a powerful rival in the witchcraft-belief, which was far more vigorously held, had Scriptural (and, in earlier centuries, legal) backing, and purported to explain a much wider range of illnesses and misfortunes. The belief in fairies, though very ancient, was comparatively functionless in nineteenth-century rural society, and so withered more rapidly than the belief in witches.

A few material items, however, served as 'evidence' to bolster it. First and foremost, of course, the obvious 'fairy rings' in the grass, but also occasional finds of small, unfamiliar objects in the ground. Leland, the Tudor topographer and antiquary, says that in his time the country people called the Roman coins they sometimes found around Kenchester 'dwarfs' money'; in modern times, H.L.V. Fletcher says that Roman coins from Bolitree were sometimes called 'fairies' money' and W.H. Howse tells how, when a Roman mosaic pavement was found at Painscastle in the nineteenth century, it had to be covered over again as soon as possible because of the fears of local people who thought it had something to do with the fairies, who would be offended at its being excavated. One of Miss Burne's informants owned a fairy's grindstone which her son had turned up when ploughing, which she said was 'about as large as a penny-piece, with a hole in the middle for the handle to go through'; this, Miss Burne judged, was probably really an old spindle-whorl. And in 1915 there was a strong belief at Prees Heath, near Whitchurch, that fairies had lived on the great peat-bog called Fenn's Moss on the border between Shropshire and Flint, because one often found their tobacco-pipes there; on inspecting these fairy pipes, Edmund Vale recognized them for what they were – small seventeenth-century clay pipes, which workmen cutting peat had dropped long ago!

Besides the usual types of fairies there were also, in some areas, a few individualized spirits lurking in lakes, ponds and rivers. They were described in frightening and repulsive terms, and young children were taught to fear them; indeed, the whole point of these tales was to ensure that youngsters did not play too near dangerous stretches of water. The best known is Jenny Greenteeth, 'an old woman who lurks beneath the green weeds that cover stagnant ponds; Ellesmere children are warned that if they venture too near such places, she will stretch out her long arms and drag them to her.' She was also known in Cheshire. Along the Welsh side of the Border, and especially in Monmouthshire, according to Miss Ruth Tongue, the water-ogre was a male figure called Nicky Nicky Nye, with ghastly green eyes, who lurked in rivers; there was a warning rhyme about him:

Nicky Nicky Nye,
He pulls you down,
Underneath the water,
To drown, drown, die.

Bogies of this type may perhaps even nowadays be taken seriously by children, but among adults the belief in any type of fairy, already fading fast a hundred years ago, must now be quite extinct. There is no reason, however, why one should not still tell as entertainment tales about supernatural beings in whom one does not believe — mermaids, giants and dragons, for instance, as stories in previous chapters have shown. Two well-known Shropshire legends involve the world of fairies. First, the story of Wild Edric's marriage, as told in the twelfth-century work of Walter Map, *De Nugis Curialis*, which is a typical medieval romance on the well-known theme of a man's love for a supernatural maiden whom he first wins but later loses. Rescued from the obscurity of medieval Latin by Miss Burne, this picturesque tale now has an assured place among English legends.

The story goes that one evening Edric lost his way in a forest where he had been hunting, and after wandering a long way with only one page to accompany him, he at length saw the light of a large house among the trees. Inside, a group of beautiful women were singing and dancing; they were taller and lovelier than mortal women, and Edric at once fell in love with the fairest of them. He forced his way into the building, broke the magic circle of their dance, and dragged the girl away with him, though her companions fought hard to prevent him. He took her home, but for three whole days she would not speak; on the fourth she broke her silence, and told him he would be lucky in all that he did, provided he never reproached her on account of her former home, her sisters, or any aspect of her past. If he did, not only would she leave him for ever, but he would lose both luck and life. He promised to observe this rule, and they were married with great splendour. For many years they were happy, till one day when Edric had again been hunting he discovered when he returned home that his wife was absent, and for some time he could not find her anywhere. When she reappeared, he burst out angrily, 'I suppose it was your sisters who kept you out so late?' At once she vanished, and though he wandered miserably in the forest, weeping and calling to her, he never found her again, but pined away and died of grief. But Walter Map adds that they had a son, Alnod, who gave the large Shropshire manor of Lydbury North to the Bishopric of Hereford, and that he was the only man of mixed human and elfin blood who had ever been known to prosper.

This legend has many parallels, both among early medieval lays and romances and among folk tales; among the latter, the Welsh stories of lake-maidens who marry mortals, but vanish if struck or accidentally touched with iron, are particularly close. In modern folklore, as was said in Chapter Two, Edric has himself taken on supernatural characteristics of various types – as a fairy-like 'knocker' in the mines, as an undying leader, as the leader of a spirit host that appears in times of danger. It was also sometimes said that he haunts the Stretton Hills in the form of a black dog with fiery eyes.

The second Shropshire legend involving the fairy world is that of the White Cow of Mitchell's Fold. This place is a damaged stone circle on the moors on Corndon Hill, very near the Welsh Border. The fullest version of the Mitchell's Fold story, which was widely known in Miss Burne's time, is as follows:

> In times gone by, before anyone now living can remember, there was once a dreadful famine all about this country, and the people had like to have been clemmed. There were many more living in this part then than what there are now, and times were very bad indeed. And all they had to depend on was that there used to come a fairy cow up on the hill, up at Mitchell's Fold, night and morning, to be milked. A beautiful pure white cow she was, and no matter how many came

to milk her, there was always enough for all, so long as everyone that came only took one pailful. It was in this way: if anyone was to milk her dry, she would go away and never come again; but so long as everyone took only a pailful apiece, she never would be dry. They might take whatever sort of vessel they liked, to milk her into, so long as it was only one apiece, she would always fill it. Well, and at last there came an old witch, Mitchell her name was. A bad old woman she was, and did a deal of harm, and had a spite against everybody. And she brought a riddle [i.e. a sieve], and milked the cow into that, and of course the poor thing couldn't fill it. And the old woman milked her, and milked her, and at last she milked her dry, and the cow was never seen there again, not after. Folks say she went off into Warwickshire like a crazy thing, and turned into the wild dun cow that Guy of Warwick killed; but anyhow they say she was sadly missed in this country, and a many died after she was gone, and there's never been so many living about here, not since. But the old woman got her punishment. She was turned into one of them stones on the hillside, and all the other stones were put up round her to keep her in, and that's how the place came to be called Mitchell's Fold, because her name was Mitchell, you see.

The magical cow was also sometimes said to have belonged to a giant, not to the world of fairies, but its sad fate remained the same. A similar tale is told at Audlem in Cheshire, to account for a huge bone displayed in the tower of Doddington Park; it is said to be that of a wonderful cow which died of grief when it failed to fill a witch's sieve with milk. It is probably relevant that milking cows dry, or milking them till blood came, was one of the evil deeds of which witches were accused in real life.

Finally, another medieval legend from the Border deserves mention, though its hero, King Herla, was not remembered in nineteenth-century folk tradition as Wild Edric was. This legend, too, we owe to Walter Map, and it gives us one of the finest early accounts of the Wild Hunt – the phantom host of huntsmen who ride through the air or haunt the woods, and who are mentioned in the traditions of many European lands; In some cases they are thought of as demons, in others as ghosts, in others as elves or other types of supernatural being; in the case of King Herla and his men, Map tells us, their strange fate resulted from an encounter with a 'pigmy', who is clearly a fairy of some sort:

> It is said that King Herla, one of the earliest of British kings, once met another king who was a pigmy, no bigger than a monkey. This little creature, so the story goes, was mounted on a large goat. He had the general features of Pan; his face was a fiery red, his head large, and he had a long red beard which reached to his chest. He was gaily attired in the dappled hide of a fawn, and his legs ended in goats' hoofs. He introduced himself to King Herla as follows: 'I am lord of many kings and princes, over an unnumbered and innumerable people, and have been sent, a willing envoy, by them to you... Let us agree, therefore, that I shall attend your wedding, and that you shall attend mine a year later.'

Sure enough, the pigmy king appeared at Herla's wedding with a huge train of followers, bringing wonderful food and drink for the feast. A year later, according to his promise, Herla went to attend the pigmy king's wedding, held in a magnificent palace in the depths of a mountain, to which the entrance was by way of a cave in a high cliff. When the time came to leave, the little king loaded Herla and his companions with gifts; among other things,

> ...he gave the king a small blood-hound to carry, strictly enjoining him that on no account should any of his company dismount till the dog had leapt from the arms of its bearer.

But when Herla came out again into the sunlight of his own kingdom and asked news from a shepherd, he found that not one year only but many hundreds of years had passed since he had last been there, and he himself was only remembered as a king of ancient times who had vanished into a cliff and never been seen again.

> The king, who thought he had only stayed for three days, could scarce sit his horse for amazement. Some of his company, forgetting the pigmy's orders, dismounted before the dog had alighted, and instantly fell into dust. Then the king, seeing why they had dissolved, warned the rest under pain of the like death, not to touch the earth

till the dog had leapt. But the dog has never alighted. And according to story this King Herla and his band still hold on their mad course, wandering with neither stop nor stay. Recently, however, since the first year of the coronation of our present King Henry [II], they are said to have ceased to visit our land in force. In that year, many Welshmen saw them plunge into the Wye, the river of Hereford.

In a later passage, Walter Map gives what appears to be a variant of the same tradition; 'Herlethingus' is probably a corruption of an Anglo-Saxon word for 'meeting, gathering, court of judgement' combined with Herla's name.

Nocturnal companies and squadrons, known as the Herlethingus, were fairly well known appearances in England until the time of our present lord, King Henry II. They were troops engaged in endless wandering, in an aimless round, keeping an awe-struck silence, and in them many persons who were known to have died were seen alive. This household of Herlethingus was last seen in the marches of Wales and Hereford in the first year of the reign of King Henry II, about noon. They travelled as we do, with wagons and sumpter horses, pack-saddles and panniers, hawks and hounds, and a concourse of men and women. Those who saw them first raised the whole country against them with horns and shouts... but they rose into the air and vanished suddenly.

In these phantom hosts, fairies, undying human beings, and the ghosts of men all meet and mingle.

SIX
GHOSTS

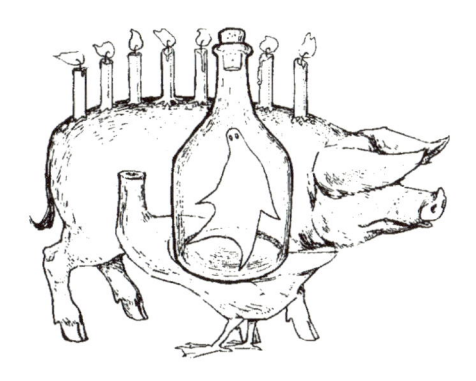

In our own times, the belief in ghosts has certainly not lost its hold on the human mind. In earlier centuries it was widespread, but not by any means universal. One of Miss Burne's informants, fortified by a robust and logical Christian faith, firmly rejected the whole idea: 'I dunna believe as there's anything in it, as the dead come back. If they bin gone to the good place, they wouldna want to come back, and if they bin gone to the tother place, they wouldna be let to!' This clear-headed attitude was rare, however, and the rich crop of ghost stories along the Welsh Border proves that many people contrived to reconcile Christian teaching with a belief that the dead can and do 'come again'.

One story, recorded by the Revd R.T. Davies of Llanishen in 1937, does reveal a certain theological unease about the true status of ghosts: A certain man had promised to watch all night beside a woman's newly-dug grave inside a church, but on the vicar's advice he had a Bible with him, and had a circle drawn round his chair. At midnight, in rushed a demon dog which dug up the corpse, skinned it, and ate the body, but left the skin whole. The man hooked the skin and dragged it inside the protective circle, where the dog was not able to get at it. When dawn had broken and the dog had vanished, the vicar advised the man to burn the skin, 'for evil spirits use those skins to appear to the relatives of the dead person, and frighten them'. We probably have in this story an echo of the views held by some Protestant theologians, in reaction against the doctrine of Purgatory, that any apparitions of ghosts are really nothing but devils in disguise, aping the features of the dead.

Few people worried about such points. Belief in ghosts was, and is, vigorous and persistent, and has given rise to tales and traditions of many different kinds. There are, for instance, the numerous legends about apparitions of people famous in history, usually those who have died tragically, and almost always located in some house or castle with which they were associated in life, or in which their descendants still live. These historical and ancestral ghosts are generally spoken of with affectionate pride, though occasionally their appearance is said to portend a death in the family, as does that of a young girl's ghost at Combermere Abbey. They are the best-known category of ghosts, being constantly mentioned by compilers of guide-books and writers of local histories.

But it is not only historical and aristocratic ghosts that are said to walk, nor are they in fact the ones that present the most interesting aspects to collectors of folklore. One way to get a representative cross-section of the great variety of spectres still remembered in popular tradition is to glance through the two volumes of *Cheshire Village Memories* published by the Federation of Women's Institutes in that county in 1952 and 1961. The range is remarkable, and many themes familiar to folklorists can be found there. Besides the story of the Headless Woman of Duddon, discussed in a previous chapter, we read that the Combermere Arms Hotel at Burleydam was formerly haunted, but that two clergymen got the ghost into a bottle which they buried under the threshold, where it will safely remain so long as the bottle is not broken (a favourite theme, of which more below.) At Gawsworth a former sexton, Mr Holland, described two ghosts. The first is that of Mary Fitton, a scandalous lady-in-waiting to Queen Elizabeth I, who haunts the church; she would come out from behind the altar, dressed in a green riding habit, and glide down the aisle looking at the monuments of her ancestors, while the church grew deathly cold. The other ghost is of a local eccentric, an eighteenth-century writer and dancing-master nicknamed 'Maggotty' Johnson, who insisted on being buried, not in the churchyard, but in a little wood, where his copiously inscribed tombstone may still be seen. Mr Holland declared that one moonlit night he had met old 'Maggotty' riding a white horse, had followed him into the wood, and had been just in time to hear the tombstone drop back into place with a loud bump. These two tales from one informant make an interesting contrast. Mary Fitton's ghost is the more dignified, though her green robe may hint (in accordance with an old system of colour symbolism) at the immorality of her life. 'Maggotty' Johnson's ghost arouses more complex reactions, for that bump of the falling stone is both humorous and alarming in its prosaic realism – one may suspect that it is this tale, focusing upon the solitary and eccentric grave, which makes the deeper impression upon local hearers.

Then there are grotesque spectral animals. One is said to haunt a lane called The Hollows at Lostock Gralam, according to an informant who was eighty when she told the tale, and who claimed that it was once seen by her own brother; it is the ghost of a pig, and its back is stuck all over with lighted candles! Another lane, from Stanney to Stoak, is haunted by a headless duck; when it was alive it used to lurk there, upsetting and alarming passers-by, until a posse of bold men ambushed it, cut its head off, and buried the corpse – but all in vain, for still the duck hurries past, though now without a head. Country lanes are a favourite setting for tales of animal ghosts in many parts of England; the most frequent are those of dogs, but black sheep and calves are also fairly common, while black pigs and sows are particularly frequent in Welsh lore. Examples of sinister black dogs will be given below; at Withington, however, there is a tradition about a helpful one: A woman missionary was once walking through the woods on her way to a prayer meeting where she was due to preach, when she saw a man who was known to be a dangerous character coming towards her; suddenly a large black dog appeared at her side, and accompanied her until she was safely out of the woods, when it disappeared as mysteriously as it had come.

At Norley there is a ghost whose coming is itself an omen of death; it is the spectre of a woman, which is said to walk up the steps of a well in Pytchley's Hollow whenever someone in the village is about to die. The association with water is interesting, since many anonymous female ghosts, often described simply as 'the White Lady', are said to haunt pools, rivers and wells; they are probably the modern counterparts of the ancient Celtic goddesses of wells and springs. At Swettenham we find another type of female ghost, associated with a tale of ghost-laying more dignified than that at Burleydam; it is that of a nun who is said to have haunted the church after being murdered for breaking her vows by marrying, until some past Rector there exorcised her spirit by reciting an Elizabethan form of absolution every night for two weeks.

Marbury Hall, near Comberbach, which was demolished in 1968, was the setting for a complex and vigorous tale which arose from the fact that a skeleton was kept there for many years. What the true history of that macabre heirloom may have been is not now remembered; instead, local storytellers have evolved explanations of their own. According to the traditions gathered in Cheshire Village Memories, long ago some member of the Barrymore family that owned Marbury Hall travelled to Egypt, where a young Egyptian girl fell so deeply in love with him that she followed him all the way back to England, and married him. For some reason she asked that when she came to die her body should be kept at the Hall, not laid in the churchyard; however, when she died (murdered, some say, on the stairs of the Hall), her request was ignored and she was given a normal funeral. Soon afterwards, bells began to ring of their own accord, and her ghost was seen riding a white horse; to put an end to the haunting, her body was brought home, and laid in an oak chest. There the skeleton was kept until the 1930s, when, it is said, it was reburied in the church at midnight.

There are alternative versions of the story where the lady simply requires her coffin, not her exposed skeleton, to be kept at home, this presumably being regarded as less gruesome. Again, some say it was an embalmed body; not knowing whose it was or why it was kept in the entrance hall, the owners of the Hall tried once to bury it in family vault, and another time threw it in Budworth Mere, but each time there was such frightful haunting that they had to bring it back. At last it was buried by the wall of the house, which satisfied the ghost.

Such tales reflect the instinctive horror many people feel at seeing human remains kept in unorthodox places rather than being given seemly burial; if, for whatever reason, a house has skulls or skeletons displayed in it, the resulting legend will often assume that only the dead person's own powerful wishes can account for such a shocking state of affairs. In the present case, the explanations are taken two stages further; in order to account for the dead woman having had so peculiar a wish, she is presented as a foreigner, from the remote and non-Christian land of Egypt, and to explain how this exotic figure came to Marbury Hall, she is credited with a romantic love-quest of a type which legend ascribes to various other heroines, including the mother of St Thomas à Becket.

The park round Marbury Hall is also reputed haunted by a more conventional ghost, a lady on a white horse, who can be seen at sunset. The starting point here is a real mare, the Marbury Dun, which famously won a wager for her owner by galloping from London to Marbury in a single day, between sunrise and sunset; tradition asserts that she dropped dead on arrival. The ghost story which grew from this claims that Lord Barrymore had bought this fine mare as a wedding present to his wife, and promised it would be there on the wedding day, and in order to keep his promise insisted on the fatal gallop. Lady Barrymore was so upset that she died soon after of a broken heart, and her last wish was to be buried by the well where the horse died, not in the churchyard. Lord Barrymore refused. Her ghost told him she would never rest, but would ride her lovely mare forever.

One more tale recently gathered in Cheshire may be quoted to illustrate another aspect of traditional lore, the difficulty there can be in defining certain types of supernatural being. It was classed by its collector, A.W. Boyd, as a ghost story, but the actual term used in it is 'boggart', and a boggart may appear in many forms, human, animal, skeletal, goblin-like; it can be either kindly or malicious; and it can be explained as a ghost, a fairy or a demon, depending on the presuppositions of the storyteller. The present boggart was described by a farmer from Frandley:

> When he was a boy, sixty years or more ago, he was walking with a farm labourer from Frandley to Barnton, crossing the fields by the footpath on the south-west side of Dog Kennel Wood. At a stile they met a little man about four feet high, and stood aside to let him pass.

When he reached the top of the stile he stood still, and they watched him grow larger and larger and larger, but he made no sound. The boy and his companion took to their heels in utter terror... My informant was perfectly confident that it was a 'boggart' that they had seen, and remained so all his life.

It would seem that stiles and gates were a favourite haunt for Cheshire boggarts; one may compare the rhyme about a gate into Pool Head Field, at Tattenhall:

Coom thou yarly, coom thou leet,
Beweer of the Buggin at th' Poo' Yed Geet.

A boggart is conceived of as a malicious, elemental creature, whose alarming manifestations require no explanation save that it is its nature to behave thus. But what causes some human beings to become ghosts, and others not? Traditional tales and beliefs offer several explanations, some of which have been already touched on, notably murder and other violent death, and the lack of proper burial. Another common traditional reason for a haunting is that the dead man is trying to redress some wrong he has done in life, such as defrauding the poor or dishonestly shifting a boundary stone ('Cursed is he that removeth his neighbour's landmark', as the Prayer Book Commination puts it). Several tales on this theme were collected by Mrs Leather and Miss Burne; in each case the remorseful spirit finds rest when some brave person speaks to him, discovers the cause of his trouble, and takes steps to put it right – although, in several cases, this leads to the depressing conclusion that the living person 'was never right afterwards', or that 'he was a very different man after that, and soon died from the effects of his fright'. The commonest cause for a ghost's remorse is that he has hidden money away in his lifetime, in which case those who would help him must find the hoard, and generally throw it into water. In Herefordshire and Radnorshire this guilt about hoarded wealth has been curiously extended to include the hiding of any metal object whatsoever, even a mere penknife; in March 1870 Kilvert was visiting a house at Llanshifr where a yew tree had just blown down, and noted in his diary:

I wonder in which of these yews Gore hid the penknife before his death, which made him restless as hidden iron is said to do, and caused his spirit to come back rummaging about the house and premises and frightening people out of their wits. Maria Lake used to tell me this story.

Similarly, in Herefordshire at the turn of this century, Mrs Leather was told how:

...people and children were warned not to put any bits of iron in walls, lest they should die and forget it, and therefore would be unable to rest. As an instance of this, only a few years ago I heard the wife of an old workman say she had to go and search under an archway for tools her husband had left there when working, as he was ill, and all his trouble was that he might have to haunt the place after death.

One tale which possibly belongs in the category of remorseful ghosts is a Roman Catholic one from Neston in Cheshire recorded by Miss Hole. A woman named Teresa Higginson, who died in 1905, used to tell how one morning early a priest arrived at the church of which she held the keys, and indicated that he wished to be let in to say Mass there. Though he was a stranger to her, she unlocked the doors, and he duly said his Mass, but then vanished from the vestry; from her description, older parishioners realised that it must have been the ghost of a former parish priest. The implication of this tale is not certain; it might mean that the priest had died without celebrating a Mass he had promised to say at someone's request, and could not rest until he had fulfilled the promise; on the other hand, it might simply reflect the common belief that ghosts revisit their former surroundings and repeat their former actions.

There are plenty of haunted churches and houses, and equally plentiful are the tales of haunted woods, bridges, lanes and stiles. Here one might meet grotesque animal ghosts, like the Cheshire pig and duck already mentioned, or another pig at Binghill in Herefordshire which used to go up an elm tree backwards, or the colt which walked at Cutberry Hollow in Shropshire 'as natural as any Christian.' The most common of all are the black dogs; thus Kilvert notes on 18 March 1871:

> Joe Phillips entertained me with the terrors of the Llowes road at night, the black dog, the phantom horses, etc., which made my hair stand on end. He said many people would not travel that road at night for £100 – Henry Pritchard, Llowes clerk, to wit!

In the Trelleck area in 1904 Miss Wherry heard several vivid descriptions of such creatures from a farmer's wife whose family seem to have seen them quite frequently; one was 'a great black beast with flaming eyes', another was seen going nine times round a tree, and yet another, which the woman had seen herself, was 'a big, big black dog, as large as a calf, an' his eyes shone like lumps of fire'. This the woman interpreted as a death omen, as the next day she got news of her brother's death in a railway accident. Similar spectral hounds were talked of round Bishop's Castle, Mountford church, Broomfield and Baschurch in Shropshire, and also on the Stretton Hills, where a fiery-eyed dog was said to be Wild Edric's ghost; in Cheshire there was said to be one at Bunbury and another in the lanes near Barthelmy, while a house at Godley Green was haunted, at the turn of this century, by a dog as big as a cow, whose colour was yellow. It is said that in 1906 a man who was coming home late one night became aware that it was beside him in the lane, keeping pace with him even when he tried to run; he tried to hit it, but his fist went straight through it and into the hedge. After a while it turned aside and vanished. The man said, 'It was the most hideous thing I ever saw. Its feet went pit-a-pat, pit-a-pat, with a horrible clanking noise like chains. I wouldn't meet it again for £20. I never want to see it again as long as I live!'

Herefordshire had several ghostly dogs, the most famous being a demonic creature at Hergest Court, which was said to appear before deaths in the Vaughan family. Some said it had belonged to the notorious Black Vaughan, who will be discussed below; it haunted both the house itself, where it clanked its chains through the upper rooms, or prowled round the moat, and also the road from Hergest Court to Kington, especially beside a certain pond. There was also a widespread belief in an even more ominous pack of spectral dogs, the Hell Hounds; they could be heard howling high in the air before the death of some particularly evil man, whose soul would be their prey. Usually their eerie howls were said to be loud and shrill, but near Trelleck some people said they buzzed like a swarm of bees.

Other terrors of the road were ghostly horses and phantom coaches, like the ones in which, they say, the ghosts of all the departed Breretons gather once a year for a midnight service in the lonely church of Shocklach. Then there are the phantom funerals – hearse, bearers, mourners and all – of which Mrs Leather had heard tell near Hay (but not in areas further from the Border), and which the father of one of Miss Burne's informants had once seen at twilight on the Long Mynd, near Ratlinghope. Such sights were feared as death omens, foretelling real funerals. But of all the perils of the dark night roads, perhaps the nastiest was the type of spook which leapt at you from behind as you rode by, and sat itself upon your horse's crupper; there were several in Shropshire, notably Madam Pigott, of whom more below, and 'a strange black creature with great white eyes' which sprang upon horses crossing a canal bridge near Woodsheaves, and was known as the Man-Monkey. It was much dreaded in the 1870s, and was said to be the ghost of a man drowned in the canal.

But all these beliefs and their supporting anecdotes seem very bare in comparison with the long, shapely and elaborate tales of ghost-layings that are one of the striking features of Border folklore. There are over a dozen of them in the region, most of which are notable for their vivid and dramatic narrative, their satisfying structure, and the deep impression they evidently made on the memories of local people. There is of course no means of telling when or where the pattern first evolved; each locality would no doubt have fiercely claimed that its own tale was true, and that any resemblance to some tale from elsewhere was simply due to the fact that all ghosts must be laid in pretty much the same way. For it is the act of exorcism which is the high point of these tales, though most of them also give details as to who the ghost is, and where and why and how it haunts.

To start with the most northerly, at Gatley, on the borders of Cheshire and Lancashire, it was said in the nineteenth century that the Gatley Carrs had once been haunted by a wailing howling ghost which used to come out from a grave in Northen churchyard, especially when the moon was full. He had been a dishonest shopkeeper, and he wailed miserably:

Milk and water sold I ever,
Weight and measure gave I never.

So he had to be laid. Fletcher Moss, who published this story in 1898 from an account which an old man had given him years before, explains the basic principles:

> The modus operandi of laying a ghost was to wait till it was on the prowl, and then a parson... got on the grave with a Bible and a lighted candle, thereby cutting off its retreat.... If the laying is to be done regardless of expense, there should be seven or even more parsons, all with Bibles and lighted candles, for there is great virtue in the light... In laying a ghost, the great thing is to corner it, keep your candles burning, and pray like fury.

How this worked in the case of the Gatley Shouter is best told in the old man's own words, as Fletcher gives them:

> 'Aye, sure, th'Gatley Shouter wur Jim Barrow's ghost. 'E come fro' Cross Acres, tother side o' Gatley. Them Gatley folk were always a gallus lot. Owd Jim were desperate fond o' brass, an' 'e stuck to all 'e could lay 'old on. 'E'd ha' flayed two fleas for one 'ide, 'e would, an' when 'e died Owd Scrat got 'im, an' 'e warmed 'im, 'e did so, an' Jim might ha' bin heard o' nights moaning "Oh dear, oh dear, wa-atered milk, wa-atered milk!", till folks got plaguey feared o' going yon road arter dark. Now there come a new parson to Northen, a scholar fresh from Oxford or Rome or someweers, chock-fu' o' book-larnin', an' 'e played the hangment wi' aw t'ghostses i' these parts, an' 'e said 'e'd tackle 'im. So 'e got aw t'parish as could read or pray a bit to come wi' their Bibles, and one night when t'moon were out Owd Scrat mun ha' bin firin' up, for t'Shouter were bein' rarely fettled, by t'way as 'e moaned. An' aw t'folks got round 'im, an' they drew towart one another in a ring like, an' kept comin' closer till at last they'd gotten 'im in a corner i' t'churchyard by t'yew tree, an' t'parson was on t'grave, an' 'e whips a bit o' chalk out o' 'is pocket an' draws a holy ring round 'em aw, an' aw t'folk join 'ands an' pray desperate like, an' t'parson 'ops about an' shouts an' bangs t'book till 'e's aw o' a muck sweat. An' 'e prayed at 'im in Latin too, mind you, as well as English, an t'poor ghost moans an' chunners an' gets littler an' littler till 'e fair sweals away, like a snail that's salted. An' at last t'devil were druv out o' 'im, an' 'e lets 'im bide as quiet as a mouse.

'E's now under yon big stone by t'parson's gate. You may see it for yosen. It's theer now.'

The tone here is none too serious and poor Shouter does not seem to have been a very alarming ghost, even before the parson started in on him. Further south, his Shropshire neighbours were more bloodcurdling. There was Madam Pigott, for instance, who in the early nineteenth century was a dreadful bugbear to villagers in the Chetwynd area. She is said to have been the wife of one of the Pigotts who owned the mansion at Chetwynd until about 1780, and to have died in childbirth – a tragedy to which her husband was callously indifferent, expressing no concern over her, provided only that the baby lived. However, it too died, and both mother and baby 'came again', and were seen haunting the house and park, and the lanes towards Edgmond. At one spot there was a twisted old tree root known as Madam Pigott's armchair; at another, a high wall from which it was said she would leap down, together with her black cat, and cling fiercely to the back of any horseman who was riding past the spot by night. If by any chance he was riding to fetch help for a woman in childbirth, her malice was redoubled. At length twelve clergymen joined forces, and laid her by incessantly reading Psalms aloud till they broke her power; it was said that a Mr Foy, a curate from Edgmond who died in 1816, was the only one whose strength held out to the end. And even so, it seems, the laying was not believed to have been fully effective; Miss Burne found, in the 1880s, that 'many a strong young groom or ploughboy still shrinks from facing Madam Pigott's Hill after dark'.

According to some gypsy storytellers, Madam Pigott was laid twice, the first time in a local pond from which she soon came again worse than before, and the second time in the Red Sea, where she still is. It took the combined prayers of twelve priests to do it; only the oldest of them could keep his candle alight, and he 'prayed till the sweat dropped off his hair'. They had a bottle with them, and little by little they forced her into it, and then threw it in the Red Sea.

A bottle is a common feature in these tales, so common that in *Precious Bane* Mary Webb amusingly describes how the fraudulent 'conjurer' Beguildy keeps one in which he claims to hold a ghost imprisoned, and how on one occasion his sceptical wife is seen shaking it 'as if it was an ill-mixed sauce'. At one time a bottle allegedly fulfilling this sinister function could actually be seen in Kinlet church, lying beneath the monument of Sir George Blount, who died in 1581, and who was said to have haunted Kinlet Hall until the eighteenth century, out of rage because his daughter had married her page-boy. It was, says Miss Burne, 'a little flat bottle seven or eight inches long, with a glass stopper in it which nobody can get out', and though it had been removed by the time she wrote, it had been in its place only a few years before, an object of awe, curiosity and terror to local schoolchildren.

Usually, the ghosts put up a terrifying resistance before they will enter the bottle, or whatever other container is chosen. They may well change shape several times, or appear in animal form; thus it is said that a ghost at Hampton's Wood near Ellesmere turned from a headless man into a cat. At Llanigon in Breconshire, an unbeliever named Joseph Arndell who died in 1768 is said to have come again as a bellowing bull, which frightened five out of six parsons into fainting fits; but the sixth read on, while the spectral bull grew smaller and smaller till it was as small as a fly, which was caught in a box and thrown into a well. There is a similar tale at Llanfair Caereinion in Montgomery, where a local wizard, not a parson, did the exorcising; at Llanfyllin in the same county the eighteenth-century poet Twm o'r Nant is credited with laying a spirit which appeared by turns as wild boar, wolf, dog and fly, and was at length put in a tobacco box and buried in a meadow.

In Herefordshire the favourite receptacle seems to have been a snuff-box, and the final resting-place was usually in water. There is said to be one at the bottom of a pool in Garnstone Park, containing a ghost which had at first appeared in the form of a bleating calf; versions differ as to whether it was the ghost of a suicide or of a man whose daughters poisoned him with stewed toad. But bottles were also used; there was said to be one buried under the tomb of Roger de Clifford in Aconbury church, so placed as to be neither inside nor outside the church, but in the thickness of the wall – a motif we have already noticed in connection with tales of how to cheat the Devil.

By far the best known Herefordshire ghost is Black Vaughan of Hergest Court, near Kington. He is usually identified as the Sir Thomas Vaughan who died at the battle of Banbury in 1469, and whose effigy lies in Kington church; some say, however, that he was a later Sir Thomas who was beheaded in 1483. Whichever he was, he made a fearsome ghost; he was said to haunt local roads even in broad daylight, overturning waggons and leaping onto the crupper of women's horses. He also haunted a certain oak tree, beneath which two bare patches where no grass would grow marked the footprints of this wicked being. Sometimes he appeared as a fly, sometimes as a bull. At length, twelve parsons gathered 'to try to read him down into a silver snuff-box'; rather unusually, they had with them a woman and a newborn baby – presumably, though Miss Leather's informant did not make the point, they had just been churched and baptized, and so were in a powerful state of grace. Even so, the exorcism was no easy one:

> 'Well, they read, but it was no use; they were all afraid, and all their candles went out but one. The parson as held that candle had a stout heart, and he feared no man nor sperrit. He called out "Vaughan, why art thou so fierce?" "I was fierce when I was a man, but fiercer now, for I am a devil!" was the answer. But nothing could dismay the stout-hearted parson, though, to tell the truth, he was nearly blind, and not a pertickler sober man. He read, and read, and read, and when Vaughan felt himself going down, and down, and down, till the snuff-box was nearly shut, he asked "Vaughan, where wilt thou be laid?" The spirit answered "Anywhere, anywhere, but not in the Red Sea!" So they shut the box, and took him and buried him for a thousand years in the bottom of Hergest pool, in the wood, with a big stone on top of him. But the time is nearly up!'

It would seem difficult to cap so fine a tale, but people in Shropshire and Montgomeryshire would claim, perhaps justly, that the Roaring Bull of Bagbury outdoes every other ghost along the Border. Both counties claim a share in him, for though he came from Bagbury it was in Hyssington church that he was laid, and the stream where some say he now lies is the actual boundary between Wales and England. There are different versions of the tale, though all agree that the ghost was that of a wicked squire from Bagbury, so mean, cruel, foul mouthed and ill tempered that when he died he turned into a monstrous and savage bull. Some informants used to add that the bull was skinless, and called it the Flayed Bull of Bagbury – 'a ghastly imagination', says Miss Burne, 'which one would have thought could only have come from the brain of a delirious butcher'. But in this she was mistaken; the gruesome concept of a flayed bull or horse as a spectre is a genuine piece of folk-tradition, and can be paralleled in Scotland and the Orkneys, Iceland, and Germany. To return to the Bagbury Bull: it would roar 'till the boards and the shutters and the tiles flew off the buildings', and would haunt the roads 'with flaming eyes and horns'. So the parson of Hyssington church (or, some say, a group of nine or twelve clergy gathering there) set up so powerful a prayer that it drew him to the church:

> 'And when they got him into the church, they all had candles, and one old blind parson, who knowed him, and knowed what a rush he would make, he carried his candle in his top boot. And he made a great rush, and all the candles went out, all but the blind parson's, and he said, "You light your candles by mine." And while they were in the church, before they laid him, the bull made such a burst that he cracked the wall of the church from the top to the bottom, and the crack was left as it was for years, till the church was done up. It was left on purpose for people to see. I've seen it hundreds of times.
>
> 'Well, they got the bull down at last, into a snuff-box, and he asked them to lay him under Bagbury Bridge, and that every mare that passed over should lose her foal, and every woman her child; but they would not do this, and they laid him in the Red Sea for a thousand years.
>
> 'I remember the old clerk at Hyssington. He was an old man then, sixty years ago, and he told me he could remember the old blind parson well.'

This version of the legend was told to Miss Burne in 1881 by an old farmer named Hayward. An earlier version which was printed by the antiquarian Thomas Wright in 1860 gives a few additional or divergent details. In this account, as in the case of the Gatley Shouter, the whole community has a part to play in the exorcism:

> They assembled all around him for miles, and drew closer and closer till they got him up to the Church. The parson read texts to him all

the way, and he continually grew smaller and tamer. Once inside the Church, the parson began to preach, and the bull was slowly but steadily decreasing, when night came on before the work was finished. Only a small bit of candle could be found, and when it was burnt out the parson could see no longer, and was obliged to stop reading. The bull was then about the size of a dog, but as soon as the parson ceased he began to grow again, till he was larger than before. The Church was not big enough to hold him, and the walls cracked around him. (You may see the cracks to this day.) Next day the parson came again, and this time the people brought a good store of candles, and the reading went on without interruption, till the bull was so small they could bind him up in a boot, which one of the congregation gave up for the purpose. They then buried him deep under the door-stone, where he lies to this day. There are believers in this story who affirm that were the stone to be loosed the bull would come forth again, by many degrees worse than he was at the first, and that he could never again be laid.

SEVEN

HOLY WELLS AND HEALING CHARMS

At first sight, the body of beliefs and practices that make up folk medicine seems a mere jumble of incongruous elements, ranging from a sensible application of homely remedies to the wildest and most arbitrary magic. In fact, many layers of cultural history have left their mark on it: the primitive principles of magic by contact, similarity or re-enactment can certainly be traced in it, but so too can medieval Catholicism with its stress on saints and miracles, the Protestant reliance on the power of Biblical texts, and various fragmentary survivals of scientific theories once current in the learned world, but long since discarded there. In addition, of course, there was a great deal of practical knowledge of the real medical value of various plants that were made up into potions, ointments and poultices, but the study of this aspect would go beyond the scope of this book.

The use of holy wells and springs for healing is one of the distinctive features in Border lore, and has in its long history been affected by several different influences. Its origins go far back into prehistoric times; there is ample evidence of a cult of wells in the Bronze Age, the Celtic Iron Age, and in Romano-British times. The powers then attributed to their waters were, no doubt, much wider than those ascribed to them in Christian times; nevertheless there is a certain continuity, exemplified, for instance, by the wooden Celtic ex-votos found some years ago at the source of the Seine – objects quite typical of the offerings made when seeking healing, or giving thanks for it, and easily paralleled in many Catholic countries. To this day, in Britain, the belief in holy wells is liveliest in the areas where Celtic influence is strongest.

Christianity did not abolish this ancient cult, but gave it a different emphasis. The important wells were now associated with various saints, often simply by being dedicated to them, but sometimes also by a legend claiming a direct link between the saint and the waters. It might be said, for instance, that a spring first appeared because the saint had been killed or wounded at that spot; probably the most famous of these is St Winifred's Well at Holywell in Flintshire, which is said to have gushed out of the ground at the place where her decapitated head touched the earth, and which has been for centuries a centre at which pilgrims sought health. At Stoke St Milborough, near Ludlow, a spring that was thought good for sore eyes is said to have been formed when St Milburga, fleeing her enemies, fell from her horse and struck her head on a rock; at her command her horse pawed the ground, releasing a stream in which she washed her wounds, but her blood left a permanent mark upon the stones. Or it may be a saint's dead body that caused the miracle; both at Marden and in Hereford there are wells named after the murdered king St Ethelbert, which are said to mark places where his body was laid down while being taken to Hereford for burial, and of which one was much valued as a cure for sores and ulcers.

Even when the medieval Life of the saint in question makes no such association with a well, later folklore will often supply it; in the nineteenth century, Oswestry schoolboys believed that St Oswald's head was actually buried behind a certain stone in the wall behind St Oswald's Well, while a recent author has heard it said that this same well originated when a raven plucked out Oswald's eye during his fight with Penda. Or again, it may be claimed that the well is holy because a missionary saint baptized his converts in it; this is said of wells at Bromborough and Plemstall in Cheshire, the saints being Patrick and Plegmund respectively.

The Romans had known and made use of the fact that water containing certain minerals drawn from the soil and rocks had medicinal qualities. In the eighteenth and nineteenth centuries the doctors rediscovered this fact with such enthusiasm that for several generations 'taking the waters' was one of the most popular forms of treatment, and spas and health resorts sprang up wherever the geological conditions were suitable. Whatever the springs contained – iron, sulphur, chalybeate, salt, or merely gassy bubbles – some doctor would come forward to publicize its merits and to explain which disorders could be cured by drinking it or bathing in it. Among wells whose reputation stood high at this period were St Stephen's Well at Tarporley in Cheshire, the Virtuous Well at Trelleck (whose 'virtues' are medical, not moral), and the three springs round which the spa of Llandridod Wells was built. To believe that such waters were curative could not, of course, be classed as folklore at that period, for the notion rested on the authority of the medical science of the times, and had a fairly sound factual basis. However, the publicity must have powerfully reinforced the older belief in holy wells; people who might otherwise have grown sceptical of their healing powers must have been persuaded that there was, after all, something in it. Occasionally, one even finds that a folktale has sprung up to explain the origin of a medicinal (as opposed to a saint's) well; it is said that the three springs of Llandridod Wells originated when a hero slew three monsters that were about to kill a girl, by crushing the first with a lump of salt, the second with a lump of iron, and the third with a lump of brimstone.

There is a distinction, too, between the type of diseases with which the spa doctors were concerned, chiefly internal ones such as anaemia, constipation, liver disorders and digestive complaints, and those which the traditional holy wells were believed to cure, which were chiefly external. By far the most common was soreness or weakness of the eyes – a notion which may once have enjoyed some medical backing, as one still quite frequently hears people assert that bathing the eyes with ordinary cold water will in some way 'strengthen' them. Next most frequent were skin troubles, such as ulcers, abscesses, and sores. Sometimes both powers were ascribed to the same well; a modern author, T.A. Ryder, describes St Anthony's Well in the Forest of Dean as:

... a stone-lined hollow fed by a stream whose water is always icy cold, even on the hottest day. It was a favourite picnic place for myself and other children years ago, and we always brought back home a bottle of the water, for we believed it would cure any eye troubles such as soreness or styes. In the eighteenth century, people used to take their dogs there to wash them if the animals had mange or distemper. Earlier still, the monks of Flaxley sent sufferers from skin diseases to St Anthony's Well with instructions to bathe in its waters on the first nine mornings in May.

The eighteenth-century reputation of this well was still remembered in 1950, when F.W. Baty was told 'That's the place with a well that cures a mangy dog if he's thrown in the waters three times at sunrise' – an interesting instance of the importance still attached to the magically potent hour of sunrise, and to the number three.

A magic hour was also crucial to the ritual connected with St Anne's Well at Aconbury in Herefordshire; in this case, midnight on Twelfth Night, which, as will be seen in a later chapter (pp. 142-45), is an important date in the lore of this county. Mrs Leather writes:

> The first water taken from this well after twelve o'clock on Twelfth Night was said to be of great medicinal value, and especially good for eye troubles. Aconbury folk used to compete for the first bucketful, which was bottled and carefully kept by the one who succeeded in obtaining it. At midnight the water bubbled up, and a blue smoke arose from it. My informant, a native of Aconbury residing at Eaton Bishop (1909), assured me he had himself seen the water do this.

Other wells and springs were held to be good for sprains, swellings, bruises, and rheumatic pains. Concerning one at Woolston in Shropshire, Miss Burne wrote:

> The water, which is singularly clear, is supposed to have wonderful powers of healing wounds and bruises and broken bones. When I visited the place in June 1885, a broken arm was in course of treatment there; the injured man coming early every morning to dip it in the well, by the advice of his doctor, who, canny man, no doubt knew that his prescription of cold water applications was much more

likely to be obeyed if he recommended recourse to a holy well rather than a common pump.

Many holy wells were not merely healers, but also wishing wells, a function which in some cases has proved the more long-lasting. Some had to be consulted with a certain amount of ritual, and to be given symbolic offerings – archaic features, with their origins undoubtedly in pre-Christian times. At Sunny Gutter, near Ludlow, you had to drop a stone in while silently making your wish; at Rhosgoch 'you could get whatever you wished for the moment the pin you threw in touched the bottom' (there seems to be a catch here, for it must be hard to judge just when a pin does touch the bottom), and its depths were bright with pins – 'it was mostly used for wishing about sweethearts'. At Gayton in Cheshire, you should toss a stone backwards into the well as you wish; at Laugh Lady Well at Brampton Bryan, people watched the water after dropping a pin in, for if bubbles rose, and especially if the water gurgled, the wish would come true; similarly at Trelleck nowadays, it is said that many bubbles indicate a rapid granting of the wish, fewer mean delay, and none at all means failure.

The most elaborate rituals are perhaps those in use at St Oswald's Well at Oswestry in the 1880s. One was to go there at midnight, scoop up water in one's hand, drink part of it while silently wishing, and then throw the rest precisely against one particular stone in the wall which forms a backing to the well; this stone had originally been carved to represent the saint's head, but even by 1842 schoolboys had 'battered it into a perfect mummy' – while still maintaining a belief that the saint's own actual head was buried behind it! Other methods were to whisper the wish into a hole in the stone archway of this wall; to wish while bathing one's face in the water; to drop a stone in with so vigorous a splash as to wet one's head; or to find an empty husk of beech-mast with markings like a face on it, drop it so that it floated with the face uppermost, and if it then stayed afloat while one could count twenty, the wish would be granted. There is much here that is remarkably archaic, for the study of Celtic myths and archaeological investigation of Celtic sites show a recurrent association between sacred wells and trees (particularly nut-bearers) and between wells and severed heads. Oswestry is in an area where Welsh influence was particularly tenacious.

Holy wells were honoured with seasonal ceremonies. The well at Didsbury in Cheshire, which was held to be good for sore eyes, was so popular in the 1890s that it was often almost choked with the flowers thrown into it in May, not to mention pins dropped in for luck. In some places it was customary to dress the wells with flowers on particular days, though not with elaborate floral pictures like the ones for which the well-dressings in Derbyshire are famous. In Cheshire the brine springs at Nantwich, Northwich and Middlewich used to be decked on Ascension Day; in Radnorshire the favourite time for dressing wells was New Year's Day, since it was thought that water drawn from them on this day was particularly potent; several wells in Shropshire and Montgomery were honoured on Trinity Sunday, when people held Wakes near them, and drank sugar-and-water. At Rorrington in Shropshire and the nearby Churchstoke in Montgomery, wells were dressed on Ascension Day until the 1830s with much merrymaking; they were covered over with bowers of green branches, rushes and flowers, and people danced round them, dropped pins in for luck and to keep witches away, and picnicked, eating spiced buns and drinking sugar-and-water.

These ceremonies have now faded from memory. Indeed, in many places the springs themselves have dried up, the water table having been lowered by increased demand, and many of those that do still remain are inaccessible to would-be drinkers, in deference to modern views on hygiene. Not long ago, the healing wells seemed doomed to extinction, but modern awareness of Celtic customs and beliefs has revived a vigorous interest in them, both as Christian holy places and as possible survivals of pagan cults. One of the first to benefit was Trelleck's Virtuous Well, whose decrepit stonework was restored in 1951 to mark the Festival of Britain. Roy Palmer reports that it is now a focus for deliberately archaic activities:

> In 1998 candles and flowers could be seen in niches of the stonework. Neighbouring trees were festooned with pieces of cloth tied there and left in a revival of a practice going back 200 years in Wales, the rags representing the survival of a belief that disease will be discarded along with a token of the sufferer's clothing. They may also embody the hope that a deeply-felt wish or longing will be satisfied.

A few other types of folk-medicine may be regarded as lingering vestiges of the scientific theories of the past. Among those current in Cheshire in 1895 were the wearing of 'galvanic rings' for rheumatism, and the belief (known in Shropshire too) that if you cut yourself you should smear not only the cut but the knife that caused it with bacon fat. The first of these must obviously reflect the great outburst of interest in the nineteenth century in possible medical applications of electricity and magnetism; the second is older, being a survival of a seventeenth-century theory (chiefly advocated by Sir Kenelm Digby) that to treat blood that has congealed on a weapon will, by 'natural sympathy', heal the wound from which the blood was drawn.

Another group of cures was based on religious beliefs, mostly survivals from before the Reformation. In the Middle Ages it was officially taught that certain specially made rings, which had been blessed by the King himself in a religious service on Good Friday, would be effective against epilepsy, convulsions, cramps, spasms, and rheumatic pains; such 'cramp-rings' were blessed and distributed each year by every King of England from Edward II to Edward VI. After the custom had been abolished by Elizabeth I, people took to making cramp-rings for themselves, out of metal that had been in some way sanctified; the most popular method was to get hold of one or more shillings that had been put in the collection plate at a Communion service, and have this 'sacramental silver' melted down into a ring, as a certain cure for fits. Folklorists of the late nineteenth century recorded several instances of clergymen in the Border counties being asked to supply shillings for this purpose. Sometimes the procedure was more complicated; in the Shropshire Collieries, one was required to beg twelve young bachelors for a penny each, and then exchange these coins for an offertory shilling. In some parts of Cheshire, money begged from people of the sex opposite to the sufferer made an effective ring, without the need for any contact with a religious service. Or again, blending the sacred with the ghoulish, some Shrewsbury people maintained that rheumatism could be cured by wearing 'a ring made of three nails taken from three coffins out of three several churchyards'.

A ritual strikingly reminiscent of medieval Catholic visits to saints' shrines was kept up until the nineteenth century in the church of Christchurch, between Caerleon and Newport. Laid flush into the floor of that church is the tombstone of a certain John and Isabella Colmer, who both died in 1376; it has a brass showing them on either side of a large, florid cross. There is nothing unusual about this brass, nor is anything known about the Colmers themselves, yet for reasons unknown their tomb became the focus of an annual healing ritual on the eve of Corpus Christi, a major medieval festival (see p. 165). At sunset sick people would gather in the church, where they would be locked in for the night, lying on the tomb, or if there were too many for this to be possible, at least resting a leg or arm on it. This, they believed, would heal them. Next day, there would be feasting in the churchyard. It is said that when an eighteenth-century squire tried to end the custom by keeping the church locked and allowing nobody in, the bells rang all by themselves at midnight, convincing him that he was wrong and the ritual should be resumed.

Bread or buns baked on Good Friday were kept all year, and crumbs grated from them and taken in water were said to cure diarrhoea in both men and animals. Rain that fell on Ascension Day would be carefully caught, bottled, and used for sore eyes; as we have seen already, this holy day was also a popular date for ceremonies at holy wells. Most potent of all the religious cures, naturally enough, were the Sacraments themselves. In Cheshire and Herefordshire, it was said that to be 'bishoped', i.e. confirmed, would cure lumbago and sciatica. In the 1880s, the wife of the Rector of Dorstone in Herefordshire found that her husband's parishioners brought babies to him as a last hope when they were ill:

> 'The child won't take nothing, don't aim to such at all, and seems always wantin', and we've tried it with potato and fat pork and all, but can't satisfy it no-way, and gran'mer says, "Go to the Reverend," her says, "and beg of him to christen it, 'twill be all right then."'

Or again:

> 'We ha' tried everything we can think of, and the doctor don't give us no hope. So I went to old Mary, and her says, "Go you to the Reverend, and ask him to give you a drop o' sacramental wine, which must be the real wine as was blessed in church – none other won't do – and you go home quiet – don't speak to nobody – and give the

child a teaspoonful in the very minute 'twixt the daylight and the dark, and if that don't cure it, nothing will.'"

Mrs Leather records that in Hereford women of the poorer classes put great faith in a broadside called 'Our Saviour's Letter', which they would hang above their beds 'for greater ease and safety in childbirth'; she reproduces one currently in use. Various texts purporting to be letters written by Jesus himself and found in miraculous circumstances had circulated in Europe since the early centuries of Christianity (with variations); the most popular one in eighteenth- and nineteenth-century England instructs all believers to keep Sundays holy, and hence is also called 'the Sunday Letter'. Although full of pious doctrine and instructions, and dire warnings to sinners, these texts also functioned as charms, promising protection against fevers, sickness, perils of childbirth, and thunderstorms to those who displayed them in their homes. Furthermore, like a modern 'chain letter', they had to be passed on: 'He that hath a Copy of this Letter, written with my own Hand, and spoken with my own Mouth, and keepeth it without publishing it to others shall not prosper,' says the Hereford broadside. Besides the printed versions, many handwritten copies were made.

Then there were verbal charms or 'blessings', which were believed to cure certain specific illnesses or injuries by repeating words which were, or were believed to be, quotations from the Bible. One of the best known was that against toothache, of which there were many slightly differing versions; a typical one was collected in Monmouthshire in the 1930s from a man whose mother had written it down in the family Bible:

> Jesus came to Peter as he stood at the gates of Jerusalem and said unto him, 'What dost thou here?' Peter answered and said unto Jesus, 'Lord, my teeth do ache.' Jesus answered and said unto Peter, 'That whosoever do carry these words in memory with them or near them, shall never have teeth ache any more.'

Often this charm was written on a piece of paper and carried in the pocket or sewn into the clothing of the sufferer. The words, though Biblical in style, are not of course really to be found in the Gospels;

other charms similarly invoked real or apocryphal details from Christ's life as precedents for whatever cure was aimed at. Mrs Leather quotes eight of them, from the notebooks of an old charmer from Weobley; one treats thorn wounds by reference to the crown of thorns, another stops flowing blood by asserting that the Jordan stopped flowing when Jesus entered it at his baptism, and another cures ague with the words:

> When Jesus saw the Cross whereon he was to be crucified he trembled and shook, and the Jews asked him 'art thou afraid, or hast thou the ague?' Jesus answered and said, 'I am not afraid, neither have the evil ague; whoever wears this about them shall not be afraid nor have that evil ague.'

There were also charms invoking saints or angels; in Shropshire, for example, one way to heal a burn was to lay one's hand on it while repeating:

> *Matthew, Mark, Luke and John*
> *Make well the place my hand is on.*

One must go on repeating this till the smarting stops. To charm a scald, one said three times:

> *There was three angels came from the west,*
> *The one brought fire and the other brought frost,*
> *The other brought the book of Jesus Christ,*
> *In the name of Father, Son and Holy Ghost. Amen.*

All these charms were regarded as holy, not as magical; sometimes they were passed on openly in families, as for instance by being written down in the family Bible, but more often they were taught in confidence, there being great reluctance to reveal them unnecessarily, or to strangers. When used, they were generally muttered too low and too fast to be heard, or else they were written down on a piece of paper which the sufferer was given, but which he was told he must not unfold and read. Some said that in order to be effective they ought only to be used by a woman to cure a man, and by a man to cure a woman, but this rule was not always followed. Many of the 'charmers' and 'conjurers' described in an earlier chapter used them, but since their effectiveness lay in the sacred words and allusions themselves, they were believed to work even when applied by ordinary people; indeed, the toothache charm was often self-administered.

When, however, it was a matter of charms based on pure magic rather than on reverence for sacred things and Biblical texts, it was often of prime importance to find the right person to perform the cure. In Radnorshire and Flint, a man who had eaten eagle's flesh, or whose father or grandfather had eaten it, could cure shingles by touching or breathing on the sufferer. There was a very widespread belief that whooping cough could be cured if the child ate, without saying 'thank you', a piece of bread and butter given him by a person peculiar in some particular way – a married woman whose maiden name had been the same as her married name now was; or one who had married twice, to men who had the same surname but were unrelated; or a married couple whose Christian names were Joseph and Mary; or a posthumous child. This illness could also be cured by the seventh son of a seventh son, or by applying any remedy whatsoever which was recommended by a man riding a piebald horse.

Contact with the dead was also, paradoxically, the basis for some cures. At Orcop in Herefordshire, it was at one time customary to make a child with whooping cough eat bread and butter that had been placed in a dead man's hand; in Shropshire, it was sometimes said that scrofula (King's Evil) would be cured by bread and butter from the hand of a person who had been killed. Even more widespread was a cure for goitre or for wens on the neck by stroking the swollen part with a dead man's hand; originally, it had been said that it must be a hanged man, and people used to go to public executions to take advantage of the opportunity. At Shrewsbury in 1828, when two murderers were hanged, the *Salopian Journal* reported:

> After they had hung the usual time, the bodies were cut down; and permission being requested that the hands of the deceased should be drawn over several individuals suffering from the affliction of wens, that operation was performed.

This gruesome prescription must originally have been based on the principle of 'sympathetic magic', the notion that 'like cures like'; the similarity between the hanged man's distorted neck and the swollen neck of the patient must have been the inspiration of the practice. In its later form, however, the curative power was simply thought to be the touch of the dead, as in the whooping cough and scrofula cures. Similar power was believed to reside in bones, coffin nails, splinters from gallows, and such-like grim objects. Writing about Cheshire in 1895, Fletcher Moss remarked:

> I have been rather surprised to hear from workmen what a large and general demand there is from the public for skulls and teeth. Common skulls are worth five shillings each ... A very old charm against toothache is to wear a sound tooth found in a churchyard, having it tied by a string and worn round the neck. If the toothache continues obstinate, an infallible cure is to have the bad tooth taken out and the sound one put in its place.

The carrying of dead men's teeth was also known in Shropshire, with the added rule that a man should carry a woman's tooth, and vice versa.

Healing could also be sought by rituals of contact with certain living trees and plants; the procedures were complicated, and imply a complex mixture of underlying ideas – imitative magic, transference of disease by contact, mimic rebirth, the importance of magic times and numbers. One example was the ash-tree cure for rupture in small children. Early in the twentieth century, at Trelleck in Monmouthshire, a woman whose child had a rupture was told by the local charmer to make use of a 'maiden ash,' by which he meant one that had grown from seed, and had never been touched by a knife. The mother and the charmer met there one Friday as the clock was striking midnight, the tree having previously been split down the middle and the cleft wedged open; standing one on either side of the tree, they passed the baby nine times through the cleft in complete silence, and then removed the wedge and bound the tree up tightly, for as the tree healed, so the child would heal. The same ritual was practised in Shropshire and Herefordshire, with minor variations; at Broxwood, for instance, instead of keeping silence, one of those taking part would say 'The Lord giveth', and the other reply 'The Lord receiveth', each time the child was passed through the cleft. At

Ludlow in 1845, a group of people were seen passing an idiot child through a split 'wittan' (mountain ash); this unusual choice of tree may reflect the wittan's supposed power against witches, for the defective child may have been thought to be bewitched.

A widespread cure for whooping cough was to creep under a bramble or briar that has formed an arch by rooting itself at the tip; since this is in itself a very common occurrence, and since folk cures often prescribe things difficult to do or to obtain, it is not surprising to find some people stipulating that the bramble arch must pass exactly over a parish boundary. Be that as it may, the afflicted child was made to crawl nine times under the arch (sometimes all on the one occasion, sometimes on nine days running). This cure was still in use in 1937 at Wolvesnewton in Monmouthshire. One suspects that a pun on 'whoop' and 'hoop' may have contributed to the popularity of the charm, but a weightier factor undoubtedly was the notion that the disease was being transferred to another creature; this comes out clearly in Mrs Leather's account (where we find, once again, the bread and butter so often used in cures for this disease):

> The bramble-bush was supposed to be quite effectual in a recent case at Weobley, but the child was passed under nine times on one morning only, and an offering of bread and butter was placed beneath the bramble arch. 'She left her cough there with the bread and butter', said my informant. At Thruxton and Kingstone, they say the Lord's Prayer while passing the patient nine times under the briar arch; he must be eating bread and butter meanwhile. On returning, the bread and butter must be given to some bird or other creature ('not a Christian'); the bird will die, and the cough will be cured. Ann P— of Kingstone told me she once got into trouble for causing the death of someone's duck in this way.

Transference and sympathetic magic are both conspicuous principles in what is certainly the best-known, most universal, and most long-lasting class of healing charms, namely the various ways of ridding oneself of warts. Again and again one finds the same basic idea: the warts are to be touched or rubbed with something, and that thing is to be buried, hung up, or thrown away, so that as it rots or shrivels the warts gradually disappear – or, alternatively, so that someone else may pick it up and thereby unwittingly 'take' the warts. Among the objects thus used are snails and slugs (to be impaled on thorns and left to shrivel); fatty bacon, raw beef (both preferably stolen), hot bread, half an apple, bean flowers, broad bean pods (all to be buried and left to rot); a notched stick, or as many stones, sticks, threads, rushes or grains of wheat as there are warts (to be made up into a parcel and dropped at a crossroads for someone else to pick up).

Gradual drying and shrivelling was also aimed at in a remedy once widely used for inflammation of the foot in cattle – for of course folk medicine was as much used for animal diseases as for those of men. In Radnorshire, where the method was still in use in the 1940s, the instructions were that if a cow was suffering from 'foul foot' one should watch her as she first rose from the ground in the morning, cut the sod of turf on which she first set her injured foot to ground, and hang it on a blackthorn bush; as it withered, so the foot would dry up and heal. With minor variations, the same charm has been recorded in Monmouthshire, Herefordshire and Shropshire too; sometimes it is stipulated that the sod should bear a visible hoof-print, or that it should be cut in the exact shape of the foot.

Another much dreaded disease of cattle was contagious abortion; to prevent the outbreak spreading, the grim remedy was to take the body of the 'piked' calf and hang it up on the cowhouse wall, where all the cows could look at it. An instance of this practice was seen by Fletcher Moss in Cheshire in the 1890s. The underlying idea seems to be that animals are capable of 'learning their lesson' by seeing what calamities have befallen others of their species – a notion also applied by gamekeepers when they strung up dead vermin on a tree or gate. There are also related practices where the thought is not so clear; in other parts of Cheshire, for instance, the calf would be buried under its mother's stall; in Shropshire in the 1930s it was said that a dead lamb should not be buried but 'put up a tree to fade away'; at St Briavels in 1902, it was said that pigs that died of disease should be buried with their toes upwards, and then the outbreak of trouble would stop. Possibly some notion of breaking a harmful spell may have given rise to these odd practices.

But when all is said and done, there remain many folk cures so very odd and arbitrary that they defy all attempts at explanation, whether on the basis of religion, old-fashioned science, or the principles of magic. To take just a few examples known from the Border counties: to carry the mossy ball from a rose-bush prevents toothache; to cut one's toe-nails while sitting under an ash tree cures it; to carry a potato or a mole's paw cures rheumatism; if you apply nine linen bandages smeared with a mixture of powdered garlic and lard to a child with measles or scarlet fever, and then bury them, this will draw the fever out of him; 'a fine fat spider, all alive and kicking', eaten with butter will cure ague; woodlice make good pills; powdered cockroaches cure dropsy; cooked hedgehog cures epilepsy; mouse pie or roast mice cure bed-wetting; eelskin garters prevent cramp; to tie a sheep's lungs or a bullock's melt to the soles of the feet of a patient with pneumonia will draw the infection out of him; live woodlice hung in a bag round a baby's neck will ease his teething pain; holding a live frog to a baby's mouth will cure him of thrush; an onion on a mantlepiece will draw infections into it. How long such ideas have existed, or how they began, is beyond conjecture, but that some are still put into practice is certain; as recently as the winter of 1967-68, a Cheshire farmer's wife claimed that the reason her farm had escaped an epidemic of foot-and-mouth disease then raging was that she had set onions all round her cowsheds.

EIGHT
FROM THE CRADLE TO THE GRAVE

Birth, marriage and death, the great turning points in the life cycle, have always had, and still do have, traditional beliefs and rituals to mark them. But even before birth there were supernatural dangers to be guarded against, for the unborn child was thought to be vulnerable to certain evil influences. Most widely known and dreaded was the hare, for if one of these crossed a pregnant woman's path her child would have a hare lip, unless she instantly made a tear in her shift, thus supplying a substitute victim. The belief (of which Mary Webb made powerful use in *Precious Bane*) obviously involves the magic principle that 'like causes like', but there must be more to it than that, otherwise rabbits would be equally feared for their split lips, and this is never so. The additional factor is probably the association between hares and witches (see above, p. 71).

Pre-natal influences were also held responsible for birthmarks, which were examined to see if they resembled anything the mother might have stared too hard at, or been frightened by, or have had a longing for. Fletcher Moss tells how his father had a birthmark shaped like a partridge behind his ear, believed to be because his grandmother, during her pregnancy, had longed to eat partridge in June, and when she could not get it, had scratched behind her ear. L.H. Hayward mentions an instance of a child in Shropshire that was born with a withered arm, which was said to be due to the fright the mother felt when a one-armed beggar cursed her. Deformities were also sometimes interpreted as Divine punishments; in 1871 the Revd Francis Kilvert was told that in Presteigne there was a deformed woman, a Miss Sylvester, who was 'part woman and part frog,' having face and feet like a frog's, and only able to hop, not to walk:

> The story about this unfortunate being is as follows. Shortly before she was born, a woman came begging to her mother's door with two or three little children. Her mother was angry and ordered the woman away. 'Get away with your young frogs,' she said. And the child she was expecting was born partly in the form of a frog, as a punishment and a curse upon her.

Another fear was that of miscarrying. One very curious notion has been recorded as an explanation of miscarriages (whether human or among farm animals), and of women dying in childbirth, when several of these misfortunes have occurred soon after one another. It seems to have been believed that lionesses and she-bears only bore young once in seven years, and that when their year came round it had a disastrous influence on pregnant women and on livestock; in Cheshire when there were losses of this type on the farms it was said that the performing bears which travelling showmen took about with them must be breeding, while in Shropshire in 1884 Miss Burne was told in four different villages that it was 'a very bad year for the women' because it was 'the seventh year, the year the lioness has her young'.

During a woman's pregnancy, and even more during her labour, her husband might suffer from toothaches, backaches, sickness, and other pains caused by his wife's condition, and if he did, her own pains would be lighter. This was quite commonly believed in Herefordshire in 1912, at least by the older generation; in Cheshire in the 1890s there was a case of a man going temporarily mad during his wife's pregnancy, which was taken to mean the child would be a boy – it was, and he recovered.

No doubt there were many beliefs and practices surrounding childbirth itself, but owing to the nature of the subject very few have been published; midwives may have been secretive about their professional activities, and in any case many nineteenth-century folklorists either did not know or did not wish publicly to discuss matters which would have been regarded as shocking or disgusting. One unusual item did get into print, in Fletcher Moss's book, concerning the alleged magic powers of the placenta:

> There is or was a belief that a man could gain the affections of a woman almost against her will by burying a placenta at the threshold of her house. This was actually done within memory at Gatley by a man named Gatley, he having procured one for two guineas. The charm failed in this instance, the woman being very self-willed.

It may be of interest to add that in the 1970s a young Sussex midwife told the present author that it used to be said that placentas were the best of all fertilizers for rose bushes, though no one ever attempts to buy them nowadays, it being well known that midwives have long been obliged by law to destroy all the birth tissues.

Beliefs concerning the caul, on the other hand, have been openly and frequently recorded. A baby born with a caul will never drown, and neither will any man who buys one, while a ship that has one in it will not sink; sailors were willing to pay several pounds to get one. No reason for this idea is given in the sources, but it is probably relevant that a baby born with a complete and unbroken caul around him will drown in the amniotic fluid, unless the midwife extricates him speedily. In contrast to the lucky caul, to be born with a tooth showing is extremely ill-omened, and means the child will grow up hard-bitten and grasping; one of Miss Burne's informants, discussing this, recalled the old tradition that Richard III had been born with teeth.

What food should first pass the baby's lips was a matter of great importance, and of some disagreement. Shropshire nurses gave a spoonful of butter and sugar, and so too did many in Herefordshire, though others there preferred to give rue pounded up with sugar; in Cheshire there were also many who favoured 'cinder-water', i.e. a spoonful of water from a glass into which a red-hot cinder had been dropped.

Many taboos surrounding a birth derived from an idea that it would be 'tempting Providence' to do anything that seemed to take for granted that the baby was going to live and thrive; thus, one ought not to bring a newly-bought cradle (or, nowadays, the pram) into the house before the baby is safe born; nor tell the chosen name to outsiders before the christening; nor weigh or measure the baby till he is a year old, lest he should stop growing. A baby must always be first taken upstairs before he is taken downstairs, to ensure that he will prosper, or to symbolize the hope that he will go to Heaven; if this cannot be done because the birth has taken place in an upstairs room, the nurse must climb onto some piece of furniture with the baby in her arms. In some families, the baby's first outing was considered important; speaking of himself and his brothers and sisters, Fletcher Moss writes:

> We were all taken dressed in our best bib and tucker, with bells and coral at our girdle, for our first visit to someone who was known to be a 'good sort'. The Good Samaritan gave us bread and salt and silver. Sometimes an egg was added, and the whole was given in a small oval basket for good hansel. The silver might be anything from a bent sixpence or old coin to a silver mug, and the giver was henceforth supposed to be interested in the little darling who unconsciously received the gift.

Other accounts give the customary gifts as an egg, a handful of salt, a piece of money, and sometimes a box of matches; obviously, they stood for wealth, food, and fire on one's hearth, and in addition the salt and the matches may have been meant to counteract witchcraft, for it is well known that evil spirits dread salt and fire. The bells and coral worn by the Moss infants, incidentally, were also originally protective amulets, though probably many Victorian parents did not know this fact.

As for the mother, it used to be strongly maintained that she must not set foot outside her house until she went to be 'churched' – a survival of the primitive notion that childbirth renders a woman 'unclean' and therefore a bringer of ill luck, until she is ritually 'purified'. Despite the efforts of the Church to present the service of 'churching' as a simple thanksgiving, the older idea lingered at the popular level. The child's baptism, too, was surrounded by popular beliefs: that it was unlucky if the baby did not cry during the service; that if it did cry, it would become a good singer; that if one of the sponsors looked into the font the child would grow up to look like him; that baptism would strengthen a sickly child; and that if the parents could coax the clergyman into giving them some of the water, this would be an excellent medicine if the child fell ill later on.

The ceremonies and rejoicings that accompanied weddings were much more public; if the young couple were popular, or of good family, the whole community might well be involved. Bell ringing was frequent; in Cheshire it might well last for as long as a week, with neighbours and friends clubbing together to pay the ringers. Arches of flowers and greenery were erected over the road leading to the church, bearing messages of good wishes, and embellished with streamers, paper hearts and gloves and sometimes flags and pennants (cf. pp. 162-63). At one wedding at Stoke-upon-Tern in 1829 there was a showy display of a type more often seen on May Day or at Rush Bearings (cf. pp. 159, 168-69):

> One went before us strewing flowers in our path; and all the silver spoons, tankards, watches and ornaments of the neighbouring farmers were fastened on white cloths drawn over hoops, so as to make a sort of trophy on each side of the gate, which is, I understand, a Shropshire custom.

During the greater part of the nineteenth century what was strewn at weddings was flowers, or sometimes ears of wheat; often, too, small posies of wild flowers were handed to the bridal party as they left the church, with good wishes from the onlookers. It is amusing to see how strongly both Miss Burne and Fletcher Moss objected to the 'horrid modern fashion' of throwing handfuls of 'rubbishy foreign rice' at the party as they left the church; one shudders to think what they would have said of the even more modern fashion of paper confetti! But at least neither rice nor confetti lent itself to a piece of symbolical ill-wishing that occurred in Herefordshire at the beginning of this century, as Mrs Leather records:

> It is only a few years since a young girl went to Cusop, to the wedding of a young man who had jilted her; waiting in the church porch till the bridegroom came out, she threw a handful of rue at him, saying 'May you rue this day as long as you live!' My informant said this caused a good deal of talk at the time, and he was told the curse would come true, because the rue was taken direct from the plant to the churchyard, and thrown 'between holy and unholy ground,' that is, between the church and the churchyard.

There were many small rules and taboos relating to weddings, some of which are still observed. The couple should not be in church to hear their banns called, lest their first child should be an imbecile. The bride should not use her married name before the ceremony (not even, for instance, for marking household linen), nor should anyone address her by it. Some girls insisted on being dressed entirely in brand new clothes, but most followed the rule 'Something old, something new, something borrowed, something blue'. Working-class girls who could not afford a white outfit usually preferred a blue dress, for blue means 'true' in the language of colours; green would certainly never be chosen, partly because it was generally considered an unlucky colour', and also because it was associated with forsaken or 'fallen' women. Some people thought it lucky to wear new shoes to a wedding, others old. In setting out for church, the bride must leave by the front door (this even applied, Miss Burne noted, when a maid was being married from the house where she worked); the front door must also be used when returning from church, and when leaving for the honeymoon or to go to the new house. It was most unlucky if the bridal procession encountered a funeral, or a woman in mourning, or passed through the lych-gate of the churchyard, or saw an open grave – any such graves would be screened off for the occasion.

On leaving the church, a wedding party in Cheshire, Radnorshire or Monmouthshire might find the porch, the path through the churchyard, or even the public road 'roped' against them by the villagers, who would not remove the obstacle until the bridegroom had distributed money to them; sometimes the rope had bunches of flowers tied to it, which the bridal party would 'pay' for. The custom is not yet quite extinct, being sometimes kept up by children in the Forest of Dean. Another very picturesque wedding custom was limited to Knutsford, the making of patterns of coloured sand in the streets, which has long been a local art in that town (cf. pp. 160-61); the town's historian, Henry Green, wrote:

> Few things please me more than to see the pavements well swept, the brown sand scattered, and then in white sand hearts and posies and knots of true love growing as it were by enchantment out of the ground.

Patterns are of course very pretty things, and the designs chosen for Knutsford wedding sandings are appropriate to the occasion; however, there may be a deeper reason for the practice, for there is an ancient belief that patterns can keep the powers of evil at bay, either by their intricacy, or by sacred symbolism. A few traces of this belief were to be found in the Border area even in fairly recent times; at St Briavels in 1902 it was said that an unbroken line of whitewash drawn all round the walls and over the top doorstep of a house would keep evil spirits out; in Shropshire up to the end of the nineteenth century both the hearthstone and the doorstep were decorated with designs made with the dye of elder leaves, to keep the Devil away and to bring luck to the house; these were simple patterns, such as rows of crosses, circles, vandykes, a design like a Union Jack, or an unbroken chain of loops. In some Herefordshire villages, doorsteps were given a neat border of white chalk after they had been washed, and nine crosses in a row were chalked inside the border; this was protection against witchcraft.

Not all weddings, however, lead to happy marriages. If a couple caused scandal by infidelity or by constant quarrels, the community might show its disapproval by the rowdy demonstration known in this area as 'Riding the Stang'. Miss Burne had heard of three cases near Shrewsbury in the 1880s, and Mrs Leather of others at Leominster and at Weobley Marsh around 1900; it is also known to have been done at Upton in Cheshire, and no doubt cases could be multiplied. The offending couple would be represented by straw-stuffed effigies like guys, which were lashed to long poles (the 'stangs') and carried through the streets, followed by a crowd yelling and whistling and banging on pots and pans. They would halt outside the culprits' home, waving the effigies and shouting out their accusations in doggerel rhymes, and making as much noise and commotion as they could. Finally the effigies would be thrown onto a bonfire, preferably in full view of the unfortunate couple's windows.

Variations naturally occurred, as at Northenden in Cheshire in about 1790, when instead of an effigy there was a proxy 'victim', mounted back to front on a donkey – a form of ritual humiliation known since the Middle Ages. The person being thus put to shame was a weaver's wife named Alice Evans, a big strong woman who had beaten her husband for getting drunk and neglecting his work. The men of the neighbourhood decided to punish her, for fear their own wives might copy her example:

> They therefore mounted one of their body, dressed in female apparel, on the back of an old donkey, this man holding a spinning wheel on his lap, and his back towards the donkey's head. Two men led the animal through the neighbourhood, followed by scores of boys and idle men, tinkling kettles and frying pans, roaring with cows' horns, and making a most hideous hullabaloo, stopping every now and then while the exhibitioner on the donkey made the following proclamation:
>
> *Ran a dan, ran a dan, ran a dan,*
> *Mrs Alice Evans has beat her good man,*
> *It was neither with a sword, spear, pistol or knife,*
> *But with a pair of tongs she vowed to take his life.*

The novelist Mrs Gaskell wrote to a friend in 1838 that Riding the Stang was 'a custom all over Cheshire', used when it became publicly known that a woman, particularly a wife, had been scolding, beating, or abusing a man. A crowd would gather in the evening, bringing 'an old, shabby, broken down horse', seize the woman, and force her to ride astride, facing the tail. They would then parade her through the village or town, drowning her angry shouts by clattering pots and pans 'just as you would scare a swarm of bees'. Mrs Gaskell wrote that in the many such cases she had known, the violence had never proceeded further, and the woman had never sought redress afterwards.

Though divorce has been available in England for several centuries, the legal expenses were so great that until recent times it was quite beyond the means of working-class couples. Instead, they sometimes had recourse to a procedure which was widely believed to be perfectly legal, the selling of a wife to another man by her own husband, whose property she was thought to be. It was, however, essential that the sale should be formally and publicly done; the woman must be brought to the market-place with a halter round her neck, and sometimes, as at Knighton in 1851 and 1854, the town crier was hired to give advance notice. The point was not so much to humiliate the woman, though presumably it did, as to ensure that there were plenty of people to bear witness to the transaction. For the same reason, a 'legal' document was often drawn up, declaring, for example, that 'We agree to part wholly and solely for life, and not to trouble one another for life'. Various other conditions were imposed locally; at Mottram in Cheshire the sales are said always to have been held on the steps of the market cross; in Shropshire the woman had to pass through a turnpike gate, duly haltered, on her way to market, and her price was fixed at five shillings and a quart of ale. In Hereford in 1802, a butcher's wife fetched a better price, £1 4s and a bowl of punch. It is from Hereford too that there comes a vivid eye-witness recollection of one such sale; the date is not given, but must have been around 1800, since the anonymous writer who describes it was in her nineties in 1876:

> I must recall to your memory my statement as to my being playfellow to Mona Delnotte Coates, for it was while walking with her that I first saw a man selling his wife. We were going from the Barton to the other side of the town, and necessarily had to pass the bottom of the pig market. Here we saw a crowd. The girl was desirous of knowing what was the matter, so she elbowed her way through the people, and was followed by the children to the open space in the centre. There stood a woman with her hat in her hand ... This woman's hat was a very smart one. She stood looking down. At first I thought she was admiring her own red cloak, but as she stood so still my eyes wandered over her to see what was amiss, and I shall never forget how surprised I felt when I observed she had a rope about her neck, and that a man was holding one end of it. 'What has she done?' we both cried out, for I believed she was going to be hanged. 'Oh,' said a

bystander, 'she has done no good, depend upon it, or else he wouldn't want to sell her.' Just then there was loud laugh, and a man shouted 'Well done, Jack, that is elevenpence more than I would give. It's too much, boy, too much.' But Jack stood firm. 'No', said he, 'I'll give a shilling, and he ought to be thankful to get rid of her at that price.' 'Well,' said the man, 'I'll take it, though her good looks ought to be worth more than that.' 'Keep her, master, keep her for her good looks,' shouted the laughing bystanders. 'No,' said he, 'good looks won't put the victuals on the table without willing hands.' 'Well,' said Jack, 'here's the shilling, and I warrant I'll make her put the victuals on the table for me, and help to get it first. Be you willing, Missis, to have me, and take me for better for worse?' 'I be willing,' says she. 'And be you willing to sell her for what I bid, maister?' 'I be,' said he, 'and will give you the rope into the bargain.' So Jack gave the man his shilling.

Even more scandalous situations could arise; according to the *Chester Chronicle* in 1799, a man called Twig, already married, bought himself not one wife but two at Macclesfield, one for a shilling and the other for half a crown, and led them home with the cattle halters still round their necks. Despite all attempts to stamp out the practice, people long remained convinced of its legality; as late as 1882 a woman maintained in the County Court at Chester that she was not living in adultery because her first husband had 'legally' sold her for 25s, and she had a stamped receipt to prove it.

But neither births nor marriages offer so ample a display of folk beliefs and practices as do deaths and funerals. For a start, there are the very numerous death omens, many of which are still dreaded to this day, though sometimes merely as bringers of unspecified bad luck rather than of death. Some are drawn from the behaviour of animals and birds: a dog howling in the night, a cock crowing between dusk and midnight; an owl screeching or hooting; bats entering the house or clinging to a window; a bird, especially a dove, entering the house or beating against the window; a raven croaking; a rook or crow perching on the roof; a frog or snake crossing the threshold; the mysterious birds known as the Seven Whistlers (possibly widgeon, curlews or golden plover) heard calling overhead; an eerie white bird, of no known species, flying round the house or singing outside a sick person's window. Other omens are drawn from household occurrences: if one of the family portraits or photographs falls from the wall; if the furniture emits loud raps; if a glass, or a glass bowl or vase, shatters for no reason; if candle wax drips to form a 'winding sheet'; if a clock falls, stops inexplicably, strikes between the hours, or even just runs down; if a bell rings of its own accord; if mirrors or china fall and break; if someone brings a spade or axe into the house on his shoulder, or opens an umbrella indoors over someone's head; if a badly folded sheet or tablecloth has a coffin-shaped crease at the centre.

Other omens are taken from incidents directly connected with death itself, with corpses, or with funerals. Thus it is thought that deaths always come in threes; that if a corpse remains limp, or if its eyes stay open, it is waiting for another death to follow in the family. Appropriately for such a keen collector of folklore, Kilvert's death was said at the time to have been preceded by an omen – on the Sunday before he died, the bell of Bredwardine church 'appeared to have an unusually heavy sound, the tone being altogether different from its usual character'. In other words, it sounded like the muffled bell sometimes tolled for funerals. Finally, there are wholly supernatural death-warnings, such as seeing one's own wraith, meeting a phantom funeral, or seeing the 'corpse candles'. This last is particularly common in Wales and in the parts of Herefordshire nearest to it, such as Hay and Kington; the 'candles' were said to be ghostly lights seen leaving a house where a death will soon occur, moving along a track to the churchyard, and hovering over the spot where the grave will be. In Cheshire, however, their course is reversed; blueish lights come out from the churchyard and move towards the doomed person's home.

It was believed that certain things would ease, and others hinder, the process of dying. Some people thought one could not die till the moon was waning, others that one cannot die while lying on a pillow or mattress containing pigeon feathers, turkey feathers, or the feathers of wild birds. So when a person's death agony was unduly long, the bystanders would sometimes pull the pillow from under him to hasten the end; it is said that at Ford, near Shrewsbury, a woman once pulled her husband bodily out of bed and onto the floor, where 'he went off as nice and easy as you please'. As soon as death had occurred, the door and windows must be opened, 'to let the soul go free', and the mirror must be turned to the wall, or covered with black drapery. The body must then be decently laid out, pennies laid on its eyelids to keep them shut, and, some said, a pewter plate containing salt placed upon its chest. This was still being done in Herefordshire in 1912, where some people also recommended that a candle should be stuck in the middle of the heaped-up salt; both there and in Shropshire there was an alternative procedure of laying a turf wrapped in paper upon the corpse. In both cases the purpose was said to be to prevent the corpse swelling, but it is very likely that in earlier periods it had been a way of keeping demons and evil spirits away. For the same reason, it used to be thought necessary to keep a light burning in the room where the body lay, and to have someone keeping constant watch beside it, or at least sitting awake in another room of the house.

All visitors who came to the house in the interval between the death and the funeral were expected to go upstairs to pay their respects to the dead man, usually by laying a hand upon his brow, or by touching his hand; this was said to ensure that one would not dream of the body. Writing in 1937, the Revd R.T. Davies noted that what he callously calls the 'insanitary custom' of keeping watch by the coffin on the night before burial was not quite abandoned in Monmouthshire, though he was 'glad to say that it had almost died out'. The watchers he so much disapproved of spent their vigil in hymn singing, and in praying for the mourners; in earlier centuries they would have been praying for the dead man himself, as is done in wakes in Catholic countries. Possibly the touching of the dead man's brow should also be interpreted as the vestigial remains of a Roman Catholic custom, the making of the Sign of the Cross over the dead; some folklorists, however, think it is connected with the belief that a murdered body will bleed if the murderer touches it (which was known and acted on in this area, as elsewhere), even though this seems rather remote from the circumstances of most domestic deaths.

Catholic practices also undoubtedly lie behind the custom, formerly well known in Wales and the Border counties, of handing beer, wine, cakes or biscuits, and sometimes cheese, across the coffin to the mourners, or to the poor. Two pre-Reformation rites are reflected here: the Requiem Mass at which mourners took Communion with the intention of assisting the dead man who was suffering in Purgatory for his sins, and the giving of alms to the poor so that they too might pray for him. Scriptural support for the latter can be found in the Book of Tobias (or Tobit), which forms part of the Greek and Latin Bible, though not of Protestant ones:

> 'Alms deliver from all sin, and from death, and will not suffer the soul to go into darkness.... Lay your bread and your wine upon the grave of a just man' (Tobias 4: 11, 18).

An interesting, though hostile, description of the funeral of a nobleman in Shrewsbury in 1671, written by a French Catholic, shows the symbolic value then attached to the wine served at a funeral:

> The relations and friends being assembled in the house of the defunct, the minister advanced into the middle of the chamber, where, before the company, he made a funeral oration, representing the great actions of the deceased, his qualities, his titles of nobility... [and saying] that he was gone to Heaven, the seat of all sorts of happiness... It is to be remarked that during this oration there stood upon the coffin a large pot of wine, out of which everyone drank to the health of the deceased, hoping that he might surmount the difficulties he had to encounter in his road to Paradise, where by the mercy of God he was about to enter; on which mercy they founded all their hope, without considering their evil life, their wicked religion, or that God is just.

The same association of ideas appears even more clearly – and this time in the words of a participant, not of a foreign onlooker – in an incident which one of Mrs Leather's informants told her had recently happened to him:

> He was invited to attend the funeral of the sister of a farmer, near Crasswall, and to his surprise was invited to go upstairs to the room where the body was lying. He went, with the brother and four bearers. At the bottom of the bed, at the foot of the coffin, was a little box, with a white cloth covering it. On it were placed a bottle of port wine, opened, and six glasses arranged round it. The glasses were

filled, and my informant was asked to drink. This he refused, saying he never took wine. 'But you must drink, sir,' said the old farmer. 'It is like the Sacrament. It is to kill the sins of my sister.'

So clear an explanation is extremely rare, but the custom itself was widespread. In 1910, the Revd D.E. Edmondes Owen found it was a 'universal and rigid' custom in Radnorshire that the mourners should gather in the house to pray for the bereaved before carrying the coffin to the church, and that they should take cake and wine while standing by the coffin. In various other parts of Wales, bread and cheese or bread and cider were handed across the coffin to poor people, either in the house or at the graveside. What type of cakes were offered depended on local convention; round Ross, they resembled hot cross buns; in other parts of Herefordshire, they were finger biscuits; in some parts of Shropshire, slices of plum cake or of seed cake; in other parts, and also in Cheshire, what Moss describes as 'small rich sponge cakes with a smell of ammonia, which were wrapped in tissue paper and then in black-edged notepaper, and addressed to those who were bidden to the burial, or sent away to those who could not come'. These special sponge cakes were no longer much in demand in either county by the 1880s, being replaced by plain biscuits. In most places, wine or hot spiced ale was also served, at any rate to the coffin-bearers and the chief mourners.

The most dramatic (and controversial) account of a ceremony of this type is that given by the famous antiquary John Aubrey in the seventeenth century, in his *Remaines of Gentilisme and Judaisme*:

> In the County of Hereford was an old Custome at funeralls to have poor people, who were to take upon them all the sinnes of the party deceased. One of them I remember lived in a cottage on Rosse highway. He was a long leane, ugly, lamentable poor raskel. The Manner was that when the Corps was brought out of the house and layd on the Biere, a Loafe of bread was brought out and delivered to the Sinne-eater over the corps, as also a Mazer-bowie of maple full of beer, which he was to drinke up, and sixpence in money, in consideration whereof he took upon him ipso facto all the Sinnes of the Defunct, and freed him (or her) from walking after they were dead....

This Custome (though rarely used in our dayes) yet by some people was continued even in the strictest time of the Presbyterian government; as at Dynder, volens nolens the Parson of the Parish, the relations of a woman deceased there had this ceremonie punctually performed according to her Will; and also the like was donne at the City of Hereford in these times, when a woman kept many years before the death a Mazard-bowie for the Sinne-eater; and the like in other places in this Countie; as also in Brecon, e.g. at Llangors, where Mr Gwin the minister about 1640 could not hinder the performing of this ancient customme. I believe this customme was heretofore used all over Wales.

About thirty years after Aubrey wrote, John Bagford declared in a letter of February 1714/15 that a parallel custom had been known in seventeenth-century Shropshire; his account, however, is not first-hand, but rests on some notes of Aubrey's that are now lost. According to Bagford:

Within the memories of our Fathers, in Shropshire, in those villages adjoining to Wales, when a person dyed, there was notice given to an old Sire (for so they called him) who presently repaired to the place where the deceased lay, and stood before the door of the house, when some of the Family came out and furnished him with a Cricket [stool], on which he sat down facing the door. Then they gave him a Groat, which he put in his pocket; a Crust of Bread, which he ate; and a full bowle of Ale, which he drank off at a draught. After this, he got up from the Cricket and pronounced, with a composed gesture, the ease and rest of the Soul departed, for which he would pawn his own Soul. This I had from the ingenious John Aubrey, Esq., who made a Collection of Curious Observations, which I have seen, and is now remaining in the hands of Mr Churchill, the bookseller.

These two remarkable accounts gave rise to vigorous controversy among nineteenth-century folklorists, especially when, at a meeting of the Cambrian Archaeological Association at Ludlow in 1852, a Mr Matthew Moggridge of Swansea claimed that Sin-Eating had existed at Llandebie 'within the last twenty years', and gave additional details, stressing the dramatic function of the human scapegoat:

> When a person died, his friends sent for the Sin-Eater of the district, who on his arrival placed a plate of salt on the breast of the defunct, and upon the salt a piece of bread. He then muttered an incantation over the bread, which he finally ate, thereby eating up all the sins of the deceased. This done, he received his fee of 2/6 and vanished as quickly as possible from the general gaze; for, as it was believed he really appropriated to his own used and behoof the sins of all those over whom he performed the above ceremony, he was utterly detested in the neighbourhood – regarded as a mere Pariah – as one irremediably lost.

Moggridge also said the practice was known in a parish near Chepstow, where the salt was marked with a cross, and a quartered apple or orange placed at the four tips of this cross; a Mr Allen of Pembrokeshire added that in that county a candle was set up in the salt.

During the next few decades, several folklorists hunted for further evidence concerning Sin-Eating; they had no difficulty in finding instances of bread and salt placed on corpses, and of distributions of cakes and wine, bread and ale, or bread and cheese, of the simpler type already described, but the human scapegoat, the Sin-Eater, remained totally elusive. Neither Miss Burne in Shropshire, Wirt Sikes in Wales, nor Mrs Leather in Herefordshire could find any additional evidence that such people had existed. But E.S. Hartland, arguing from anthropological parallels, found the accounts by Aubrey and Moggridge convincing; in his opinion, they represented something far more archaic than distorted memories of Catholic doctrines and practices, for to him the Sin-Eating was a survival of a primitive cannibalistic communion rite. Few would now accept so extreme an interpretation. Then, in 1924, Mary Webb's best-selling novel *Precious Bane* gave a central place to a powerful episode involving Sin-Eating, describing it so soberly and realistically that most readers have taken it for granted that this was a quite normal and well-attested procedure in nineteenth-century Shropshire. In fact, however, as we have seen, the only really solid evidence, Aubrey's, refers to Herefordshire and Wales in the seventeenth century; Bagford's second-hand reference to Shropshire must be treated with caution, and so too must the later survivals claimed for Wales. The Sin-Eater who appeared briefly in the televised version of *The Diary of a Farmer's Wife* must be dismissed as fictitious (see Introduction, pp. 12-13).

An amusing sidelight on this issue is that local tradition long identified the Sin-Eater's 'cottage on Rosse high-way' mentioned by Aubrey with one called The Black House on the road from Ross to Ledbury, used as a blacksmith's shop and situated near a pub, The Traveller's Rest (it has been demolished, and the old pub replaced by a modern one). One correspondent assured me in 1982 that in the 1950s a local historian, passing this cottage, said, 'The last Sin-Eater I knew lived here', which he took to be proof that the custom persisted into living memory. Yet it seems virtually certain that the local historian was simply passing on Aubrey's information, and that some ambiguity of phrasing led his hearer to assume he was speaking from personal knowledge, and thus to update the tradition by two hundred years or more.

To revert to more normal funeral customs: as the procession left the house, one of the mourners would stop beside the beehives, if the dead man had owned bees, and shake or lift or tap them, and would tell the bees that their master was dead; some said the hives must be lifted at the same moment as the coffin was raised from the table or trestles where it had rested. If this was not done, the bees would either die or leave their hives. There were, however, people who thought it more correct to inform the bees secretly, in the middle of the night; instances of this are known from Shropshire, Cheshire and Montgomery.

In some districts it was traditional that as the bearers carried the coffin to church (which was done on foot, the mourners walking behind), they should set it down at certain specified spots, or should carry it round some particular stone or tree, or turn it round before bringing it into the churchyard. Thus at Trelleck until about 1930 the coffin-bearers used always to pause to set their burden down as soon as they came in sight of the church, while in earlier times those coming by the road from Park House to Trelleck church used to carry the coffin round the stump of an old wayside cross. Others, when crossing Pennallt Common, used to stop and sing a psalm while the coffin rested on a stone bench under a certain oak tree. At Pembridge in Herefordshire, coffins were always brought to the church by a roundabout route, the bearers halting for a few moments at each crossroads, and then carried sunwise round the church before entering. At Brilley coffins were carried three times round the 'Funeral Stone' in the churchyard, which may have been the base of an old cross, in order to prevent the Devil from getting the dead man's soul. In Shropshire there do not seem to have been fixed stopping places of this sort, but in many villages 'the neighbours set their tables and benches, sometimes covered with white cloths, in the roadway, that the bearers may lay down their burden and pause for a moment's rest'.

The choice of bearers was a matter of considerable importance; usually they were kinsmen or close friends to the dead man, and to be asked to perform this office was a compliment. There was a tradition, still in force in many rural areas towards the end of the nineteenth century, that the age and status of the bearers should reflect that of the deceased; older people, especially if married, would be carried to their grave by married men; unmarried girls by young women (unless the distance was too long and tiring, in which case young men would do); babies and young children by little boys or little girls dressed in white. Round Edgmond, it was customary to wear white scarves and hat bands for all unmarried people, of whatever age, but elsewhere this type of mourning was worn for children only. The bearers were generally given mourning gloves, scarves and hat bands; sometimes a dole, which might be anything from a penny to half-a-crown, would be slipped inside the gloves.

Round Rhayader, and in a few other places in Radnorshire, there was an unusual and very characteristically Celtic custom: the mourners in a funeral procession would each be carrying a small pebble, and as they passed a certain spot they would throw it onto a pile of stones left there from previous funerals, saying 'carn ar dy ben', i.e. 'a stone on thy head'. These cairns were still being occasionally added to at funerals up to 1910.

Far more common, till late in the nineteenth century, was the custom that each mourner should carry with him a sprig of rosemary, which was given him as the procession set out; usually this would be thrown into the grave after the coffin had been lowered in, but some people took their rosemary home to dry it as a keepsake, while others planted the cutting to grow into a bush in memory of the dead – 'Rosemary, that's for remembrance', as Ophelia said. In Monmouthshire in 1905, Miss Wherry observed that people sometimes put rue, hyssop or wormwood into the coffin itself; she did not record whether they deliberately chose these herbs as being all three symbolical of repentence, but this seems likely. In north Shropshire, in contrast, the coffin would be filled with wallflowers, roses, or other blooms. But the laying of flower wreaths on top of the coffin and then on the filled-in grave, so common nowadays, only came in towards the end of the nineteenth century; Miss Burne dates its beginning to the 1870s, and Fletcher Moss writes:

> In my memory it was considered heathenish to put flowers on graves or in them, and I believe it was on my father's grave, in December 1867, that the Rector of Didsbury first consented to having plants or flowers planted on a grave.

Bell ringing at funerals took various forms. Strictly speaking, the term 'passing bell' referred to the tolling of a single bell shortly after a death had occurred, in order to announce it to the community; however, the phrase was also sometimes loosely used for the tolling that greeted the approaching funeral procession. There were different ways of ringing it. At Didsbury the code was eight strokes for a child, twelve for a woman, sixteen for a man; at Great Budworth, until about 1930, a muffled bell would be rung for about half an hour on the evening before the funeral, and again for an hour before the funeral itself, starting at three-minute intervals but gradually speeding up till the strokes came every half-minute, at which point the vicar would know it was time for him to prepare to meet the cortege. In Shrewsbury in 1879 the ringing code was highly elaborate; at ten o'clock on the evening of the death, the sexton would first toll seventy strokes (since 'the days of our age are threescore years and ten'), pause, toll for ten minutes, then pause again, and then give the strokes that revealed the age and sex of the deceased – nine for a child, nine and a pause and then ten for a woman, nine and a pause plus ten and a pause plus eleven for a man. On the evening before the funeral there would again be ten minutes of tolling, then the sex given out as before, and finally as many strokes as the precise age of the deceased. In several Shropshire villages the tolling would speed up as the procession drew near the church, in the same way as at Great Budworth; at Edgmond and Morville, instead of tolling a single bell, the whole ring would be chimed together, a practice known there as 'joy bells', or as 'ringing the dead home'. The chief purpose of all these customs was, obviously, to honour the dead, but the old belief that the sound of church bells drives evil spirits away was not wholly forgotten.

A custom that attracted unfavourable notice at the time of the Reformation, as savouring of Popery, was that of taking a collection across the coffin or at the graveside; one presumes this had originally been for paying for Requiem Masses, since if it had only been to defray funeral expenses it is hard to see why anyone should have objected. There was also sometimes a distribution of money as alms, originally no doubt as a payment to 'bedesmen', poor people who undertook to pray for the dead man. At Tarvin in Cheshire money was given out at funerals till 1659, but was then abolished on the grounds that it caused unseemly uproar as people scrambled for the coins. But other forms of this collection persisted for a long time; in 1875 Kilvert wrote:

> William Boscawon told us of a curious custom which is still kept up in many parts of Wales. At the funerals offerings are made at the graveside to the clergyman by the mourners, and the offerings are collected upon the grave shovel. This is a relic of the old Catholic custom of offering money to the priest to say Masses for the soul of the departed.

It was still customary in some parts of Radnorshire in 1910 for the gravedigger to hold out his spade across the open grave, and for each mourner to lay a coin in it as his fee.

Any startling incident occurring at a funeral was naturally remembered, discussed, interpreted, and made the subject of local storytelling. Any untoward hitch in the proceedings might be held to mean that the dead man had led an evil life, and was bound for an unpleasant destination. A thunderstorm, for instance, boded ill for the fate of his soul, though a gentle rain was a good sign; in Cheshire it was said, if the horses drawing a hearse sweated heavily, that it was a sign that the dead man 'had had too much brass, or had done summat wrong', since it was always very difficult to get a wicked corpse to church. At Orcop in Herefordshire people long remembered the funeral of one old lady who had refused to pay certain charitable dues to which her farm was liable; as her coffin was being carried through the church a fine embroidered shroud which hung from it caught on the chancel rails and 'ripped from end to end and hung down round the coffin, that was because she had defrauded the poor'. Most macabre of all is a tale from Cheshire; as the coffin of a certain Captain Whittle was being carried along the particularly windy ridge of Mottram Hill, a terrible gust snatched it from the grasp of the bearers and sent it rolling down the hillside – and to this day, they say, the wind still howls there, and is known as Captain Whittle's Wind.

The observances due to death did not end with the burial. Quite apart from the elaborate etiquette of Victorian upper and middle-class mourning (too vast a subject to be discussed here), there lingered in the Welsh districts and in parts of Herefordshire a faint recollection of the pre-Reformation custom of observing the thirtieth day after a death by offering Mass for the dead, and observing the anniversary in the same way. In Herefordshire the memory was verbal only; the term mouzend denoted the 'month's end' after a funeral, and the twelve months following the death was known as the deathzearr. In Radnorshire and Monmouthshire, however, an actual commemorative service was held, called the 'Month's Mind' or the 'Month's End'. Originally it was held one month after the death, but later more usually on the second or third Sunday after either the death or the funeral; in the nineteenth century it was thought to be unlucky for the closest mourners to leave the house before this, and even in the 1930s, according to the Revd R.T. Davies, they would certainly not come to church on the intervening Sundays.

A few Shropshire villages in the eighteenth century had a picturesque way of honouring a girl who died unmarried, particularly if she had been betrothed at the time of her death, by displaying a 'Virgin's Garland' on her coffin, and then hanging it in the church as her permanent memorial. The 'garland' is a structure rather like a crown, made up of two intersecting arches on a hoop base, the whole thing being about a foot in height. The framework is covered with white linen, onto which are sewn pink paper roses and white paper lilies, or, in other examples, black and white ribbon rosettes; ribbons hang down from it, and sometimes also one or more pairs of white gloves, whether real or made of paper. The girl's name and dates are usually indicated, either on small wooden labels, hanging from the garland, or by inscriptions on the bracket that supports it. There are still seven of these garlands to be seen in Minsterley church, another at Astley Abbots, and another at Acton Burnell. There are known to have been others, now lost, at Shrawardine, Hanwood, and Little Ness chapel.

Once the dead have been laid to rest, it is reckoned both wrong and unlucky to disturb their resting places. In his *History of Kington* in 1845, Richard Parry deplored the way in which tombstones had been moved from their places and used for paving the church floor; a local sexton, however, had taken measures of his own to avert evil consequences, and told Parry: 'They be quite se'af, the owd gravestones. Mr —— had they to lay flurs wi', they be quite se'af wi' their faces down'rts.' The method seems based on a traditional way of stopping potential ghosts from walking, by burying the bodies face down, so that if they do move, they only go deeper underground.

A final instance of these eerie notions was encountered by Mrs Leather in 1926: an old man told her that 'queer flowers with black blooms' grow if the bones in a churchyard are dug up and thrown on a rubbish heap, as had happened at Grosmont when he was a boy – 'nobody had seen the like before, and the flowers were just like the plumes they used to have on a hearse.'

NINE

THE TURNING YEAR: JANUARY TO MAY

It has always been common for people to mark the beginnings and ends of periods of time by rituals, often believed to ensure luck. The New Year is one such turning-point, and so all along the Border people would remain awake till after midnight to 'let the New Year in' by welcoming into their homes the first visitor of the year – a visitor who, if he was to bring luck with him, must fufil certain conditions. It must be a man or boy, preferably dark-haired. In Cheshire it was added that he must not squint, nor be flat-footed, nor have eyebrows joining over his nose, and that he must silently lay gifts of bread and whisky on the table, and a coal on the fire; he would then be given wine and cake, and would wish everyone in the house a happy New Year. In Shropshire, round Shrewsbury and Clun, it was once usual for men or boys to walk right through the house, entering by one door and leaving by the other; the first to pass through would be given a silver coin, a mince pie, and mulled wine; the second, a copper coin; any others, just beer.

The strongest belief associated with this custom, which has remained vigorous to this day, is that it would mean very bad luck if the first visitor on this day should be a woman. Indeed, in the Stretton

Valley in the 1880s it was held unlucky for a woman to enter anyone's house before noon on New Year's Day, no matter how many men had preceded her. Similarly, when the Revd Francis Kilvert was at Clyro in the 1870s, old Hannah Whitney told him that her mother's death had been caused by two girls breaking this rule. The mother had been quite well up to the moment when the two girls called, wanting to borrow some horseradish:

> It was before noon, and the sight of the girls gave her a turn. It was very unlucky. 'Name of goodness,' she screamed, 'what ails the girls to come about folks' houses on New Year's Day in the morning? Sure as fate, something will happen before twelve months are out!'

And sure enough, she fell ill of a fever that very day, and she and her sister and her old father all died of it.

The first water drawn from a well on New Year's Day was thought to give beauty and good luck, and was known as the 'cream of the well' or the 'crop of the well'. In Herefordshire servants would sit up to see the New Year in, and on the stroke of midnight would race to draw water from the well; whoever drew a pailful and brought it to the mistress of the house would get a shilling. Similar ideas existed in Radnorshire and Monmouthshire, where as recently as 1900 two old men used to dress Llanishen well with sprigs of box on New Year's Eve, and then race to get its 'crop' at midnight, to make tea with! What special qualities they thought this tea would have is not recorded.

Another custom which must be carried out before dawn on New Year's Day was 'Burning the Bush'. This was common on farms in Radnorshire and Herefordshire in the nineteenth century, and still persisted in a few areas of the latter when Mrs Leather was writing in 1912. The purpose of the procedure was to protect the wheat against evil spirits, or against the disease called smut. All the men of the farm would go out very early, around five in the morning, carrying a hawthorn 'bush', i.e. a branch whose twigs had been forcibly bent into a rough globe. Sometimes this had been freshly made for the occasion, but in most places it was a year old, having been made on the previous New Year's Day and kept hanging in the kitchen ever since as a luck-bringer. It was burned on the wheatfield in a straw fire; in some places it was carried, blazing, across twelve ridges, and if it went out before passing the twelfth, this boded ill for the crop. Meanwhile, a new bush was being prepared and its end would be singed in the fire that destroyed the old one; it might also be doused with cider 'to varnish and darken the bush, like.' The ceremony ended with a hearty drink; at Brinsop in Mrs Leather's time:

> The men stand in a ring round the fire and 'holloa old cider'. They sing, on a very deep note, very slowly, holding each note as long as possible, 'Auld Ci–der'. The 'der' becomes a sort of growl at the end, and is an octave below the first two notes; it has a weird dirge-like effect. This is repeated thrice, bowing as low as possible as each note is sung, nine bows altogether. Then follows cheering and drinking, cider and cake being provided for the purpose.

These farming rituals are now extinct, but it is still common for groups of children to go from house to house on New Year's morning singing or reciting short verses, in order to get money, apples or sweets. Like so many children's customs, it must only be done before the hour of noon, so those taking part would start early, even sometimes at dawn, so as to visit as many friends and neighbours as they could. At Presteigne in the 1940s one of the verses ran:

> *Master and mistress sit by the fire,*
> *We poor boys are out in the mire,*
> *A penny apiece is our desire.*
> *Please to give us a New Year's gift!*

Elsewhere in Radnorshire in the 1950s a schoolgirl described how she and her sister and a few friends reckoned to collect nine or ten shillings every year, plus apples and mince pies; their song was:

> *I wish you a merry Christmas, a happy New Year,*
> *A pocket full of money and a cellar full of beer,*
> *A good fat pig to last you all the year.*
> *Please give to me a New Year's gift for this New Year.*

Some generations earlier, New Year Gifting was not confined to children. In 1822, *The Gentleman's Magazine* reported that in

Herefordshire the 'peasantry' were calling at houses with 'a small pyramid made of leaves, apples, nuts etc., gilt, in the hope of receiving gifts in exchange for the luck this conferred'. Generally these apples were mounted on three wooden legs and decorated with sprigs of box and hazel nuts; they were still common in Monmouthshire and round St Briavels in 1900, and according to one author could still be seen at the latter place as recently as 1950, being carried by children. Another author, Edmund Mason, writes of it in 1987 as being 'still kept up' at Devauden in the Wye Valley.

In Chepstow before the First World War such an apple was called a Monty, and the children who carried it chanted:

Monty, Monty, Happy New Year,
A pocket full of money and a cellar full of beer!

They also used oranges as Monties, mounting them on three legs in the same way, but choosing holly as the decoration; tinsel, raisins, and gold or silver glitter were added.

In a few districts of Herefordshire and Monmouthshire, New Year's Day was the time for wassailing fields and cattle, but this was more frequently done on 5 January. This was a very widespread custom in the first half of the nineteenth century, and did not wholly die out till about 1910. The first part of the ritual consisted of the farmer going out, towards six in the evening, with his friends and his farm labourers, to a field where wheat was growing. There they made a circle of twelve small bonfires round one larger one, the latter being variously known as 'old Meg', 'the witch', 'the Virgin Mary', or 'Judas'; in the latter case, the twelve little fires would of course be 'the Apostles', and the big one would be soon kicked out. The men formed a ring round the big fire, shouting and cheering and toasting one another in cider; they called this 'burning the witch', and said that if it was not done there would be no crop. When the fires had died down, the men returned to the farm for a good supper. The second part of the ritual took place later that evening, when they all went out again in procession, this time to the cowsheds to toast the cattle, and in particular the oxen that drew the plough. Each would be pledged by name in ale or cider, with some such verse as:

Here's to thee, Brownie, and to thy white horn;
God send thy master a good crop of corn,
Of wheat, rye and barley and all sorts of grain;
You eat your oats and I'll drink my beer,
May the Lord send us a happy New Year.

Then a large plum cake with a hole in the middle was placed on the horn of the finest ox, and he was pricked and tickled to make him toss his head; if he tossed the cake forwards it was a good omen for the harvest, but not if it fell behind him. Others said that in the first case the cake must be given to the head cowman, in the second returned to the mistress of the house.

These farming rituals gradually died out during the first part of the twentieth century, but in more recent times similar rituals have been recreated in several places, drawing both on the memories of the elderly and on written descriptions such as Mrs Leather's, frequently echoed in books and magazines of local interest. Morris dancers and others who consciously encourage traditional aspects of country life often play an active role in these revivals. Thus, at the present time at Aymestrey in the cider-making area of Herefordshire, the Leominster Morris Men take the lead in wassailing apple trees on 6 January, in a ceremony clearly drawing upon features of the old wassailing of wheat and cattle. A recent (2002) participant captures the emotional significance of the occasion, and the pagan mysticism which some read into it; he writes of local people gathering at an inn, and eventually forming a procession:

> Torches were lit, one from another. The drum beat a simple rhythm, the accordion played in two-time, the fiddler joined in, and we walked away from the inn, a long, long line of us, along the road, through the village, the band and Morris men leading, the line of torches following for 150 yards behind, carrying the warmth and light of fire to warm the Cider-God back to life from his midwinter slumber.
>
> In the orchard, a circle of circular bonfire heaps, twelve of them, one for each month, around the hub of the central and ancient apple tree. Darkness except for the torches; cold except for their little radius of heat. Together, we lit the fires; there was a thirteenth fire, for Judas,

quickly stamped out, and a symbolic 'bush', to tell the Sun to wake up, that winter had begun to end. Now there was warmth and light and music and dancing; they brought mugs of cider so we all joined in sharing the hopes and aspirations of the centuries, of the generations, of the British and the Norsemen and the Shetlanders and the Northumbrians, all with their midwinter fire rituals to drive out the cold and dark and replace them with warmth and light.

There were no tourists; no foreign visitors; no promoters or profiteers; just us and our past, present and future.

Many of the beliefs connected with Twelfth Night reflect the stubborn conviction that 6 January is the 'real' Christmas Day, and that the adjustment of the calendar in 1752 must be ignored. In 1822, according to *The Gentleman's Magazine*, people in the Forest of Dean utterly refused to observe 25 December, while as late as 1850 some Herefordshire parishes insisted on holding special services on 6 January; indeed, H.L.V. Fletcher found that the underlying conviction persisted in this county in the 1930s and 1940s. Both here and in Monmouthshire it was said that various plants and animals knew this was the 'real' Christmas and would show homage to the Christ-child at midnight; rosemary would blossom, bees would leave their hives and hum, cattle would kneel and weep in the stalls.

The best known of these 'miracles' was the blossoming of the Holy Thorn, of which there were, and are, many specimens in Herefordshire, all said to be descended from cuttings taken from the famous Glastonbury Thorn. The blossoms are thought to open exactly at midnight, the hour when Christ was born, and to drop off an hour later; sprigs picked during this time bring luck, if kept for a year. On 7 January 1878, Kilvert visited a farm at Dolfach where a Holy Thorn had bloomed at midnight on Twelfth Night, watched by fifteen people; the farmer's daughter gave him a spray in bud, assuring him it would come out in water, and explaining that she set great store by it and always gathered and kept a piece every year. Kilvert later had a cutting grafted in his own garden, and on 6 January 1879, he notes with pleasure that it had indeed just bloomed, despite intense frost. In milder years this early flowering is quite common; Mrs Leather was one of a group who watched it happen at Wormesley in 1908 (she wondered whether the warmth of their candles might have helped), but a crowd of 100 who visited the same place in 1934 were disappointed. However, in 1949 a correspondent wrote to *The Times* to say that many buds of the Orcop Thorn had burst into flower within a few minutes of midnight on Old Christmas Eve. Nowadays the presence of Holy Thorns in several Herefordshire places has been forgotten, and the custom of watching them has therefore lapsed.

The first Church feast in February, Candlemas or the Feast of the Purification (2 February), has little importance in this region. A few proverbs allude to it, notably the Cheshire saying:

A farmer should on Candlemas Day
Have half his corn and half his hay.

The point of this lies in warning that winter is only half over, so provisions must be used sparingly. In Shropshire, the date is associated with the coming of snowdrops, known as 'Christ's flowers', 'Candlemas Bells', 'Fair Maid of February' or 'Purification Flowers'; some people used to bring a bunch into the house on or around this date, though to do so at other times was believed to be unlucky.

It is more startling to find that St Valentine's Day, after its great popularity in the nineteenth century, passed into a period of complete eclipse. In 1912 Mrs Leather noted that in Herefordshire 'the custom of sending Valentines is dying, but not yet extinct'; in Radnorshire in 1949, said W.H. Howse, the day 'has now fallen almost out of remembrance', not having been celebrated since the 1890s. Modern commercial publicity, spreading out from the cities to the countryside, has now ensured that Valentines are even more widespread than in their Victorian heyday, and are hardly likely to be forgotten again.

A movable feast normally falling in this month is Shrove Tuesday, on which the essential food is the pancake. Again, modern publicity has done much to spread the custom, but it has always had firm roots in the Border area, particularly in Cheshire, where it was common for a church bell to ring at 11.00 a.m. as a signal to housewives to start frying. This Pancake Bell has been kept up or revived at Audlem, Congleton and Tarvin. In the nineteenth century the day was sometimes known in Cheshire by the robust name of Gutsing Tuesday, in honour of the good feeding, and the previous day as

Collop Monday, on which occasion collops of fat bacon were eaten 'to lubricate the inside as preparation for the pancakes'.

Shrove Tuesday was also for many generations a day of general merrymaking, with public dancing, fairs and games, the latter being often rather rough and aggressive. One early example was the wild game of football played in the sixteenth century by crowds who surged through the streets of Chester, with a hearty disregard for life and limb; it was later alleged that it had originated when a party of Cheshire warriors captured a Dane, killed him, and played football with his head. Owing to what was officially said to be 'inconvenience' caused by 'evil disposed persons' taking part, this game was suppressed in 1540, and foot-traces substituted.

Equally fierce was a tug-of-war formerly held at Ludlow, in which teams representing two wards struggled over a rope thirty-six yards long, with a blue knob at one end and a red one at the other. Tradition asserted that it originated in a siege of the town by Henry VI, when one group of citizens who wished to admit the King struggled against others who supported the Duke of York. The game was started off by the Mayor, who dangled the rope from an upper window of the Market Hall, while two men and a woman from each team stood on one another's shoulders to reach it. Then the serious tugging began; the Reds tried to pull the rope into Mill Street and dip it in the Teme, while the Blues tried to get it to the Bull Ring and dip it in the Corve. Each time one team scored, the rope would be brought back to the Market Hall and the sport would start again, until the same team had scored twice running. Finally, the rope would be sold by public subscription, and the money spent on beer. The event gave rise to so much fighting and so many injuries among the crowds that it was suppressed in 1851; at Presteigne, however, a similar tug-of-war was able to continue till the end of the nineteenth century.

Other traditional but brutal Shrove Tuesday sports were cock-fighting and cock-shies; the latter, in the eighteenth and early nineteenth centuries, meant hurling short heavy sticks at a live cock or hen tethered by a short rope, whoever stunned the bird having it as prize. Later, more humane substitutes were adopted, such as shying at a lead cock. At the 'Hen Fair' at Wildboarclough in Cheshire, which was kept up till 1900, competitors shied at a bobbin on a stick in the ground, and whoever broke the bobbin won a hen. As for cock-fighting, despite official disapproval it long remained popular; it was clearly very familiar to the Cheshire author Fletcher Moss, who in 1898 writes about gamecocks with enthusiasm, and records some of the curious practices connected with cock-fighting:

> There is, or lately was, for I have known it done, a strange custom of placing hen's eggs in a magpie's nest, so that the devil's own bird could hatch a chicken which would grow into a gamecock which would be endowed from its birth with some of the supernatural sharpness of the devil's own. On the other hand, the dust has been swept off the church altar and preserved to strew over the cockpit, to give better luck or supernatural strength to the fighting cock, and even consecrated bread is said to have been secreted to give to some favourite bird.

At Kington in Herefordshire crowds gathered on Shrove Tuesday, early in the nineteenth century, to enjoy various rowdy amusements, including cock-fighting; in 1845 Parry noted with distaste how 'men paraded the town on this day with fire engines, the water going into the dwellings and on the heads of passers-by; in the evening the boys assembled in large parties, paying rude visits to the houses of the townspeople, demanding beer and cider.' A rather more sympathetic reference in the *Hereford Journal* of 1868 shows that the night was then being celebrated by men and boys carrying a boy on a pole, with his face blackened, who would utter 'some nonsensical rhyme' at every house as a way of asking for drinks; they called this 'Blackamoor Night'.

After such rowdyism, it is pleasant to read that at Ellesmere and Wellington in Shropshire children used to play 'Thread the Needle' in the churchyard, and then do 'Clipping the Church' – that is, a long line of them would link hands in such a way as to encircle the church with their backs to it, and then walk sideways round it. This pretty custom was discontinued in 1817 at Ellesmere and around 1854 at Wellington.

Mothering Sunday, the middle Sunday of Lent, normally falls in March, and has been a popular feast day for several centuries along the Welsh Border, especially in Herefordshire, Monmouthshire, and the southern part of Shropshire. Like St Valentine's Day, however, it has had its ups and downs. From the mid-seventeenth century till late in the nineteenth it only concerned working-class families whose sons and daughters had left home to live as servants or apprentices. On this one day of the year, they would be given enough time off to be able to return home and spend a few hours with their parents, and share with them a special dinner of which the traditional ingredients were roast veal (possibly in allusion to the Biblical fatted calf), rice pudding and mince pies. The returning youngsters would bring their mother presents of various sorts. A correspondent to *The Gentleman's Magazine* in 1784 noted the custom round Chepstow:

> The practice hereabouts was for all the servants and apprentices, on Mid-Lent Sunday, to visit their parents and make them a present of money, a trinket, or some nice eatables.

The popularity of these family reunions grew rapidly, and spread up the social scale; Kilvert notes in his Diary on 19 March 1871:

> All the country is in an upturn, going out visiting. Girls and boys going home to see their mothers and taking them cakes, brothers and sisters of middle age going to see each other. It is a grand visiting day.

The cakes vary locally; round Chepstow people use iced buns sprinkled with the tiny coloured sugar grains called 'hundreds and thousands', but in Shropshire they devised the famous Simnel Cakes, which are now enjoyed far beyond the borders of that county. These are rich fruitcakes contained in a hard crust of saffron bread, and topped with almond icing. The name is humorously (but mistakenly) said to derive from an imaginary old couple, Simon and Nell, who once wanted to use up some unleavened dough, and also the remains of their Christmas pudding. They quarrelled over whether to bake or to boil it, smashing a stool, a broom and some eggs in the scrimmage. In the end they did both, using the broken furniture as fuel, and glazing the crust with the eggs. The result was called by their combined names, Sim-Nel.

Gradually the observing of Mothering Sunday began to lose popularity; Mrs Leather noticed its decline in Herefordshire in 1912, and A.R. Wright in 1936 said that everywhere it was 'rare or discontinued'. Suddenly in the 1950s it sprang again into vigorous life and spread like wildfire all over England, even in areas where it had previously been unknown. This was due to the influence of the American 'Mother's Day' (a purely modern institution, arbitrarily invented by a Miss Anna Jarvis in 1906, and held on the second Sunday in May), which American servicemen stationed in England had brought with them in the Second World War. The result has been a blending; as now practised, Mothering Sunday keeps to the English date and the Simnel Cakes, but has elaborated the traditional English bunch of wild violets into a more expensive florist's bouquet, and has also adopted the American custom of sending greeting cards. Another innovation is the idea that children should take over the housework on this day; a Cheshire teacher reported in 1953 that his boys all found this a great burden, but 'one ray of brightness is the Simnel Cake'.

On Palm Sunday, the last Sunday in Lent, people used to go out into the countryside to pick twigs of willow and sallow, these being regarded as suitable English substitutes for the palm branches carried at Christ's entry into Jerusalem, and consequently much used for decorating churches on this day. At Pontesford Hill in Shropshire the 'palming' expeditions developed into a search for a mysterious golden arrow which was said to have been dropped somewhere on the hill in some battle long ago, or lost by a fairy, or hidden by a king. To find it would bring great good luck, but some said that only the seventh daughter of a seventh son could do so, while others said the finder would be the lost heir to some great estate, who would thereby win back his lands. Young people would climb the hill looking for the arrow, or would try to be the first to pluck a twig from a haunted yew on the top, and then run headlong down the slope and dip a finger in Lyde Hole, a pool which was alleged to be bottomless. Up to about 1855 the custom was observed with large-scale picnics, dancing and general merrymaking; by the 1880s, however, it had become too rowdy for respectable girls to take part in it, and by 1914 it had almost died out. It is now a thing of the past; but readers of Mary Webb will recall how in *The Golden Arrow* she transformed this simple country festival into a symbol of sacrificial loyalty and true love.

Three Herefordshire churches, Hentland, King's Caple and Sellack, keep a tradition of distributing small buns on Palm Sunday after the morning service; they are called Pax Cakes, and symbolize reconciliation and the forgiving of old grudges, in preparation for Easter Communion. 'Friends who have been estranged by a petty quarrel ... are invited to share their cakes and let bygones be bygones,' said an eyewitness in the *Hartford Journal* in 1907; he also recorded that until a few years previously beer had been provided too — originally by the churchwardens, but later by the congregations themselves. At Sellack, nowadays, cider is given, and in both places the accompanying words are 'Peace and good neighbourhood', or 'Peace and good will'. It is not known how old the custom is, nor who were the original benefactors who provided funds for it; at Hentland some say it was begun by Lady Scudamore in 1570, others by an eighteenth-century farmer, while others claim it to be five hundred years old. There may be a grain of truth in this last claim, in the sense that we may see here a remote survival of a pre-Reformation custom; in periods when extreme reverence for the Sacrament discouraged people from taking Communion frequently, the blessing and distribution of ordinary bread after Mass was sometimes adopted as a pious substitute.

Another Palm Sunday tradition in some areas was to deck the graves in the churchyard with flowers; this was done round Chepstow till the 1580s, round St Briavels, in Radnorshire, and in some villages in Herefordshire and Monmouthshire. Most districts, however, preferred to deck their graves on Easter Saturday.

Many striking customs are attached to the period of Holy Week and Easter. Good Friday is marked out by a curious medley of precepts and taboos, implying that it is a day of particular sanctity. Thus in Herefordshire it was said to be the only safe day for shifting beehives, but also a most unlucky day for working a team of horses; in Shropshire, people said sewing done on Good Friday would never come undone; in Cheshire, it was the best day to start weaning a baby (because it was a fast day, possibly?), to set potatoes, and to plant parsley and stocks if you wanted them to grow curly leaves and double flowers. Some beliefs had explanatory legends attached to them, as in the following Herefordshire story which explained why it was unlucky to do any washing on this day, but very necessary to bake bread:

As our Blessed Lord was carrying His Cross on the way to His Crucifixion, a woman who had been washing came out of her house and threw her dirty water over the Saviour; another woman who was standing near with some freshly baked bread said to her 'Why do you treat that poor man like that, one who never did you any harm?' And she gave Our Blessed Lord a loaf, which He ate, and said 'From henceforth blessed be the baker, and cursed be the washer.'

Nowadays the Hot Cross Buns eaten on Good Friday are bought ready made, but up to the end of the nineteenth century it was more usual for each household to bake its own small loaves marked with a cross. Some of them would be kept all year for luck, and would be used as medicine, grated up and mixed with water, being particularly recommended for intestinal disorders in men and animals. It was said that Good Friday bread would never go mouldy, though Radnorshire people added the proviso that the dough must be set to rise before seven and to bake before eleven. A Herefordshire baker who still kept up these traditions explained to H.L.V. Fletcher in the 1940s:

'We'm important men, us bakers. The birth of Our Lord and His death – we'm at both. We makes mincepies for His birthday, and hot cross buns for His death day.'

In some Border areas Easter Saturday was devoted to decorating not only the churches but the churchyards in preparation for Easter Day. Kilvert gives a charming description of the scene in Clyro churchyard on 16 April 1870, when women and children came all day with flowers and evergreens to deck the graves of their families, and worked late into the night by moonlight. They cut slots in the turf of the graves and stuck the flowers in, using primroses, daffodils, flowering current, laurel and box; Kilvert was keen that they should set the primroses in the form of a cross, but found that despite his urgings many were still 'sticking sprigs into the turf aimlessly anywhere, anyhow, with no meaning at all'. He also commented that the custom had almost died out a few years previously, but that it was now reviving rapidly; certainly he did all he could to encourage it – a pleasing contrast to the clergy of Chepstow, who in 1885 were expressing from the pulpit their disapproval of putting flowers on graves on Palm Sunday. Nowadays the custom of decking graves for Easter is still practised, not only at Clyro but at many country churchyards in Radnorshire and Herefordshire, though vases of daffodils frequently replace the earlier way of pricking flowers directly into the turf.

Up in Cheshire, groups of children used to spend the few days preceding Easter in following the northern custom of pace-egging, i.e. going from house to house asking for eggs, which would then be hard-boiled and used in various games on Easter Sunday and Monday. The children used traditional rhymes for this; one, recorded in 1876, ran:

> *Eggs, bacon, apples or cheese,*
> *Bread or corn, if you please,*
> *Or any good thing that will make us merry.*

A later generation of Cheshire children, in the Wirral between the two wars, used to go round on Easter Monday collecting pennies, but their verse still alluded to eggs:

> *Please, Mrs Whiteleg,*
> *Please to give us an Easter egg.*
> *If you won't give us an Easter egg,*
> *Your hens will lay all addled eggs,*
> *And your cocks lay all stones.*

At one time pace-egging had been an adults' custom, and had included the performance of the Pace-Egging Play – a variant of the widespread Mummers' Play, in which men with their faces blacked or otherwise disguised represented various grotesque figures. Usually these included Lord Nelson, a comic devil named Old Toss Pot, and a ludicrous 'woman', played by a man. Sometimes, according to Fletcher Moss, they took with them 'a real horse's head got from the neighbouring tanyard, that snapped its jaws (worked by strings) at the girls' legs, who would scream and want to be taken care of.' The 'Wild Horse' and the mummers will be discussed more fully below (pp. 180–83), in connection with the November custom of going Souling. A few verses of a song with which the actors in the Pace-

Egging Play introduced themselves were still being sung by children during the years 1895-1900, according to the recollections of an eighty-year-old man from Marple, in 1966:

Here comes three or four jovie lads all in a row,
We've come a pace eggin', we hope you'll prove kind;
Prove kind, prove kind, with your eggs and small beer.
We hope you'll remember it's pace eggin' time.
For the diddle dol, for the day, for the diddle dol de day.

The next that comes in is Lord Nelson, you see,
With a bunch of blue ribbon tied under his knee;
With a star on his breast, like a diamond do shine.
I hope you'll remember it's pace eggin' time.
For the diddle dol, for the day, for the diddle dol de day.

The next that comes in is the miner, you see,
With his round hat and candle, he works underground:
He works underground, to get neighbour's coal,
At six in the morning he pops down yond hole.
For the diddle dol, for the day, for the diddle dol de day.

The date for collecting the eggs, or the money substitute, is flexible; instead of occurring before Easter Day, it may be done on the more convenient Easter Monday. In the same way the egg games, originally played on the Sunday, may spread into Easter Monday too. The sport consists in rolling coloured hard-boiled eggs down a slope, the winner being he whose egg is the last to break; sometimes pegs are placed at the foot of the slope, in which case the aim is to make the egg pass between them without smashing. These games are still played in some places; in Pontypool in the 1950s children were still dyeing their eggs by one of the traditional methods, that of boiling them wrapped up in brightly-coloured cloth, and then competing in rolling them down a slope. One earlier record mentions an amusing variation: at Chester in 1839 the Bishop and Dean themselves played with the choirboys inside the cathedral after Morning Service, tossing the eggs from hand to hand, 'after which they all retired to dine upon gammon of bacon and tansy pudding'. All this may at first seem startlingly frivolous, but

Continental parallels make it clear that the egg is a widespread symbol of the Resurrection; sometimes egg-rolling is specifically explained as an allusion to the rolling away of the stone from Christ's tomb.

Another custom inspired by religion was that of rising before dawn on Easter Day and climbing a hill to see the rising sun dance in the sky in joy at the Resurrection; this was quite commonly done in Shropshire and Herefordshire in the nineteenth century, but has now died out. In other districts, for instance round Clyro in Kilvert's time, it was held that one must look at the sun reflected in a pool, in order 'to see the sun dance and play in the water, and the angels who were at the Resurrection playing backwards and forwards before the sun'. This method is certainly to be preferred; the quivering surface of the water would favour one's chances of observing an effect of 'dancing' in the reflection, and furthermore there is no risk of damage to the eyes.

It need hardly be said that churches were, and are, lavishly decorated for Easter. In the nineteenth century evergreens predominated, particularly box and yew, for they were symbols of everlasting life; nowadays colour schemes in white, gold and green are probably the most favoured. Texts from the Scriptures were formerly much used; the lettering might be worked in cotton wool on red cloth, or in straw, or in flowers against a background of moss, and the texts were then hung on the walls. An old example of a cloth text was still in use at Aberedw in the upper Wye Valley in 1947. Various beliefs were attached to Easter Sunday, for instance that it was lucky to hear the cuckoo, but very unlucky to lie late in bed; it is still a normal practice to wear something new on this day, often a pretty hat.

To ensure the well-being of the crops, there was a custom in the nineteenth century known in Herefordshire as 'corn-showing', and in Monmouthshire as 'walking the wheat'. The farmers or farm-bailiffs would walk up and down the wheat fields with their workmen and all their families on the afternoon of Easter Sunday, carrying plum cakes and cider. In Monmouthshire 'they ate a little, buried a little, and flung a little piece abroad', saying as they did so:

A bit for God, a bit for man,
And a bit for the fowls of the air.

In Herefordshire they buried a small piece of the cake, pouring some of the cider over it, and ate and drank the rest; after this, all would join hands and march up and down the field, repeating:

Every step a leap, every leap a sheaf,
And God send the master a good harvest.

Like many rural customs, this fell victim to a combination of economic changes and Victorian respectability; one of Mrs Leather's informants explained that it had been discontinued in the Golden Valley about 1880 'when owing to the importation of the wheat from abroad the crop had no longer so much importance, and also it gave rise to a noisy assemblage on Easter Sunday'.

Another entertaining but controversial custom was the 'lifting', 'heaving', or 'hoving' which took place either on Easter Monday and Tuesday or, particularly in Cheshire, on the Monday and Tuesday of the following week, known as Hocktide. On the Monday, groups of men went round the houses carrying a chair covered in greenery, ribbons and flowers; they would get each woman in the house to sit on it in turn, and then lift her as high as they could. Some said this was a way of honouring the Resurrection, and sang an Easter hymn. In Herefordshire and Shropshire one would also sprinkle the woman's feet with water, using a bunch of flowers as sprinkler. Finally, the men would claim a kiss, or a sum of money as forfeit; in her account book for 1718, the wife of Mr Charles Cholmondeley of Vale Royal in Cheshire notes that she 'gave for lifting me at Easter, 2s and 6d'. On the Tuesday, the process was reversed, with women invading houses to 'heave' and kiss the men. Maids in hotels sometimes played this trick on unwary travellers, who reacted with pleasure, indignation or antiquarian curiosity, according to temperament; it was also common for servant girls in private homes to lift their masters or the male visitors – or rather, to claim tips from them as an alternative to lifting. Another tactic sometimes used was to rope off one of the main streets in a town, and to demand that any man wishing to pass through should either pay a fee or submit to being lifted; at Chester in 1771 a letter published in *Adam's Weekly Courant* complained that 'a number of females stand at all gates of the city' demanding money from every passing man, on penalty of being tossed or having his shoes removed.

Male 'lifters' could be equally troublesome; in Shropshire in the 1870s, 'a maidservant of the Vicar of Ketley... was incautiously sent to the Post Office on Easter Monday, and was so beset by heaving parties in the street that her master... was obliged to go out and rescue her from their hands'. Gradually the custom faded, blighted by public disapproval. In Herefordshire by 1869 it was said to have 'degenerated into wickedness' and to be discontinued; in Cheshire, where it lingered longest, it had died out by about 1900.

The last few evenings of April were devoted to preparing for May Day, the chief secular spring festival. Groups of singers used to call at every house, singing their good wishes to its owner and his family. A typical Cheshire May Song opens:

> *All on this pleasant evening together come are we,*
> *For the summer springs so fresh, green and gay,*
> *To tell you of a blossom that hangs on every tree,*
> *Drawing near to the month of May.*
> *Oh this is pleasant singing, sweet May-flower is springing,*
> *And summer comes, so fresh and gay.*

Subsequent verses are addressed individually, to the master of the house, to his wife ('Rise up, the mistress of this house, with gold upon your breast'), and to their children ('Oh rise up, all the little ones, the flower of all your kin'). Needless to say, those who brought these good wishes expected to be tipped.

Also to be found in Cheshire in the earlier part of the nineteenth century were groups known as May Birchers, who carried out their functions more secretly. Coming to a house after dark on May Eve, they would quietly leave a branch of some tree or shrub on the doorstep, to be discovered by the inhabitants next morning; this conveyed a message, complimentary or insulting, according to the plant chosen. The code was based on rhyme; nut for a slut, pear if you're fair, plum if you're glum, bramble if you ramble, alder (pronounced 'owler') for a scowler, and gorse for the whores. There was also hawthorn, which did not rhyme with anything but counted as a general compliment.

This Cheshire practice is only a particular application of a more widespread habit of decking doorways with flowers or greenery for

May Day. Sometimes these would be placed in position on the Eve, but more often parties of young people would rise at dawn, and go out into the woods, returning with boughs of green birch which would be propped up against the door all day. In parts of Cheshire and Shropshire the marsh marigold was called the May Flower and used in the same way; Miss Burne writes that 'on May Day every house in Edgmond used to be adorned with a bunch of these flowers hung, stalk uppermost, on the doorpost, where they remained withering for two or three days'. Similar bunches were to be seen in Shrewsbury in 1878.

This greenery was often thought of as being more than mere decoration, rather a method of driving away witches, fairies, and the power of an Evil Eye. For this purpose, birch and mountain ash ('wittan' or 'witty', as it is known in this region) were used; thus at Clyro Francis Kilvert frivolously entered in his Diary for 30 April 1870:

> This evening, being May Eve, I ought to have put some birch and wittan over the door to keep out the 'old witch'. But I was too lazy to go out and get it. Let us hope the old witch will not come in during the night. The young witches are welcome.

Though he himself was by no means in earnest, he did also record on another occasion that a few farms both in Radnorshire and Herefordshire had birch and wittan over their doors. Once put up, generally in the form of two crossed twigs, they would be left in place all year. In 1912 Mrs Leather noticed these little crosses at Llanveyno and Michaelchurch, and was told they were there 'to counteract the influence of a malicious neighbour, whose evil eye was much feared'. She also noted:

> A tall birch tree, decorated with red and white rags, may still be seen occasionally, fastened near the door of the stable. It is placed there early on May Day, and usually left up for the whole year. Its purpose is to avert ill luck, and to prevent witches or fairies from riding the horses at night, or plaiting their manes and tails so that the waggoners cannot comb them.

Indeed, round Chepstow the same practice continued as late as 1928, when one could still occasionally see crosses of hawthorn or birch over house doors and stable doors, and hawthorn twigs stuck in seedbeds to nullify witches' spells.

On May Day itself, it was common for children to go from house to house carrying garlands of flowers, or small home-made Maypoles covered with flowers and ribbons, in the hope of collecting pennies, or dainty foods. The flower arrangements might be dispensed with, especially by poorer children in the towns; in Chepstow in the 1890s girls went about the town calling themselves May Queens, 'but only as a pretext for asking for money.' Writing in 1937, Miss Hole describes how:

> In Chester, Stockport and many other towns, pathetic little bands may be seen in the streets during the last week of April and the first week of May. A little girl with a veil made from an old lace curtain represents the Queen of the May, and her attendants usually carry a thin stick with a few ribbons on it. With them goes a boy with blackened face, whose duty it is generally to collect pennies from the passers-by.

An interesting survival of these simple and individualistic ways of celebrating May Day was observed in the Monkmoor area of Shrewsbury in 1952. Groups of little girls aged between five and eleven were going about with Maypoles made by fixing a pram-wheel to a pole, in such a way that it could revolve, and covering it with crêpe paper and streamers. The girls' dresses were also adorned with crêpe paper. Each group had its Queen, who sat on a stool holding the Maypole, while the rest danced round her and sang:

> *Round and round the Maypole*
> *Merrily we go,*
> *Singing hip-a-cherry,*
> *Dancing as we go.*
> *All the happy children*
> *Upon the village green, Sitting in the sunshine,*
> *Hurrah for the queen!*

The May Queen then sang a solo, after which the group hopped round her, singing patriotic ditties ('Three Cheers for the Red, White and Blue', and 'Rule Britannia'). Finally, one of the company would take the collecting tin to the house outside which the performance had taken place.

In the eighteenth and early nineteenth century, a period when the celebration of May Day was not much in favour, there were nevertheless certain groups of adults who made the day peculiarly their own. At Boughton, a suburb of Chester, the chimney sweeps used to parade in their best clothes, all decked with ribbons, while in Hereford in the 1790s:

> ...the milk women used to dance with the milk pails on their heads. They used to dress the pails with all sorts of beautiful silver things which they borrowed, and they used to shine in the sun as the women danced. So the spoons, the cream jugs, and all these things used to make music along with the fiddle. Oh, there was some pleasure then for young and old, for rich and poor, for everyone who could used to go a-maying.

In *William Hone's Every-Day Book* (1827) a correspondent reports delightedly on seeing in Chepstow on May Day 'one of the prettiest processions I ever enjoyed'. A group of milkmaids and young men, about thirty in number, were dancing and singing as they went from house to house, their arms, heads and necks garlanded with lilies-of-the-valley and wild roses. An old man went with them, blowing a cow's horn; he too wore a wreath of wild flowers and carried a hawthorn branch in one hand and a staff adorned with flowers in the other. An older woman offered strawberries and cream to all comers [presumably, though the writer does not say so, in exchange for donations]. There was a hurdy-gurdy, six goats 'harnessed in flowers' and carrying milking pails and butter churns, and a farmer riding a placid bull 'also tastily dressed with the produce of the fields and hedges'. The whole party ended up in a pub.

One custom that is still sometimes kept up is for young girls to go out early on May Day to wash their faces in dew, believing that this will rid them of pimples and freckles, and give them good complexions for the rest of the year; others drink the dew at sunrise, hoping this means they will marry in May. May dew has long been believed to give beauty, and luck in marriage; sometimes it was also valued as medicine, as at Edgmond in 1883 in the case of 'a little idiot boy whose mother, fancying it was weakness of the spine that prevented him from walking, took him to the fields nine mornings running, to rub his back with May dew'.

These individual practices and beliefs are mostly fading or forgotten nowadays, but large communally-organized May Day celebrations have been revived in some places. They have had a chequered history, for though they were popular in Tudor times they incurred the grave displeasure of the Puritan clergy, who regarded Maypoles in particular as vile and dangerous idols. Typical of these hostile critics was Adam Martindale, Presbyterian minister at Rostherne in Cheshire in the seventeenth century. From his pulpit he denounced a 'rabble of prophane youths and doting fools' for setting up a Maypole on a certain bank 'where in times past the Sabbath had been woefully prophaned by musick and dancing'; when his words had no effect, his wife herself went out with three young women 'and whipt it down in the night with a framing-saw'. This, not surprisingly, 'made them almost mad', and a magistrate sent a constable to arrest two pious women; but in vain, for he was himself forced to admit that their action 'was against no law that this gentleman could find, so nothing was made of it'.

With the revival of interest in folk customs towards the end of the nineteenth century, May Day recovered its importance; it offered a splendid occasion for picturesque celebration at every level from the village school to a full-scale civic display. Largest and most famous of all is the Royal May Day at Knutsford, first held in 1864; however, it does not necessarily fall on May Day itself, but on any convenient date in May or early June. It draws thousands of visitors to see its elaborate procession, including such traditional figures as Robin Hood and Maid Marion, Morris Dancers, a Jack-in-the-Green, and the Queen of the May with her attendants; there is also, in honour of Mrs Gaskell's *Cranford*, an ancient sedan chair. An old and interesting feature is the sanding of the streets; it had long been a custom in Knutsford to make patterns of brown and white sand on the pavements in honour of weddings, jubilees and so forth, and this pleasing decorative art is now associated with Royal May Day. Sanded patterns are made outside St John's church in front of the Sessions House (where the procession now starts), and outside the May Queen's home; some shopkeepers also pay to have the pavement sanded in front of their premises. To 'explain' both the sanding custom and the name of the town, it is sometimes said that King Canute (or Knut, to spell his name the Scandinavian way) once forded the river at Knutsford, but got sand in his shoes, and had to stop and shake it out. A wedding party was just passing, and the King wished them as many children as the grains of sand – hence the sanding at weddings, as described earlier (above, p. 123).

In some areas May Day was less important than 29 May, Oak Apple Day. This date was Charles II's birthday, and also the day on which he re-entered Whitehall at his Restoration in 1660, and for several generations it was observed as an official public holiday; since Charles had saved his life by hiding in an oak tree after the battle of Worcester, the feast was known as Royal Oak Day or Oak Apple Day, and oak was the characteristic decoration. One of Mrs Leather's informants told her how in the middle of the nineteenth century 'The 29th was our real May Day in Bromyard; you'd see Maypoles all the way down Sheep Street, decorated with oak boughs and flowers, and people dancing round them, all wearing oak leaves.' At Kingsland, said another, 'there were great doings that day; we used to climb up and put a great bough of oak on the church tower.' Children gathered oak twigs, especially those with oak-apples on them, and sold them for a few pence; those who refused to buy were jeered at:

Shig-shag, penny-a-rag,
Bang his head with Cromwell's bag,
All up in a bundle!

Judging by a related custom at Tiverton in Devon, the mysterious 'Cromwell's bag' may have originally been a bag of soot with which to smear the faces of those who would not honour the day. As it was, anyone not wearing oak leaves in Herefordshire would be suspected of being anti-royalist, and might be kicked, pinched, or pelted with eggs. Similar customs were observed in Shropshire, notably in Shrewsbury and Newport, where horses had their harness decorated, and even railway engines had oak branches fixed to them. Across the

Border, one could see houses with oak-leaf garlands and people wearing sprays of oak as late as 1900 in Radnorshire. Possibly the only adult celebration of the day now extant is the annual parade of the Heart of Oak Friendly Society at Fawnhope, Herefordshire, on or about 29 May; the members carry staves decorated with wooden oak-apples.

As so often, however, a custom dropped by adults remains active among children. It was very frequent in the 1920s and 1930s that schoolchildren had to wear oak on this day, on pain of being pinched or stung with nettles by their companions, at any hour up to noon. In fact, this still happens at some places in Cheshire and northern Shropshire, for instance at Warburton and Waverton. At Antrobus and Great Budworth in the 1940s, even the stroke of noon did not bring peace, since during the rest of the day the children did their best to trip one another up – a sport which they called 'legging-down time'.

Until the mid-1990s, a unique ceremony was observed on this same date at Aston-on-Clun in Shropshire. A tall black poplar called the Arbor Tree was kept permanently decorated with flags hung from long poles fixed to its boughs, and these were renewed every 29 May. Sadly, the tree rotted and fell in September 1995, and only a sawn-off stump remains. However, it had been obvious for some years that its days were numbered, and the local Parish Council had grown a young tree from a cutting; this was ceremonially replanted at a site near that of the old tree on 16 December 1995. The sapling was at that time only sixteen years old, and not strong enough to carry the weight of the flags, which were consequently fixed to railings round it. It will not be regarded as a true Arbor Tree until flags are actually attached to it.

It is not clear how old the ceremony is. There seem to be no references to it before 1912, neither in general books on British customs nor in those specifically about Shropshire; Charlotte Burne's classic account of Shropshire lore says nothing about it, even though she has a section on Oak Apple Day. However, the 1912 reference, which is in the Revd J.E. Auden's *Shropshire*, speaks of it as if it were well established:

> At Aston on Clun, where five roads meet, stands a large poplar tree decorated with flags every 29th of May, which remain till the same

day next year, to commemorate the marriage, and a bequest to the poor, of a lady who once resided at Aston House.

It is locally said that this refers to the marriage of John Marston, lord of the manor at Oaker, to an heiress named Mary Carter on 29 May 1786, and that flags were hung out on the tree to mark the occasion. Presumably the wedding had been timed to coincide with this widely celebrated public holiday, and there is even a local belief that the Aston tree-dressing actually goes back to the Restoration of 1660. It is said that the sight pleased Mary so much that she gave money to pay for the same thing being done every year. The Marston family ensured that the custom continued unbroken through the twentieth century, at which point, the Marstons having died out, Hopesay Parish Council took over the ceremony.

Stimulated by the enthusiasm of a local resident, Tom Beardsley, the event became more elaborate in 1954, with much pageantry and publicity. At about the same time new theories and customs developed; it was suggested that an alternative name for the tree was 'The Bride's Tree', and that this referred not to Mary Carter but to the Irish Saint Brigid or Bride, and through her to the ancient Irish goddess Brigid whose cult is supposed to underlie hers. Because of this speculative and unwarranted association, it became popular around 1954 for brides at Aston to be given a rooted cutting from the poplar on their wedding day, to ensure the blessing of a family. Unfortunately, the ensuing press publicity stressing 'pagan fertility rites' proved an embarrassment, especially to the Rector, and in 1959 the Parish Council stopped handing out cuttings. For some years only small-scale local celebrations took place, but currently a pageant and a fête are once again the norm.

Two movable feasts of the religious calendar normally fall in May: Ascension Day, and Whitsun. Both are often the occasion for local wakes, fairs, and other festivities. Several Shropshire places used to choose Ascension Day for their well-wakes. Thus at Rorrington until about 1834 people decorated the Holy Well on the hill with flowers, greenery and a bower of rushes; they walked to the well in procession, tasted its waters, and threw pins into it as protection against witchcraft. The rest of the day was spent dancing on Rorrington Green, drinking ale and eating special flat buns marked with a cross which, like Good Friday buns, brought good luck if they were kept. A rather similar feast used to be held at the salt spring at Nantwich in Cheshire, known as Blessing the Brine; the spring would be adorned with ribbons, branches and flowers, and people danced round it all day. This custom, however, had died out by the middle of the eighteenth century.

As for Whitsun, its most striking traditional ceremony in this area is the bread and cheese dole still given at St Briavels, Gloucestershire. Originally the dole was distributed inside the church itself, immediately after Morning Service on Whitsunday; several baskets of bread and cheese, cut into small squares, were brought into the upper galleries of the church, from which the churchwardens would toss them down to the congregation, 'who', wrote *The Gentleman's Magazine* in 1816, 'have a grand scramble for them in the body of the church – there is as great a tumult and uproar as the amusement at a village wake'. The earliest writer to describe the dole, Samuel Rudder in 1779, explains that the expense was met by a levy of one penny on each householder in the parish, and adds that the custom was traditionally believed to be connected with the woodcutting privilege which a Countess of Hereford is said to have won for the people of St Briavels (see above, p. 46). Naturally such disorderly behaviour inside a church struck a later generation as irreverent; by 1857 the distribution was transferred to the churchyard, but even so it eventually was allowed to lapse. In the present century, however, it has been enthusiastically revived; crowds gather to receive the dole, which is now thrown from the top of the churchyard wall on to the public road, and a collection is taken for charity. Some people keep their bit of bread or cheese for a year, for luck.

TEN

THE TURNING YEAR: JUNE TO DECEMBER

The month of June was once rich in fairs, wakes, and civic festivals, of which some were held on fixed dates, while others followed the religious calendar. In some cases, a modern secular festival can be traced back, through various intermediate stages, to the medieval religious processions and plays held on the feast of Corpus Christi, the first Thursday after Trinity Sunday. At Hereford, Chester and Shrewsbury before the Reformation there were elaborate religious processions in which the Sacred Host was carried through the streets; at Chester there were, in addition, plays on Biblical subjects which were performed by actors standing on high, decorated carts which moved slowly through the town, like the floats of a modern carnival pageant. After the Reformation the feast of Corpus Christi was abolished; the Chester plays were transferred to Whit Week, but Puritan opposition to them was intransigent, and the last performance was in 1574.

At Shrewsbury the Corpus Christi procession had evolved into the civic pageant by the end of the sixteenth century, this being held on the second Monday after Trinity. The Mayor and Corporation and all the trade companies went in procession, with banners and emblems, to the common at Kingsland. The pageant included tableaux vivants mounted on carts, often representing the saints, kings, queens and other figures regarded as patrons of the various trades. At Kingsland the rest of the day was spent in feasting, games and sports. One of these was 'Running the Shoemakers' Race'; competitors had to run through a labyrinth cut in the turf, whose zigzag path was exactly a mile long, and end by leaping into a space in the middle which was so cut as to represent a giant's face, landing with their feet squarely on the giant's eyes. A connection with the local legend of the giant of the Wrekin seems probable. The entertainment as a whole was known as the Shrewsbury Show. In the course of the nineteenth century its character changed from a civic celebration to a mere funfair, full of sideshows and drinking booths which attracted low-class trippers. It was officially abolished in 1878, though still in 1885 'a miserable pretence of a procession makes its way through the streets'. Meanwhile official support had been transferred to a more decorous event, the Musical and Floral Fête, which was begun in 1874 and still continues; it takes place in August.

At Chester in the late fifteenth century a pageant was held on Midsummer Day; on this date, as well as at Whitsun, some of the tableaux represented scenes from the former Corpus Christi plays – for instance, Christ as a child among the Doctors in the Temple. Much information about the pageant can be found in the old city records; in 1498, for example, two artists were hired to repaint the processional figures annually, these being listed as four giants, a unicorn, a dromedary, a camel, a luce, an ass, a dragon, six hobby horses, and sixteen naked boys. The Puritans, needless to say, found all this most offensive. Henry Hardware, the Mayor of Chester in 1599, made himself unpopular because:

> He caused the giants in the Midsomer Show to be put downe and broken, and not to goe, the Devil in his feathers which rode for the Butchers he put away, and the cuppes and cannes, and Dragon and Naked Boys, but caused a man in complete armour to goe before the Show in their stead.

In order to pacify such critics, the Show was often given a markedly patriotic content. The one in 1608 celebrated the elevation of Prince

Henry (a great favourite with the Puritan party) to the rank of Prince of Wales, but it also contained many of the popular old spectacles, notably the dragon:

> ...very lively to behold, pursuing the savages, entring their denne, casting fire from his mouth; which afterwards was slaine, to the great pleasure of the spectators, bleeding, fainting and staggering, as though he endured a feelinge of paine even at the last gaspe and farewell.

But not all its patriotism could save the show from being suppressed under the Commonwealth; it was briefly revived at the Restoration (when it cost £1 6s to make a new dragon and get 'six naked boys to beat at it'), but did not continue beyond 1678. Some of the traditional features reappeared as part of a historical pageant in 1910; a further pageant was held in 1937, but apparently without any of the old-style Midsummer Day spectacles.

Several old fairs were formerly held in Cheshire round about Midsummer. The Barnaby Fair at Macclesfield was kept on its correct date, 22 June, till 1948; it is still customary for local schools to have a two weeks' holiday at this season, and for many of the local mills to make this their main holiday period. What the entertainments at such fairs were like in their heyday is well conveyed by a handbill of 1808, advertising for a Master of Ceremonies to organize Bunbury Wake:

> It is necessary that he should have a complete knowledge of pony and donkey racing; bag, cock and peg racing; archery, singlestick, quoits, cricket, football, cocking, wrestling, bull and badger baiting, dog fighting, goose riding, bumble-puppy, etc. In addition to the above qualifications, he must be competent to decide in dipping, mumbling, jawing, grinning, whistling, jumping, jingling, skinning, smoking, scaling, knitting, bobbing, bowling, throwing, dancing, snuff-taking, singing, pudding-eating, etc.'

One is left somewhat breathless – unless, indeed, this hand-bill is not so much a genuine attempt to find a single omni-competent organizer, as a clever way of advertising all the fun of the fair!

Another June event that deserves mention is 'Barning the Thorn' at Appleton in Cheshire on St Peter's Day, 29 June. The hawthorn tree in question stands between the church and the pub, and is often said to be descended from a sprig of the Glastonbury Holy Thorn; it is the most recent in a long series of Appleton Thorns, the first of which local tradition declares was planted in 1178 by Adam de Dutton, an ancestor of the Egerton Warburton family who are lords of the manor at Appleton. The ceremony consists in dancing round the tree and decorating it with ribbons and flowers; the word 'barning' or 'bawming' means 'adorning'. Up to the middle of the nineteenth century this was a popular festival for the local villagers, but then rowdy spectators from nearby towns began causing trouble, and by 1866 it had been dropped. In the 1930s, however, it was revived as a children's affair, and so continued till shortly before the Second World War, when it again lapsed. It has since been once more revived in 1972, and is flourishing at the present time.

From medieval times until the eighteenth century it was common to cover the floors of churches (and indeed sometimes of houses too) with a layer of rushes to make the stone flags less chilly to the feet. The process of clearing out the old rushes from a church and laying down fresh ones developed a festive character; at some date during the summer, usually in July or August and preferably on the patronal feast of the church, there would be a ceremonial 'rush-bearing'. A harvest cart loaded with a steep pile of rushes would be dragged to the church – often by the men themselves, not by horses – with an escort of musicians, Morris dancers, and people carrying garlands. The pile of rushes would be brightly decorated with flowers or ribbons, or with a white sheet to which were pinned, in a glittering mass, all the silver spoons, jugs, mugs, goblets, tongs and watches which could be borrowed for the occasion, as a way of displaying the wealth of the parish. Often the load was topped by a leafy bough, and by a man sitting astride the ridge of the pile. Even after rushes were no longer used as floor coverings, the tradition was maintained; the rushes were brought to the church to be sold by auction, and in some places sheaves and garlands of them were used to decorate the church.

This custom is particularly characteristic of the industrial areas of north-west England; in our region, therefore, it is to be found in north Cheshire. It was at its peak in the mid-nineteenth century, and continued in many places up to the 1890s; the two villages that still keep it up are Farndon, where both church and graves are decked on the second Sunday in July, and Lymm, where it is done on the second Monday in August, and marks the opening of the local Holiday Week. At one time Lymm could proudly boast of a fine team of six grey horses to draw their rush cart – a team so famous that to this day the people of the village affectionately adopt the nickname 'Old Lymm Greys.' Nowadays the procession there consists of civic dignitaries and members of the public, together with dancers and a Rose Queen, all carrying rushes that have been locally cut; when they reach the church, where the bells are ringing, they lay them at the Chancel step. A short service follows, after which people adjourn to the village hall for refreshments and entertainments – the rushes, meanwhile, being hastily removed from the church before their smell gets too fierce!

Many towns and villages celebrate their Wakes during these summer months, the dates being originally fixed by reference to the feast of the patronal saint of their church. The basic pattern in the nineteenth century consisted of a procession of local dignitaries and club members, a church service, a meal at the inn, and then an afternoon and evening spent at a small fair, with sideshows and possibly a circus. Special foods were often sold, especially furmenty or frumenty, that universally popular country dish made of boiled wheat and milk, with sugar, spices and treacle. In earlier times there were the savage but popular sports of cock-fighting, bull-baiting, bear-baiting and prize-fighting; also various ludicrous competitions and games, like those already quoted from the Bunbury handbill.

Among individual variations on this pattern, Congleton Wake deserves special mention for its custom of Ringing the Chains, which originated in medieval times and lasted till about 1860. Congleton church is dedicated to St Peter ad Vincula, and the Wake consequently is held on or near 12 August, the feast that celebrates Peter's miraculous rescue from prison by an angel who broke his chains. In the Middle Ages, three acolytes used to dance through the streets of Congleton on the eve of the feast day, wearing leather straps hung with bells whose jingling represented St Peter's chains. After the Reformation a local family named Stubbs took it on themselves to keep up the tradition; most of them were chimney sweeps, a trade which is also in many places associated with the folklore of May Day. For 300 years the Stubbses always marched through the town in

Wakes Week, wearing the three leather sashes laden with bells; unfortunately a feud developed between two branches of the family as to who should own them, leading to fights and drunken brawls which spoilt the festivities. Eventually the town clerk took custody of the three sashes and deposited them in the town hall, where they may still be seen.

Congleton's other claim to fame concerns bears. Bear-baiting was extremely popular there, as in many other places, and tradition alleges that when the town bear died just before the Wake in 1662, the citizens diverted money which had been earmarked for buying a new Bible, and bought a new bear instead. Hence a mocking rhyme:

Congleton rare, Congleton rare,
Sold the Church Bible to buy a new bear.

The various cruel but popular blood-sports began to rouse opposition in the early nineteenth century, and both cock-fighting and the various forms of 'baiting' were made illegal in 1835. In some places they had already been dropped; it is said that the last bull-baiting at Ellesmere was in 1813 and at Kington in 1815, while the last bear-baiting in Cheshire was at the Middlewich Wakes of 1834. At Bunbury, however, there was a public bull-baiting as late as 1848, and the 'sport' is said to have continued in secret for some years more. Cock-fighting and badger-baiting, which were easier to keep secret, continued to a much later date; indeed, it may be that 'cocking' has never quite died out.

Even after it had ceased, bear-baiting was fondly remembered, and many amusing stories circulated about famous bears who had survived many fights, and developed strong personalities. One such was Old Nell of Middlewich, who used to accompany her master into the pub when the baiting was over, and drink beer with relish. It is said that her owner was once told by the constable that his goods had all been seized because he had not paid his rates; that night he brought Nell round to the constable's house, saying she was valuable enough to settle the debt. The constable took one look at the unmuzzled Nell, and swiftly sought refuge up the chimney; thereupon the bearward gathered up his other possessions and went home, with Nell lumbering at his heels. At Prestbury, which was also a great place for bear-baiting, it was believed that to ride on the bear's back would cure whooping-cough, and 'many distressed youngsters were put through the ordeal'; similarly, Miss Burne tells of a Shropshire child supposedly cured of measles by being passed three times over the back and under the belly of a dancing bear. These trained animals, which danced and performed tricks in the streets under the guidance of their itinerant owners, were a familiar sight until 1914, and they too were a topic for storytelling. A recent Monmouthshire writer relates the tale of how one travelling bear-master killed another, and tried to cover up the crime by forcing the bear to maul the corpse, but in vain, since 'bayers 'on't touch the dead, everybody do know that'. Instead, the bear turned on the murderer and tore him to pieces, and 'the yells of that bloke was horrible'.

With September, the harvest month, folklore interest shifts back from the towns to the countryside. Harvest suppers were a universal custom to mark the end of the corn cutting (and also, in some places, of the hop picking), and were always marked by copious drinking, often with elaborate sung toasts. In Herefordshire and Shropshire the main dish was often roast goose; as late as 1938 farm workers might jokingly remark to a stranger watching them bring in the last load that he ought to stand them a goose.

A picturesque custom very characteristic of the Border counties was that known in Shropshire as 'Cutting the Gander's Neck' (presumably the gander in question being the one about to be eaten at the Harvest Supper), in Herefordshire as 'Crying the Mare', and in Cheshire as 'Cutting the Neck'. Two distinct elements are involved, the ceremonial reaping of the last few ears of corn in a manner requiring unusual skill, and the ritual mocking of any other farmer whose harvest is not yet completed, by loud shouts, and ironic offers to send a mare to help in his harvesting. Each element may occur separately. In Herefordshire, for instance, it was only the cutting that Mrs Leather's informants remembered, even though their name for it was 'Crying the Mare.' She describes it as follows:

> At the conclusion of the harvest, before the days of reaping machines, the reapers left a small patch of corn standing. This was tied up into four bunches, 'the four legs of a mare, like,' my informant explained. These were again tied at the top. Then the reapers tried to cut off the

ears of corn by standing at a certain distance and throwing their sickles at the 'mare', holding them by the point to throw. In some places the men stood with their backs to the mare, but this required great skill in throwing the sickle. It sometimes took two hours to accomplish the feat; the man who succeeded sat at one end of the table, opposite the master, at the harvest supper. As for the mare, or last sheaf, it was carefully plaited in a variety of ways... and hung up in the farmhouse kitchen... to be kept till next harvest for luck.

The custom in Monmouthshire was similar, with the last tuft being called 'the harvest mare' and plaited in the same pattern as a mare's tail would be. The man who managed to cut it had to bring it into the farmhouse without being caught and drenched by the womenfolk, who lay in ambush with pails of water. If he succeeded, this was a good omen for the year and he would be given the seat of honour at the harvest supper, but if the mare was wetted the farmer might refuse to accept it because of the ill luck it brought, and the man who brought it would be jeered at.

In Shropshire the reapers threw their sickles at the tied or plaited tuft in much the same way, and when the field had been cleared of all sheaves the man who had cut this last tuft cried out that he had 'got the mare'. The others would then ask what he meant to do with it, and he would reply that he was going to send it to Mr X, naming some farmer whose harvesting was not finished yet. In Cheshire, the sickle-throwing was well known, but there were also some farms where only the 'crying' or 'shutting' was done. There, the reapers would gather in a circle, and one of them would shout loudly 'Oyez, oyez, oyez! This is to give notice that Mester A has gen the sack a turn, and sent th'old hare into Mester B's standing curn.' (To 'give the sack a turn' meant to steal a march on one's rivals, and 'hare' was a more realistic variation on 'mare', since hares were common in cornfields and would flee as the harvesters advanced.) Then they would all bend down, link hands, and let out a long unearthly yell of triumph, after which they would have a drink of beer all round, and set off back to the farm for the harvest supper.

The last sheaf, whether or not it had been cut with these ceremonies, was very frequently plaited into traditional shapes and kept all year for luck. These ornaments are known as corn-babies or corn-dollies; some do look like human figures, others are twisted bell-like cages, while others again, from Radnorshire, are plaited in the same way as mares' tails traditionally were. Originally the corn ornaments had been plaited from the growing tuft, before it was reaped; mechanized harvesting has of course rendered this impossible now, but the making of 'dollies' from pre-cut wheat is now a highly popular craft in Young Farmers' clubs and Women's Institutes, where very elaborate examples are produced.

As regards the fixed festivals in September, the only one of importance is Michaelmas, 29 September, commemorating the celestial battle in which St Michael drove Lucifer out of Heaven. In many parts of England it is believed to be unlucky or unhealthy to eat blackberries after this date (or, more often, after 10 October, which is in fact the corresponding date since the eleven-day calendar change of 1752); the explanation given is that the Devil has spat or stamped on them during the night, or waved his club over them. This belief is known in some parts of Shropshire, especially near Tong, while in Herefordshire there used to be a dislike of eating blackberries at any season; one informant told Mrs Leather this was because 'the serpent had left his mark on them'. Michaelmas was also formerly a frequent date for the paying of rents and customary dues, and also for holding hiring fairs – that is, fairs where servants and farm-hands wanting a change of job would stand in the marketplace holding the emblem of their trade, such as a carter's whip or a shepherd's crook. Hiring fairs were also held on other dates, notably 1 May.

The Revd Francis Kilvert describes a rather unusual begging custom carried out in his part of Radnorshire 'between and about the two Michaelmasses', by which he presumably means 29 September and 10 October. In his diary for 14 October 1870, he noted:

> At Wern Vawr... Mrs Morgan of Cold Blow was waiting to have her gallon tin filled with milk. It is an old custom in these parts for the poor people to go round the farmhouses to beg and gather milk between and about the two Michaelmasses, that they may be able to make some puddings and pancakes against Bryngwyn and Clyro Feasts, which are on the same day, next Sunday, the Sunday after Old Michaelmas Day or Hay Fair, October 10. The old custom is still kept up in Bryngwyn and at some hill farms in Clyro, but it is honoured

at comparatively few farms now, and scarcely anywhere in Clyro Vale.... Besides being given a gallon of milk to carry away, the poor people are fed and refreshed to help them on their way to the next farm, for they wander many miles for milk, and it is a weary tramp before they reach home.

This description drives home the realization that many folk customs were of great economic importance to the rural poor, who at times lived on the margin of starvation, and certainly had no reserves of food with which to honour a feast; nobody would go tramping 'many miles' across the Welsh hills carrying heavy buckets of milk merely for the pleasure of keeping up a tradition. Other examples of customs with the practical function of transferring some of the autumn surpluses from the store-rooms of big farms and houses to the poorer cottages will be found below, in the description of November and December.

October itself is a month somewhat bare of customs in the Border regions. Mobberley in Cheshire used to hold its Wake on the next Sunday after St Luke's Day, the 18th, and up to the 1880s used to mark the day by pelting the parson with crab apples – a rather painful form of sport which was once quite common at wakes and fairs, though not directed at parsons! Another saint's day, that of Saints Crispin and Crispian on 25 October, had once been the craft festival of all shoemakers, but only faint traces of this survived into the late nineteenth century at Cross Keys in Shropshire and at Ross, where cobblers took the day off, and boys sang:

The twenty-fifth of October
Cursed be the cobbler
Who goes to bed sober.

But the month does at least end memorably, with Hallowe'en. From early Celtic times 1 November and its Eve had been a major turning point in the year, a time when the supernatural denizens of the Otherworld, whether fairies, ghosts, demons or witches, were close at hand and could irrupt into human homes. By choosing 1 November as All Saints' Day and 2 November as All Souls' Day, the Church gave its powerful approval to the association of this season with the dead.

Consequently, Hallowe'en figures in folklore as the most opportune moment for making contact with the supernatural in its darker aspects, and in particular for performing various eerie rituals in order to obtain a glimpse into the future. Typical examples, all current in the nineteenth century, include: a girl wanting to know who her future husband was to be would see his wraith appear if she went into the garden and picked a cabbage as the clock struck midnight, or if she plucked nine leaves of sage on the first nine strokes; if she was not destined to marry, she would see a coffin instead. Or she might pick a sprig of yew from some churchyard where she had never been before, and sleep with it under her pillow; or she might walk through a churchyard sowing hempseed behind her, and call on her true love to appear and mow it; or she and her friends might hang up their shifts in front of a fire, wait in silence till midnight struck, say a charm, and then watch to see whose shift would move first, for the girl who owned it would be the first to marry. To know if her present lover was true to her, a girl could roast two nuts on the bars of the grate; if they stayed together, all was well, but if one fell off, it was a bad omen.

According to an article written by Kilvert's niece Mrs Essex Hope after his death, there was one occasion which 'came within his own knowledge' where a divination came true in eerie circumstances. However, the tale is most unlikely to be factually true, and is certainly not unique, for precisely similar anecdotes (punch-line included) have been recorded elsewhere in Britain; one must suppose that it reached Kilvert at second hand, but that he trusted whoever told it to him was reliable:

> A servant girl at a country farm went out as usual on Llanhallan Eve [Halloween] to sow hempseed, and suspecting that some trick might be played on her, said to her mistress, 'Don't send master out after me'. The mistress promised not to, and the girl went out and began sowing the seed and singing the song. In a few minutes she became aware of the figure of her master raking the earth after her. She threw down the rest of the seed angrily, and ran in, crying, 'Why did you send the master when you promised not to?' The mistress turned deadly pale and cried, 'He has never left the house! Oh, Gwenny, be kind to my poor children!' She died soon after, and the master married the girl before a year had passed.

Other divinations were aimed at finding out who would die during the coming year, and these naturally were regarded as more sinister. In Herefordshire in 1909 people practised an old custom of each putting an ivy leaf in water overnight, to see which, if any, would have a mark like a coffin on it by morning; Mrs Leather was also told a tale about a man who listened at a church door on the eve of All Souls' Day:

> There once lived in Dorstone a man called Jack of France, an evil-doer, and a terror to all peaceable folk. One night, the Eve of All Souls, he was passing through the churchyard, and saw a light shining in all the windows of the church. He looked in, and saw a large congregation assembled, listening apparently to the preaching of a man in a monk's habit, who was declaiming from the pulpit the names of all those who were to die during the coming year. The preacher lifted his head, and Jack saw under the cowl the features of the Prince of Darkness himself, and to his horror heard his own name given out among the list of those death should claim. He went home, and repenting too late of his evil deeds, took to his bed and died.

'Jack of France' is an odd name. Perhaps there was confusion with Jack o' Kent, though his magic is not normally represented as sinister.

Kilvert came upon a rather less grim version of this at Clyro in 1873, where he was told that at Hallowe'en:

> ...people used to go to the church door at midnight to hear the saints within call over the names of those who were to die within the year. Also their heard the sound of pew doors opening and shutting, though no one was in the church.

Most Hallowe'en customs, even when ostensibly festive, had a certain spice of fear in them. The Welsh custom of lighting bonfires, for instance, was also common in the Border areas; the merrymaking often ended in a wild rush for home as the fire burnt down, for fear that a ghostly black sow would take the hindmost, since, so it was said, on this night there was 'a little black sow with a ringed tail sitting on every stile'. In Radnorshire there were family parties with fortune-telling and traditional games, and also much telling of alarming tales about fairies, ghosts and witches.

Nowadays, Hallowe'en is very much a children's feast. In a few places in north-east Shropshire and in Cheshire groups of them go round the streets 'souling', in the manner which will be described below at its more typical dates of 1 and 2 November. More widespread are the parties and games, the guising and the turnip lanterns. In their survey of schoolchildren's lore in the 1950s, Iona and Peter Opie collected much information on Hallowe'en from this area. A girl from Griffithstown described how to make a lantern from a hollow swede with a candle in it and take it out into the street, 'and if anyone comes along, you pop out from round a corner and frighten them'. A Knighton boy went one better – he fixed his lantern onto a long pole and made it bob about outside people's bedroom windows. At Pontypool, the 'Jack-o-lanterns' are put on gateposts 'to keep evil spirits away'. Everywhere it is common for groups of children to be out on the streets, with blackened faces, or wearing weird clothes and masks, asking passers-by for pennies, apples, oranges or nuts; they call themselves 'guisers', which is an old dialect term for people disguised by fancy dress. There are also many fancy-dress parties, at which one plays traditional games involving apples; using only one's teeth, one has to pick up an apple floating in a pail of water or balanced on a mound of flour, or else one has to get a bite from an apple swinging on a string. So important are these games that in Monmouthshire the feast is actually called Bob Apple Night or Crab Apple Night. A few traces of the old divinatory rites were also to be found in the 1950s; at Hay, girls said they caught snails and kept them all night under a lid, so that by morning their tracks would have formed the initials of their future husbands.

The 1st and 2nd of November, dates long associated with the dead, are still marked in some Cheshire villages and in the area of north-east Shropshire round Oswestry by the custom known as 'souling'. Originally, in Roman Catholic times, alms were given to the poor at this season on the understanding that they in return would pray for the souls of the dead kinsmen of their benefactors; despite the horror which such notions evoked after the Reformation, it was still possible in Monmouthshire in the 1880s to hear the poor begging for bread 'for the sake of the souls of the departed'. In most areas, however, all memories of this aspect of the matter had faded by the nineteenth century, leaving only the name 'soul-cake', which referred to little buns, fruit-cakes or spiced cakes which were baked for the occasion and given to singers who came round from house to house. Soon even this term lost its specific meaning, the special cakes were no longer made, and instead the gifts handed out were apples, pears, beer, and money – though all these items collectively were still called soul-cakes.

The singers, who were known as 'soulers', were at first groups of adult men; their proceedings, like those of the May Day singers, combined luck-bringing and ritualised begging. Two versions of the Cheshire Souling Song recorded in 1819 by George Ormerod run:

Step down into your cellar and see what you can find,
If your barrels are not empty I hope you will prove kind;
I hope you will prove kind with your apples and strong beer,
We'll come no more a-souling until another year.

Cold winter is a-coming on, dark, dirty, wet and cold;
To try your good nature this night we do make bold;
This night we do make bold with your apples and strong beer,
We'll come no more a-souling until another year.

Similarly, Miss Burne records that at Edgmond around 1850 farm labourers used to sing outside their master's door a song beginning:

There's two or three hearty lads standing hard by,
We are come a-souling, good nature to try;
We are come a-souling, as well doth appear,
And all that we soul for is ale and strong beer.

In Cheshire, but not elsewhere, the soulers were sometimes accompanied by a 'hodening horse', i.e. a man carrying a decorated horse-skull on a short pole, and himself hunched up under a horse-cloth or other rug, so that the whole thing looks like a grotesque three-legged horse. This creature still plays a vital part in the Mummers' Play of this area, as will be described below.

By the latter part of the nineteenth century, however, it was more usually children who went souling. In some Cheshire villages they have kept up the custom to this day, either on Hallowe'en or on the first two nights of November; since the various November feasts fall so close together, it is not surprising that the reason the children of Waverton now go souling is to raise money with which to buy fireworks for Guy Fawkes Day.

The ditties children chant when souling are varied. Some include fragments of the old song for adult soulers, as in two recent examples from Budworth and Comberbach, of which one begins:

> *Tonight we come a-souling, good nature to find,*
> *And we hope you'll remember it's soul-caking time,*

and the other:

> *Look down into your cellar and see what you find*
> *For the best of all ale and the best of stone wine.*

Another very widespread type is:

> *Soul! Soul! A soul-cake!*
> *Good missis, gi'us a soul-cake!*
> *One for Peter, one for Paul,*
> *And one for Him as made us all.*
> *An apple or a cherry,*
> *Or anything else to make us merry.*

To which in Shropshire may be added:

> *Up with your kettle and down with your pan,*
> *Give us an answer and we'll be gone.*

Various all-purpose tags of begging rhymes may follow, such as:

> *The lanes are very dirty, my shoes are very thin,*
> *I've a little pocket, to put a penny in.*

Or even, inappropriately:

> *Christmas is coming, the geese are getting fat,*
> *Won't you put a penny in the old man's hat?*

If you haven't got a penny, a ha'penny will do;
If you haven't got a ha'penny, God bless you!

Two features of outstanding interest characterise the Cheshire souling customs: the Soul-Caking Play, which is a local variation of the basic Mummers' Play with its combats and comic resuscitation (such as is performed in other parts of England at Christmas), and the accompanying 'hodening horse', variously known as Old Hob, Dick, Ned, or the Wild Horse. In origin, the two were distinct; the horse may well have been inspired by Welsh hobby-horses which accompanied house-to-house singers, but its crazy antics and the boasts of its driver are now regarded as the climax of the play.

The custom is not evenly spread across the county, but limited to the area around Northwich, where some two dozen villages are known to have observed it in the period from the mid-nineteenth century to the First World War. The earliest allusion to a horse figure in Cheshire comes from 1819, but implies that it appeared independently of the play and over a longer period; the author, George Ormerod, first describes the play and then adds: 'Old Hob, or the custom of carrying a dead horse's head, covered with a sheet, to frighten people, is sometimes a frolic between All Soul's Day and Christmas.' The more regular procedure, well attested later in the century, was that young men used to make up a band of Soul Cakers and go round the houses performing the play. F.H. Crossley, who himself belonged to one of these groups in the 1890s, describes how its members (all farm workers, like himself) found welcome relief from the monotony of their work in secretly preparing for it and rehearsing, and above all in perfecting their horse, which was made from a real skull:

> The essential thing was the horse's head; this was procured from a knacker's yard, and the bones strung together so that the mouth could be worked and the teeth snapped. The head was painted and decorated in traditional colours and was carried on a short pole, its carrier wrapped in a horse-cloth. At the time several companies of soulers were upon the roads at nights, and if two companies met it was a fight to the finish, the victorious company taking the horse's head as trophy, when they carried two horses' heads. The usual procedure was for a

company to march up to a farmhouse, hammer at the door, and demand entrance. This granted, they trooped into the kitchen, the 'Letter-in' introducing the company, who immediately commenced the play in a ranting, shouting tone of voice.

Details recorded from other villages broadly confirm this account. The head was almost everywhere a real skull, only three or four places opting for a wooden one or even a brush; however, the Antrobus team prefer a donkey's skull as being lighter in weight, though it is called 'horse' for the purposes of the drama. The skull would be cleaned by boiling or by burying it for some while; its jaws would be wired up for snapping; it would be blackened and varnished, given leather ears and bottle-glass eyes, and decorated with rosettes, ribbons, horse-brasses, and so forth. Two villages (Frodsham and Higher Whitley) are known to have regularly buried the head after the season for performances was over; at the latter place, a mock funeral was held. It is unclear whether this was simply a way of preventing rivals from stealing it in the course of the year, or whether it was part of the ritual.

The First World War put an end to all this in almost all the villages, but at Comberbach the old tradition survived into the 1920s, when it attracted the sympathetic attention of Major A.W. Boyd, who published the text of the play in 1929. Following his encouragement, several Young Farmers' clubs in the Antrobus area undertook to carry on the performances, which are now given at various pubs and private houses at this season, and also during the Great Budworth Wakes in the second week of November.

The players begin by singing a version of the old Souling Song quoted above, as a way of asking admittance. Then the Letter-in, a compere in evening dress, announces 'a dreadful fight between King George and the Black Prince', after which the two antagonists enter and hurl defiance at one another in boastful verses; they fight, and King George kills the Black Prince. In comes an Old Woman (played by a man, of course), who falls over the corpse, reproaches King George, and summons a comic Doctor, who boasts of his wide travels and marvellous cures. At length he consents to revive the Prince. He is followed by two other comic personages, and finally by the grotesque three-legged Wild Horse and his Driver – who is clad in the pink coat with green collar of the exclusive Tarporley Hunt Club. The

Driver's lengthy rigmarole is the highlight of the entertainment; the Horse, meanwhile, prances, bows, snaps his jaws, tries to bite his Driver, bites and kicks people, sits on the knees of girls in the audience, and so forth. The Driver praises the Horse's outstandingly good points:

> *Now this horse has an eye like a hawk,*
> *A neck like a swan,*
> *Every tooth in its mouth stands rank-gank like a regiment of pickled onions,*
> *Tongue like a lady's pocket-book,*
> *And his ears are made out of an old box-hat.*
> *Whoa, boy!*

This Horse, he declares, 'was bred from Marbury Dun' – this being a famous mare which once belonged to one of the Smith-Barry family that owned Marbury Hall at Comberbach. It is said that she won a wager for him by galloping from London to Marbury between sunrise and sunset, and that she has been buried in the park 'with silver shoes upon her feet, and lapped in a linen sheet'. She can certainly rank as a local heroine, and it is only fitting that the Comberbach Wild Horse should claim descent from her.

Similarly, at Antrobus the Groom who leads the Wild Horse boasts of its many fine points, while it rears and stamps, clashes its jaws, and threatens the audience:

> Now ladies and gentlemen just look around, and see if you ever saw a better class of beast out of England's ground. He has a h'eye like a hawk, a neck like a swan, a pair of ears made from an old lady's pocket book, so read it if you can. Every time he opens his mouth his head's half off. Tell you what, if you look down his mouth you can see the holes in his socks. Whoa, stand still. On Antrobus oats this horse has been fed. He's won the Derby, and the Oaks, and finished up pulling an old milk float. So stand round, Dick, and show yourself. Whoee now, stand still, stand still.

At Great Budworth, more attention is given to the Horse's alleged destructiveness and mock aggressivity, in a passage of rapid nonsense patter:

'As me and Owd Dick was going up Bud'orth Hill, he ran away and left the cart standing with the wheels going round. He run into Bill Wright's drawing-room and worried three leather ladies and a silk footman and bust twenty spun-new calico ale barrels. This horse can plough an acre a day with his head in a sling, and had to have his farther foot strapped up to keep him from going too fast. We feed him on paving stones, and we have to have him rugged up to keep the hay from burning his inside.'

These quotations are from the versions published by Major Boyd, but the play does not always follow a fixed text throughout. On the contrary, there is room for slight variations, local allusions, mimed actions and impromptu jokes, all within the broad limits of tradition; not only does each company evolve characteristic details, but the same company can modify its performance to suit different audiences, for example as regards the broadness of its humour. Whatever the variations, the play ends with the taking of a collection; as they say at Great Budworth:

Poor old Ned, he stands on one leg,
For his living he has to beg.
What he gets it is but small,
And it's obliged to keep us all.

The historian Ronald Hutton thus analyses the overall impact of the play:

Its action is characterised by a very powerful internal logic; weak on narrative and social or moral sense, it depends upon the fielding of an increasingly outrageous set of characters who evoke laughter, but also fear, surprise, and questioning. All are peripheral to the community, all economically unproductive; they are either menacing outsiders or internal misfits, all the more unsettling for the fact that they are so highly stylised and the action is deliberately not naturalistic. In this context the misbehaviour of the Wild Horse makes a perfect climax to the presentation, being literally bestial and yet acted by a human, and so the end-product of a continuous deliberate disharmony between jest and earnest.

The next November feast is Guy Fawkes, whose familiar bonfires and fireworks can be seen almost anywhere, as can the gangs of children roaming the streets demanding pennies, or collecting fuel for their bonfires. In earlier and less safety-conscious times, the festivities could be distinctly alarming. At Newport in Monmouthshire burning tar-barrels used to be rolled down Stow Hill, a steep street in the town, and it is said that this was only stopped after the crowd had on one occasion thrown a policeman into the fire for trying to interfere. At Chepstow too there were some memorably violent scenes:

> In 1863 a fireball blazed on top of the Beaufort Arms Assembly Room, and tarbarrels were rolled down from Thomas Street, where a policeman was stoned and injured. The culprits were looked upon as heroes and defended by lawyers paid by means of a public subscription. In 1874 some boys stole 24lbs of blasting powder from a local contractor, and were given eight days in prison and twelve strokes of the birch. Year after year the magistrates tried to punish the trouble-makers, but were defeated by mass perjury and the shortage of policemen. Mobs threw mud and stones, kicked one constable's door in, and soaked another in paraffin and tried to burn him. Even the *Advertiser*, which had condemned the custom in 1855, declared in 1882 that it would be better if the police kept the streets clear on Sundays instead of 'battering the heads of people indiscriminately on Guy Fawkes' Day.' But from 1892 Harry Gorman and others organized torchlight carnivals, and marched the potential rioters to the safety of a fireworks display in the Meads near the river.

December customs in the Border area all relate to the Christmas season and the end of the old year. In order to lay in a little extra food for the festivities, poor women used to go 'Tomassing,' 'gooding' or 'corning' on 21 December, St Thomas's Day. This, as one writer explained in 1850, meant that 'the poor people go from farm to farm, and generally carry a bag or a can, in which meal, flour or corn, and milk are put; begging on this day is universal in Cheshire and the neighbouring counties.' The normal thing was for each farmer to give each cottager's wife a pint or a quart of corn, which the miller then ground free of charge, so that every family might have a cake at Christmas. At Clun in Shropshire there was an additional gift of barley for the cottagers' pigs, and there the gifts were distributed centrally from the Town Hall; at Edgmond there was no begging for food, but the Rector and Churchwardens distributed warm clothes instead. These charitable doles were of considerable value to people whose income was low at the best of times, and who in a bad year were faced with grave hardship.

In Herefordshire, Shropshire and Radnorshire the custom of the Yule Log was observed. A huge log was dragged into the kitchen on Christmas Eve, laid on the open hearth, and lit from a fragment of the previous year's log; to keep such a fragment all year was said to bring good luck and to keep the house safe from lightning and fire. Houses were decorated with holly, ivy and mistletoe, as they still are; sometimes greenery was tied to a hooped frame and decorated with oranges, apples and ribbons, to form a globular 'kissing bough'. None of these decorations must be brought into the house before Christmas Eve, and none must be left on display after Twelfth Night; opinion differed sharply as to whether they should then be burnt, as in Herefordshire and some parts of Shropshire, or whether on the contrary they must never be burnt, on pain of grave ill-luck, as in other parts of Shropshire and in Cheshire. In Radnorshire, W.H. Howse tells us that the holly at any rate was kept till Shrove Tuesday, when it was used to kindle the fire for frying the pancakes. Churches were naturally decorated too; at Presteigne in 1864 a great hoop hung from the arms of each gas burner, 'elegantly dressed with moss, ivy, holly, and other evergreens'. The range of Christmas decorations in customary use widened considerably in the nineteenth and twentieth centuries, with the introduction of the Christmas tree and its glass baubles, candles and tinsel, the Christmas card, the Crib, and innumerable forms of streamers, table decorations, and so forth; nevertheless, the holly and the mistletoe are still indispensable, both for their symbolic value and as reminders of the time when every home was decorated simply from the resources of the surrounding woods and fields.

Various beliefs were held in the nineteenth century about what was and was not lucky to do on Christmas Day. In Herefordshire it was unlucky for a woman to enter the house unless she had slept under its roof that night, and farmers' wives often paid a dark-haired man to be the 'first foot,' just as on New Year's Day. Both there and in Shropshire it was very unlucky to 'lend' fire, i.e. to give glowing coals from one's own hearth to a neighbour whose fire had gone out; if it had to be done, the fire must be paid for, if only with a pin. In Cheshire, the rules seem to have been stricter; neither fire nor light must be given out of the house for the whole twelve days of Christmas. Often it was considered wrong to do any avoidable work on the farm during the twelve days, and particularly on Holy Innocents' Day (28 December), an extremely ill-omened date, or on New Year's Day. In Cheshire the farm-hands kept complete holiday from Boxing Day, when their old contract of service expired, to 2 January, when the new one began. Referring to the end of the nineteenth century, F.H. Crossley writes:

> I have known unmarried farm-hands spend their entire week card playing, hardly even going to bed during the time, and losing the whole year's earnings which they received upon termination of their hire.

On the Welsh side of the Border, in Radnorshire and Monmouthshire, it was once customary to hold a service in the very early hours of Christmas morning, known as plygain (a Welsh word for 'dawn' or 'cock-crow'). People, whether Nonconformist or Church of England, would gather at five or six in the morning at their church or chapel – or at a farm, if need be – and pray, sing carols and sing hymns till dawn broke. The custom obviously derives from the ancient Roman Catholic one of holding first a Midnight Mass, then a Dawn Mass, and then the Mass of Christmas Day. However, when the old Dawn Mass had been forgotten, various fanciful explanations were given to account for the plygain, as that it was held in memory of the angels who woke the shepherds, or that the purpose was to try and wake the Devil so that he would be driven away by the crowing of the cock. Plygain now only survives in the Tanad Valley, south-west of Oswestry, in the form of an evening carol service held on any date between mid-December and mid-January; the local churches and chapels hold them on different dates, so that the same singers can attend several plygainiau. They perform as groups of three or four, almost always all-male, and sing unaccompanied. Until the 1920s they also went carol-singing from door to door during Christmas Night, to collect money.

The plygain custom was enthusiastically encouraged during the nineteenth century at Llanofer Court in Monmouthshire, home of Augusta, Lady Llanover, who was 'passionately devoted to Welsh music, customs, and language'. She also supported the Mari Lwyd ('Grey Mare'), a midwinter custom once widespread in South Wales, and first recorded in 1800. A hobby-horse similar to the Soulers' horse described above (pp. 180-81), accompanied by costumed guisers, would call at a house, whose doors would be locked against it. The horse's attendants would chant Welsh verses demanding admittance, to which those inside would reply, also in verse; eventually the doors would be opened and the Mari Lwyd would enter, frisking about and chasing girls. This was done every year at Llanofer Court up until Lady Llanover's death in 1896. Roy Palmer notes that when the contents of Llanofer Court were sold in 1934 they included 'two carved wood horses' heads, as used in the old Welsh Christmas custom known as Mari Lwyd', and that a mid-Victorian painting showing the horse at the door of Llanofer Court can still be seen in the village post office.

Kilvert gives a first-hand account of how he encountered it, possibly at Clyro; the year is not given:

> It was between the Christmasses [i.e. between 25 December and 6 January] and at eight o'clock I was sitting with some other people around the fire, when we heard tramping outside, and a loud knocking at the door, which was locked. There was the sound of a flute a moment later, and a man began singing – then a few minutes later another man, inside the room, went to the door and sang what was apparently an answer to the song without. Then the door was thrown open, and in walked about a dozen people, headed by a most extraordinary apparition, an animal covered by a flowing sheet, and surmounted by a horse's skull, to which a bridle was attached. This apparition, I saw a moment later, was really a man covered with a sheet; his head was bowed down, and a skull had been fastened to it. The people sang, collected some money, and then went off. They ought by rights, apparently, to have had an ass's skull, but then, dead donkeys are proverbially hard to come by.

This season was also the time when mummers went round inns and large houses, performing their doggerel play about Saint (or King)

George and his various adversaries. This custom, very popular in other regions, is rarer here; only two instances are known from Shropshire, one from Herefordshire, and a few in Cheshire, where, as has already been shown, versions of this play were done instead at Easter and in early November. An incomplete text has recently been found in a Monmouth bookshop; the play used to be performed there in the Punchbowl Inn up to the 1880s. It would seem that in some places the slapstick combats were far more appreciated than the words; Mrs Leather prints a rather corrupt version she collected from an informant in Ross in 1908, in which St George massacres no fewer than six miscellaneous opponents (Prince Valentine, Captain Rover, Turkey Snipe, Little John, Bonaparte and Black Sambo), and is finally himself killed off by the Doctor, who is angry with him for refusing him his ten guinea fee for reviving the victims! Again, we learn that at Chepstow till about 1910 a party of men dressed up as Robin Hood's band used to fight mock battles in the bar of the Greyhound Inn. No doubt it is as a last faint echo of this tradition that at Bridgnorth in the 1950s boys came out in pairs on the morning of Boxing Day, their faces blacked with soot and their jackets inside out, and fought mock duels in the streets with broomsticks (which they wielded as in the old sport of singlestick), while singing 'This old Man, he played one...'.

31 December brings us full circle, for some customs already described for New Year's Day could also be done on the Eve; at Trelleck in 1904 the Monty apple was being taken round on New Year's Eve, and at Leominster in 1895 this was the date for Burning the Bush. And as night drew on, everywhere people would be waiting up to let the New Year in.

NOTES

Books and articles frequently cited are given their full titles only when they are first mentioned in these notes; thereafter they are referred to by the author's surname only, but full titles and other details can be found in the Bibliography (pp. 208-10). If there are several books or articles by the same author, these are identified as 'Bett (1)', 'Bett (2)' etc., in order of publication date. The two volumes of the Cheshire Federation of Women's Institutes' *Cheshire Village Memories* are referred to as *C.V.M.* I and II.

INTRODUCTION, pp. 11-16
Anne Hughes' Diary: For the controversy, see 'Another Diary of Another Nobody', *Private Eye*, 4 December 1981; correspondence in *The Times* on 9, 15, 23, 26 and 29 January and 4 February 1982.
Pub talk: H.L.V. Fletcher, *Portrait of the Wye Valley*, 1968, 40. The same author in his *Herefordshire*, 1948, 126-13 l, describes an encounter with a surly old man whose conversation consisted mainly of those traditional jibes which one village or county makes at another's expense, but who also told him a grimly humorous ghost story and cracked macabre jokes about how to lay a ghost by turning the corpse on its belly. Most of the material here, however, merely elaborates on that recorded in Mrs Leather's book.
Place names and landscape: Wulvarn Brook, Cheshire Federation of Women's Institutes, *Cheshire Village Memories* I 30; Wildboarclough, J.H. Ingram, *Companion into Cheshire*, 1947, 8; submerged forest, Ingram 15; squirrel rhyme, Ingram 79 and (a variant) 5.
The making of the Wrekin: Oral information from Sister Mary Joseph of Sion, formerly of Acton Burnell, 1974.

1. THE LANDSCAPE, pp. 17-30
The Skirrid: J.H. Matthews, 'Collecteanea,' *Folklore* XV, 1904, 349. E.M. Leather (2), 'Scraps of English Folklore: Monmouthshire and Radnorshire', *Folklore* XXIV, 1913, 110; J.H. Massingham, *The Southern Marches*, 1952, 13.

The Wrekin: C.S. Burne, *Shropshire Folk-Lore*, ed. from the collections of G.F. Jackson, 1883-6, 2-4.

Herefordshire hills: E.M. Leather (1), *The Folk-Lore of Herefordshire*, 1912, 1-2.

Outcrops of rock: The Stiperstones and Titterstone Clee, Burne 4-5, 198; the Devil's Pulpit near Tintern, F.W. Baty, *The Forest of Dean*, 1952, 40, and I. Waters, *Folklore and Dialect of the Lower Wye Valley*, 1973, 5; the Devil's Pulpit near Bream, T.A. Ryder, *Portrait of Gloucestershire*, 1966, 26, 80, and L.M. Eyre (1), 'Folklore Notes from St Briavels', *Folklore* XIII, 1902, 171.

Stones flung by the Devil or giants: The Lea Stone, M. Fraser (2) *Welsh Border Country*, 1972, 114; at Stockport, at Arden Hall, and at Bluestone, C.M. Hole, *Traditions and Customs of Cheshire*, 1937 (reprinted 1970), 192, 197; at Bartestree, Leather (1) 3; on Brown Clee, Burne 6; at Beeston Castle, H. Bett (1), *English Legends*, 1950, 72; at Trelleck, R.T. Davies, 'The Folklore of Gwent,' *Folklore* XLVIII, 1937, 43; Moll Walbee's Stone, Fletcher (2) 95, Fraser (2) 176, W.H. Howse, *Radnorshire*, 1949, 320; giant at Painscastle, F.R. Kilvert, *Diary*, ed. W. Plomer, second ed. 1960, I 70-1; Robin Hood's Stone at Arden Mill, Hole 197.

Stones flung by Jack o' Kent: From the Skirrid to Trelleck, B.A. Wherry (1) 'Wizardry on the Welsh Border', *Folklore* XV, 1904, 86; from Trelleck Beacon, Davies 41; at Stroat and Thornbury, Waters 4; Robin Hood's Butts and Garway Hill, Leather (1) 2 and 164; stones at Grosmont, Davies 42; Jack's stones can't be shifted, L. M. Eyre (2) 'Folklore of the Wye Valley', *Folklore* XVI, 1905, 164.

Devil's Rocks at Downton Castle: Leather (3) 'Scraps of English Folklore: Shropshire', *Folklore* XXV, 1914, 372.

Hills and stones linked with history: Robin Hood shooting from a tumulus near Ludlow, Burne 21; from a tumulus at Tilston Fearnall, Hole 197; Harold and the Trelleck stones, Eyre (2), 164; Saxons at Willaston, *C.V.M.* I 122; Vikings at Irby, Hole 63; Viking at the Bridestones, Ingram 215; Arthur's Stone at Dorstone, Kilvert III 399, Leather (1) 5.

Stones that move or bleed: Stones feared by farmers, Howse 204; the Four Stones near Walton, Howse 204, A. Watkins, *The Old Straight Track*, 1925 (reprinted 1974), 18; the Whetstone near Kington, Leather (1) 6; the Long Stone near Staunton, A. Watkins 26, Baty 108, Fletcher (2) 147; the Lea Stone, Fraser (2) 114; the Colwall Stone, Leather (1) 5-6;

an unnamed stone in the Forest of Dean, Eyre (1) 171, who adds that it was put up to commemorate the murder of one of the Constables of the Forest.

Lakes with sunken buildings: The story of Llangorse Lake is discussed by F.J. North in *Sunken Cities*, 1957; he regards it as the oldest of the Welsh legends of this type; it is first recorded in a manuscript of about 1700. He also discusses the story of Llynclys Lake, which is first alluded to in Humphrey Llwyd's *Breviary of Britayne*, 1573, and given more fully in *Y Brython* V, 1862, 338. See also J. Rhys, *Celtic Folklore, Welsh and Manx*, 1901, 403. For Shobdon Marshes and the pool at Dorstone, see Leather (1) 11; the pool at Trelleck, Eyre (2) 166; Colemere, Crossmere, Bomere and Ellesmere, Burne 64-66, 69-73; Rostherne Mere, Hole 58, and Egerton Leigh, *Ballads and Legends of Cheshire*, 1866, 233-5, 278-9.

Lost bells: In Cheshire, Hole 58-9, Leigh 233-5, 278-9, *C.V.M.* I 128, F. Moss, *Folklore, Old Customs and Tales of My Neighbours*, 1898, 100. In Shropshire, Burne 66-8, H. Bett (2) *English Myths and Traditions*, 1952, 85. At Marden, Leather (1) 168-9.

Mermaids: In Rostherne Mere, Hole 58; at Child's Ercall, Burne 78. The Asrai, R.L. Tongue, *Forgotten Folktales of the English Counties*, 1970, 24-6.

Fish: In Bomere, Burne 80. At Peterchurch, Leather (1) 12; Readers' Digest, *Folklore, Myths and Legends of Britain*, 1973, 327; Massingham 5-6, on information from the Revd George Powell, Rector of Dorstone; Kilvert III 266-7. The Man who went fishing on Sunday, Tongue 28-30; she says the story was also told of the Severn, and along the Welsh Border.

Buried treasures: At Stokesay Castle, Burne 7-8; at Bronsil, Peynard and Longtown Castles, Leather (1) 8; at Skenfrith Castle, K. Thomas, *Religion and the Decline of Magic*, 1971, 236; at Wormelow Barrow, Bett (1) 98; at Clun, Burne 640; at St Weonard's Tump, Leather (1) 9; at Llanymynech Hill, Burne 6.

Tunnels: At the Hermitage near Bridgnorth, Burne 85-6; from Tintern Abbey to Trelleck, Eyre (2) 165; from Orleton Hall to Woofferton, Leather (1) 4; the fiddler of Llanymynech, Burne 57; the old men of Trelleck, B.A. Wherry (2), 'Miscellaneous Notes from Monmouthshire', *Folklore* XVI, 1905, 64.

Towns that have moved: Oswestry, Burne 9 n.3; Ross, Fletcher (1) 78.

Church sites shifted: At Clodock, Leather (1) 214, Massingham 132;

at Kilgwrrwg, Davies 55; at Bebbington, Ingram 36-7; at Ince, Hole 192, Ingram 78; at Over, Leigh 191-6, Hole 192, Ingram 112; at Stock, Hole 192, Ingram 78; the four Shropshire churches, Burne 8-10; the three in Herefordshire, Leather (1) 10.

2 RUMOURS OF WAR, pp. 31-43

Bloody rivers and fields: At Dorstone, Massingham 164-5; the Dulas Brook, Leather (1) 3; at Trelleck, Eyre (2) 163; at Barber's Bridge, Baty 64. See also Burne 22-3.

Place-names and battles: The Slaughter, Fletcher (2) 146; Scotland Bank, Massingham 164-5; Beachley and Hewelsfield, Eyre (2) 163.

Llewellyn: Fletcher (2) 74, 86.

Harold: S. Baring-Gould, *Curious Myths of the Middle Ages*, 1901 ed., 118; S. Hartland, *The Science of Fairy Tales*, 1925 ed., 205; Hole 186-7; Ingram 60.

Wild Edric: Burne 25-9; Fraser (2) 111-12; L.H. Hayward, 'Shropshire Folklore of Yesterday and Today', *Folklore* XLIX, 1938, 238; J. Hughes (1), *A Light-Hearted Look at our Shropshire History*, 1969, 18.

The sleeping warriors: Arthur in Wales, Rhys 462-3, T. Gwyn Jones, *Welsh Folklore and Folk Custom*, 1930, 89-90. The Wizard of Alderley Edge, W.E.A. Axon, *Cheshire Gleanings*, 1884, 56-8, 60; Leigh 102-11 quotes an anonymous poem printed as the Alderley guide; Hole 185-6; Ingram 147-8; oral informant, 1973. 'King George's Men' at Penlascarn, Jones 88-9. For the Scottish parallels, see E.B. Lyle, 'Thomas of Erceldoune, the Prophet and the Prophesied', *Folklore* LXXIX, 1968, 117-21.

Treasures: At Arthur's Cave, Massingham 273; in Beeston Castle, Hole 67, Ingram 97, *C.V.M.* II 32; at Guildon Sutton, *C.V.M.* II 56; at Birkenhead, Ingram 8; at Abbey-cwm-hir, Fletcher (2) 40, from oral informants in the 1960s; at Easthope, Hayward 241.

Monks' curses At Combermere, Moss 140-5; at Abbey Grange, Ingram 78; at Llyn Gwyn, Howse 17 and 200; on the Scudamore family, Fletcher (2) 129 – but contrast Fletcher (1) 172-4, where he states that at that time (1948) he had not found such a legend, though he had expected to. An influential book on the topic was Henry Spelman's *The History and Fate of Sacrilege*, compiled early in the seventeenth century and published in 1698; the fourth edition in 1895 was brought up to date by the addition of many local traditions.

The silent woman: *C.V.M.* II 44, 89; H. Hughes, *Cheshire and its Welsh Border*, 1966, 38 (with photograph of the figurehead); oral information from Mr E.L. Povey, 1973.

The drummer boy of Hereford: Leather (1) 225.

The Civil War: At Llansilin, Readers' Digest *Folklore, Myths and Legends of Britain*, 1973, 396; at Acton, *C.V.M.* I 15; at Wem, Burne 585.

Nixon: All texts quoted are from the edition by W.E.A. Axon, *Nixon's Cheshire Prophecies*, 1873, which includes three pamphlets about Nixon (John Oldmixon, *Nixon's Cheshire Prophecy*, 1714; W.E., *The Life of Robert Nixon*, 1719; Anon., *The Life of Robert Nixon of Bridge House*, c. 1800), and also the actual prophecies, *The Original Predictions of Robert Nixon, as Delivered by Himself in Doggrel Verse*, c. 1800. The latter are also in Leigh, 177-85. See also the article on Nixon in the *Dictionary of National Biography*; G. Ormerod, *History of Cheshire*, 1819, II 100 ff.; Thomas 392 n.19; Hole 166-71; Ingram 36, 117 for the sayings about Bebington and Northwich; Kilvert III 154-5 for 'Saxon'; Dickens, *The Pickwick Papers*, ch.43. On the general topic of political 'prophecies', see Thomas 389-415; M.E. Griffiths, *Early Vaticination in Welsh*, 1937. On Thomas of Erceldoune, see E.B. Lyle, *Folklore* LXXIX 1968, 117-21.

3 LOCAL HEROES, ROGUES AND VILLAINS, pp. 44-58

Effigies: Owd Scriven at Berrington, Burne 13; Sir Hugh Calverley at Bunbury, Ingram 93-4; Constantia Pauncefoote at Much Cowarne, Leather (1) 223-4; Sir Ralph de Stavelry at Mottram, Ingram 172-3.

Coats-of-arms: The Vaughans' snakes, R. Parry, *History of Kington*, 1845, for the first version, and Fletcher (2) 144 for the second; the Venables' dragon, Leigh 223-7; the Breretons' bear, *C.V.M.* I 34.

The naked ride: S. Rudder, *A New History of Gloucester*, 1779, 307; Fletcher (2) 180. A legend told to explain why a piece of land at Bromfield in Shropshire is called the 'Crawls' is of a related type, but is not connected with any charitable endowments: an heiress wished to marry a poor man, and her angry father swore her only dowry would be as much land as she could crawl round on hands and knees in one night, so she did this, and her father relented. Burne 91.

Almshouses and curfews: At Monmouth, Fletcher (2) 151-2, 182; at Tong and Shrewsbury, Burne 602; at Aymestrey, Leather (1) 48; at Chepstow, Waters 6-7.

Dragons: At Grimesditch, Hole 199; at Brinsop, Leather (1) 11; at

Deerhurst, Rudder 402-3, and R. Atkyns, *The Ancient and Present state of Gloucestershire*, 1712; at Llandeilo Graban, D. Edmondes Owen, 'Pre-Reformation Survivals,' *Transactions of the Honourable Society of Cymmrodorion*, 1910-11, as quoted by Howse, 201. At Mordiford, Lipscombe, *A Journey into South Wales*, 1802, 71; J. Dacres Devlin, *The Mordiford Dragon*, 1848, 1-70; Leather (1) 24; Massingham 256-8, from information from Mr and Miss Hereford, whose uncle was Rector of Mordiford in 1875.

Fools: Burne 97-8; John Aubrey, *Brief Lives*, 1669-96, pub. 1949, 114-15.

Highwaymen and poachers: The gibbet on Trafford Green, Hole 135-6; inns on the Macclesfield to Buxton road, Ingram 188-9; Higgins of Knutsford, H. Green, *Knutsford, its Traditions and History*; the blacksmiths at Mollington, *C.V.M.* II 24. Dick Turpin at Hoo Green, Hole 199; at Ashley and Bollington, *C.V.M.* II, 17, 25; at Lostock Gralam, *C.V.M.* I 83. The horse-thief and the ground-fairies, *C.V.M.* I 107; the buck in the cradle, *C.V.M.* I 89 and Ingram 137.

Outlaws and bandits: Wild Humphrey Kynaston, Burne 15-19; Ippikin, Burne 14-15; the bandits of Bloody Bones Cave, *C.V.M.* II 92.

Murders: At Plaish Hall, Burne 99-100, Hughes (1) 14, Hayward 240; at Condover Hall, Burne 80-1, 114-15, 642. 'Revenge House' at Capel-y-ffin, Palmer (1) 187-8. 'No grass will grow' at Nass, J.H. Peele, *Portrait of the Severn*, 1968, 49; at Black Hill, Hole 158-9; at Godley, Ingram 185; at Montgomery, R.M. Price, *The Robber's Grave*, 1852.

Telepathic warning: Palmer (2) 90-1.

Ravens reveal murder: Richard Gough, *The History of Myddle*, 1702, ed. David Hey, 1981, 122. Burne 225, Leather (1) 168.

Quakers and tithes: Ingram 152.

Trade unionists and folk customs: On disguises, see A.W. Smith, 'Some Folklore Elements in Movements of Social Protest', *Folklore* LXXVII 1966, 244-5; on Masonic rituals at Nantwich, H. Pelling, *A History of British Trade Unionism*, 40; on the 'Scotch Cattle', M. Fraser (1), *West of Offa's Dyke*, 1958, 59; for 'General Ludd's Wives' at Stockport, Darvall, *Popular Disturbances in Regency England*, 1934, 98.

Rebecca rioters and Rebecca poachers: David J.V. Jones, *Rebecca's Children*, 1990; G. Borrow, *Wild Wales*, Everyman edition, 86-7; Howse 86-7; Fletcher (1) 50-1; Fletcher (2) 64-6; Fraser (1) 29.

4 WIZARDS AND WITCHES, pp. 59-74

Jack o' Kent: For possible historical identifications, see I.C. Peate, *Folklore* XLVIII, 1937, 218-19; for Anthony Munday, see Lord Raglan, *Folklore* XLVIII, 1937, 334. The main collections of tales about him are in Wherry (1) 85-6, Leather (1) 163-6, Davies 41-3; additional details in Baty 100-1 and Massingham 295. See also the references in Ch. 1 to Jack as outdoing the Devil in stone-throwing. Jack's black stick is from Leather (1) 165, and the crows from Wherry (1) 85.

Davies the wizard: W.J.H. Watkins, 'A Cycle of Stories Current in Radnorshire', *Folklore* XLIII 1932, 424-7; also K.M. Briggs, *A Dictionary of British Folktales*, 1970, B I 65-7, quoting *Bye-Gones*, Second Series, 1888, IX 106, and 1889, I 242. The good and the evil bird are also mentioned by Moss, 112-13, in connection with a Cheshire wizard named John of Hale Barns, who ordered that his heart 'or a piece of beef similar to it' be placed in a tree; in his case the evil bird was a magpie (regarded as the Devil's bird in Cheshire), while the good one, unexpectedly, was a crow.

Cheating the Devil: The Vale Royal monk, K.M. Briggs, *A Dictionary of British Folk-Tales*, London 1970-1, B I 83, from the Norton Collection; the doctor's race, Woods 21.

Conjurers as healers and hypnotists: For Nicholas Johnson of Devauden, see Davies 46; for Jenkyns of Trelleck, Wherry (1) 76-81 (from whom the quotations were taken) and Wherry (2) 66-7. Davies 44-5 gives anecdotes about a Jenkins of Tregare who may be the same man, though the date of his death, around 1900, seems a little later than the dates implied by Miss Wherry; Waters, however, treats them as identical. The 'Jenkins' whom Mrs Leather describes (pp. 53-9) is a pseudonym for a different man, living between Hereford and Bromyard. For the conjurers at Ross and near Hereford, see Leather (1) 60 and 57. Other stories about such men will be found in Howse 198 and Eyre (2) 167-70; the latter refers to Luke Page of St Briavels, who died in 1905.

Magic books: For the Vicar of Beguildy, see Owen, quoted by Howse 196; for the servant and the book, Davies 50. In Murray-Aynsley, 'Scraps of English Folklore XVI: Herefordshire', *Folklore* XXXIX, 1928, 382-3, there is a story of schoolboys who raised the Devil by opening their master's book, and could not lay him till he returned.

Thief-catching How wizards punish thieves, Leather (1) 60, Howse 197, Wherry (1) 77; the stolen ram at Longtown, Leather (1) 59; the rick-burners at Twemlose, E. Vale, *Shropshire*, 1949, 13-14. For other Shropshire conjurers, see Burne 169-72. For James Jones of Clyro, Kilvert I 300-1, III 273-4.

Wise women as healers or thief-catchers: Burne 146, 149, 169; Hole 175; Murray-Aynsley 383.

Witches dreaded in the Wye Valley: Eyre (2) 171.

Curses: Thomas 506-8; Lead tablet from Dymock, T.A. Ryder, *Portrait of Gloucestershire*, 1966, 95; doll from Hereford, *The Hereford Times* 22/1/1960; miniature coffin, Palmer (2)156-7; the Image House, Hole 14.

Ill-wishing: Davies 47, 49; Howse 196; Murray-Aynsley 390.

The witch and the waggon: Burne 152-3; for the witch and the calves, Burne 151-2. Other tales of witches stopping waggons, though without the 'My God' motif, are in Leather (1) 55 and Davies 47-9.

The witch as hare: Leather (1) 52, Burne 156, Waters 3-4, Eyre (1) 175-6. Transformation to other animals, Leather (1) 52, Davies 50-1.

The witch as crow: Palmer (1), 81.

Witches riding: Wherry (1) 80, Eyre (1) 176; also Leather (1) 53 for three witches riding a grindstone, a broom, and a hurdle. The man who followed a witch, Davies 51-2; the boy who followed fairies, Leather (1) 176-7.

Witches in stables: Eyre (1) 175, Davies 51, Murray-Aynsley 382-3, Burne 157.

Charms against witches: Birch and/or mountain ash, Howse 196; Kilvert I 119-20, 135, III 268; Leather (1) 18; Murray-Aynsley 382, 387-8; Burne 246-8; Massingham 42. Hawthorn, Eyre (1) 175, Davies 51; yew, Eyre (1) 175; holly, Hole 13, 120; various, Leather (1) 53; parson's wig, Moss 207.

Breaking a witch's power: Knife or nail in footprint, Wherry (1) 80; the Nanny Morgan case, Burne 160-2; heart and pins, Leather (1) 51-2, 54-5, Davies 52-3, Moss 112-13.

The 'Maynons' charm: Howse 199.

5 FAIRIES, pp. 75-86

Belief in fairies: Kilvert I 281 (conversation with David Price); I 247 (information from Hannah Whitney); II 81 (from Mrs Meredith); II 130 (from Hannah Jones). Fairies in Monmouthshire, Wherry (2) 63; in Shropshire, Burne 55-6; girl taken by dancing fairies, Leather (1) 45-6;

other fairy beliefs in Herefordshire, Leather (1) 43-5, 48; the changeling, Leather (1) 46-7.

The bogeys and the salt-box: Burne 45-7.

Material evidence for fairies: Coins, Leland's *Itinerary* VII, 152, quoted in Leather (1) 44; Fletcher (1) 83. The Roman pavement, Howse 28; spindle-whorl, Burne 369; pipes, Vale 16-17.

Water spirits: Jenny Greenteeth, Burne 79, Hole 60; Nicky Nicky Nye, R.L. Tongue, *Forgotten Folktales of the English Counties*, 1970, 108-16.

Wild Edric: Burne 59-60, from Walter Map, *De Nugis Curialium*, c. 1190, Distinctio II, ch. XII. For Edric as a knocker and as a dog, Burne 28, 105.

The fairy cow: At Mitchell's Fold, Burne 39-40; at Audlem, Ingram 102.

King Herla: Walter Map, *De Nugis Curialium*, Distinctio I ch. XI and Distinctio IV ch. XIII, ed. and transl. M.R. James, J.E. Lloyd and E.S. Hartland, 1923, 13-17, 206-7.

6 GHOSTS, pp. 87-101

Disbelief in ghosts: Burne 129.

The dog and the skin: Davies 58-9.

Combermere Abbey ghosts Hole 144-5.

Cheshire ghosts: In bottle at Burleydam, *C.V.M.* I 40. Mary Fitton and Maggotty Johnson at Gawsworth, I 65-6; pig at Lostock Gralam, I 83. duck at Stanney, II 87; dog at Withington, II 107; woman at well at Pytchley Hollow, I 96; nun at Swettenham, I 110; skeleton at Marbury Hall, II 43; Other Marbury Hall tales, Woods 51-3. The boggart at Frandley, A.W. Boyd, *A Country Parish*, 1951, 66; boggart rhyme at Tattenhall, *C.V.M.* II 93.

Remorseful ghosts: Leather (1) 32-4, Burne 117-19; hidden iron, Leather (1) 33-4, Kilvert I 58, Murray-Aynsley 386; the ghostly priest, Hole 150.

Animal ghosts: Pig at Bunghill, Leather (1) 35; colt at Cutberry Hollow, Burne 106 (it was said to be the ghost of a woman whose corpse had been dug up and robbed of its jewels by a sexton); dog and horses on Llowes road, Kilvert I 313; dog and other beasts at Trelleck, Wherry (1) 83-4; dogs in Shropshire, Burne 104-5; in Cheshire, Hole 163-5; in Herefordshire, Leather (1) 38-9, Parry 204. Hell Hounds at Trelleck, Davies 57.

Phantom funerals: Hole 162, Leather (1) 37, Burne 104.
Ghosts leaping on horseback: Burne 106-7, 124, 125, 128.
Exorcisms: The Gatley Shouter, Moss 133-5; the rhyme was also ascribed to other ghosts at Shrewsbury and at Burslem in Staffordshire, see Burne 120. For Madam Pigott, Burne 124-7; three other female ghosts laid in bottles are described in Burne 111 n.2, 124, 128. For Sir George Blount, see Burne 122-3, 642; for the ghost at Ellesmere, Burne 114; for the bull-ghosts at Llanigon, M.E. Hartland and E.B. Thomas, 'Breconshire Village Folklore', *Folklore* XXIV, 1913, 505-6; bull-ghosts at Llanfair Caereinion and at Llanfyllin, Readers' Digest *Folklore, Myths and Legends of Britain*, 393, 394; the calf at Garnstone Park, Leather (1) 33, 35, and Fletcher (1) 128-30; Black Vaughan, Leather (1) 29-30; Roaring Bull of Bagbury, Burne 107-11, 642, and T. Wright, *Collecteanea Archaeologica* I, part 1 (summarized in Burne). Other exorcism tales from this area that follow the same pattern are those of Mr Hoskins' ghost, Leather (1) 30-1; the Great Giant of Henllys, *Athenaeum*, 1847, reprinted in Briggs B I 487; 'Tommy and the Ghost,' *Folklore Record* II 1879, 76-7, reprinted in Briggs B I 592.

7 HOLY WELLS AND HEALING CHARMS, pp. 102-16

Saints and Wells: St Winifred, Jones 115-16; St Milburga, Burne 417-18; St Ethelbert, Leather (1) 11-12; St Oswald, Burne 482, and Hughes (1) 62; Sts Patrick and Plegmund, Hole 63, 68.
Llandridod and Trelleck: Some eighteenth-century advertisements are given in Waters 20. Monsters slain, Fletcher (2) 75.
Healing wells: Lists of wells in Herefordshire and their properties are given in Leather (1) 11-14, and Murray-Aynsley 391-2; in Shropshire, Burne 416-30; in Cheshire, Hole 62-9; In Radnorshire, Howse 211. For St Anthony's Well in the Forest of Dean, see Ryder 87 and Baty 22; St Anne's Well at Aconbury, Leather (1) 11; the well at Woolston, Burne 430.
Wishing wells: At Sunny Gutter and Rhosgoch, Burne 422-3; at Gayton, Leigh 230; at Brampton Bryan, Leather (1) 13; at Trelleck, A.D. Hippisley-Coxe, *Haunted Britain*, 1973, 156; St Oswald's Well, Burne 428-9.
Well dressing and well wakes: At Didsbury, Moss 110; at Nantwich, Northwich and Middlewich, Leigh 62, F.H. Crossley, *Cheshire*, 1949, 50; in Radnorshire, Howse 211; at Rorrington and Churchstoke, Burne 433-4.

Modern rituals at Trelleck: Palmer (1), 112-13.
Treating the knife: Moss 167, Burne 198-99.
Rings: Galvanic, Moss 167. medieval cramp-rings, Thomas 198-9; sacrament rings, Leather (1) 79, Burne 192-3, Murray-Aynsley 387; ring from bachelors' pennies, Moss 166; ring from coffin nails, Burne 193.
The Colmer tomb: Palmer (1), 133-4.
Good Friday buns and Ascension Day rain: Burne 191, Leather (1) 78, Eyre (1) 173.
Baptism, Confirmation, Communion wine: Moss 167, Murray-Aynsley 388 (from whom the quotations are taken), Leather (1) 80.
Our Saviour's letter: Leather (1) 112, 259, ill. at end of book; Owen Davies, *Witchcraft, Magic and Culture 1736-1951*, 1999, 126-30.
Scriptural charms: Against toothache, the version quoted is from R.T. Davies 54; other versions are in Howse 198, Leather (1) 74-5, Burne 181-2, Hartland and Thomas 507. Against ague, Leather (1) 73-4; against burns and scalds, Burne 183-4. More charms of this sort will be found in Eyre (1) 173, and Boyd 65-6. Leather and Burne both contain additional scriptural charms besides those quoted here.
Eagles' flesh: Howse 205, Burne 185-6.
Persons who cure whooping cough: Burne 186, 203-6; Hole 10-11; Leather (1) 83; Eyre (1) 172; Leigh 44.
Dead man's hand: For whooping cough, Leather (1) 82; for wens and goitre, Leather (1) 84, Burne 202, 645, Moss 168-9.
Dead men's teeth: Moss 20, Burne 193.
Split ash: Wherry (2) 64, Leather (1) 80-1, Burne 196; split rowan at Ludlow, Burne 196-7.
Arched bramble: Quotation from Leather (1) 82; other instances, Burne 195-6, Davies 53-4, Eyre (1) 172, Moss 10, Murray-Aynsley 389.
Warts: Hole 12, Leather (1) 83-4, Davies 47, Hayward 226-7, Howse 206, Murray-Aynsley 389, Waters 19-20, *C.V.M.* I 93.
Foul foot: Howse 206, Davies 53, Murray-Aynsley 389, Burne 202, Leather (1) 78.
Dead animals displayed: Aborted calf, Moss 87, Hole 23-4; lambs, Hayward 232; pigs, Eyre (1) 172.
Miscellaneous cures: Eyre (1) 172-3 (ball from rosebush, trimming toenails, mole's paw); Moss 11 (garlic bandages), 166-7 (spider, woodlice as pills, cockroaches, roast mice); Leather (1) 78, 80, 82 (eelskin garters,

sheep's lungs, woodlice for teething, frog for thrush); Hole 10-12 (bullock's melt, hedgehog); Boyd 64 (onion on mantlepiece, mole's paw); M. Baker, *Folklore and Customs of Rural England*, 1974, 39 (onions round cowshed). Other cures besides these will be found in Leather (1) 77-85 and Burne 189-206.

8 FROM THE CRADLE TO THE GRAVE, pp. 117-38
Dangers in pregnancy: Hares, Burne 213; birthmarks, Leather (1) 112, Moss 6; the beggar's curse, Hayward 229; the frog-woman, Kilvert I 380-1; miscarriages caused by bears or lions breeding, Hole 24, Burne 286 n.2.
Husband's sickness: Leather (1) 111-12, Moss 6-7.
Placenta: As love charm, Moss 169; as fertilizer for roses, information from Miss Cheryl Ingram, 1975.
Baby born with caul or teeth: Burne 285, Leather (1) 112, Moss 4-5.
Baby's first food: Moss 1-3, Burne 284, Leather (1) 112, Boyd 64, Hole 8.
Other rules and taboos about babies: Burne 285-7, Leather (1) 113, Moss 8, Hayward 224, Hole 8.
Churching: Burne 286, Leather (1) 113.
Baptism: Burne 286, Leather (1) 113, Murray-Aynsley 388.
Wedding rejoicings: Bell ringing, Crossley 48; arches over road, Burne 293-4, Leather (1) 115; display of silver, Burne 293, quoting Hare, *Memorials of a Quiet Life* I 245; posies and strewing flowers, Moss 13, Burne 293, Leather (1) 115.
Rules and taboos at weddings: Leather (1) 114-15, Burne 289-95, Moss 12-16, Hole 4-5.
Roping the road: *C.V.M.* I 22, II 53, 95, 103; Howse 214; Jones 190; Wherry (2) 65-6; M. Baker, *Folklore and Customs of Rural England*, 1974, 141; E.J. Dunhill, 'Welsh Folklore Items: Monmouthshire', *Folklore* XXIV 1913, 109-10.
Sanding at Knutsford: Crossley 48, Hole 4. For a legend 'explaining' the custom, see pp. 161.
Protective patterns: Eyre (1) 172, Hayward 236-7, Leather (1) 53.
Riding the Stang: Axon (2), 330-1; A.V. Chappel and A. Pollard (eds), *The Letters of Mrs Gaskell* (1966), 29-31. Burne 295-6, Leather (1) 160, *C.V.M.* I 117.

Sale of wives: At Knighton, with 'legal' document, Howse 217-18; at Mottram, *C.V.M.* I 92; passing through a turnpike, Burne 295; at Hereford, Leather (1) 117-18, with quotation from the *Hereford Times*, 20/5/1876; in Cheshire, Hole 7-8.

Omens of death: From birds and animals, Burne 209, 211, 225-32; Leather (1) 25; Hole 16; Moss 88, 97; Hayward 224; Eyre (1) 172; Davies 56-7; Boyd 60-1. From household objects, Burne 280-1, 296; Leather (1) 118-19; Hole 16; Hayward 225; Eyre (1) 172; Davies 56-7. From corpses and deaths, Burne 297, Leather (1) 119, Boyd 61. For the omen preceding Kilvert's death, see the newspaper report of his funeral quoted in Plomer's Introduction to Vol. III of the *Diary*.

Corpse candles: Howse 208, Leather (1) 119, Hole 16; George Borrow, *Wild Wales* ch. 11 (Everyman edition 64-5) reports a conversation with a woman who had seen them at Llangollen.

Rules and taboos concerning death: Feathers, Burne 297, n.3, Leather (1) 119-20, Hayward 225 (at Ford). Waning moon, Hayward 225. Windows and mirrors, Moss 122, Hayward 225, Burne 229.

Laying out the corpse: With salt, Burne 299, Leather (1) 120, Hole 17, Moss 19; with candle in salt, Leather (1) 120; with turf in paper, Burne 299, Leather (1) 120 (the latter also mentions putting a pail of salt water under the bed); with bread, Leather (4) 'Scraps of English Folklore, Herefordshire', *Folklore* XXXVII, 1926, 296. Vigil kept and lights burning, Burne 298-9, Leather (1) 120, Howse 209, Davies 56, Hayward 225, Hole 17.

Touching corpse: Burne 298, Leather (1) 120, Hole 17, Davies 56.

Wine and cakes beside coffin: The account in 1671 by M. Jorevin de Rocheford is quoted by Burne, 309-10. Wine at Crasswell, Leather (1) 121. Wine and biscuits or cake, or ale and cake, are described in Burne 304-5, Leather (1) 121, Moss 28, Hole 18, Owen (quoted by Howse, 136-7), Jones 214, Wherry (2) 66, and G. Hope, *Folklore* IV, 1893, 392.

The Sin Eater: John Aubrey, *Remaines of Gentilisme and Judaisme* (1686), ed. J. Britten, 1881; his account of the Sin Eater, and also John Bagford's, are quoted in Burne, 306-7, and the former partly quoted in Leather (1) 121 n.2. For Moggridge's and Allen's statements in 1852, see Wirt Sykes, *British Goblins*, 1880, 322-4. E.S. Hartland, *The Legend of Perseus*, 1895, II 291-4 discusses the custom from an anthropological point of view. A parallel belief from Derbyshire is recorded in S.O. Addy, *Household Tales*, 1895, 123-4: when drinking at a funeral, 'every drop you drink is a sin which the deceased has committed, you thereby take away the dead man's sins and bear them yourself.'

Telling bees: Leather (1) 123, Burne 235-6, Eyre (1) 173, Howse 209, Moss 28, Boyd 63.

Funeral procession: Coffin laid down and/or turned, Davies 55, Waters 7, Leather (1) 122-3, Burne 134. Choice of bearers, Burne 300-1, Leather (1) 122, Wherry (2) 66, Hole 19. Cairn, Owen, quoted by Howse 209-10, and Fletcher (2) 61. Rosemary, Burne 304, Leather (1) 123, Moss 28-9; rue, hyssop and wormwood, Wherry (2) 66; flowers, Burne 299, Moss 18-19.

Passing bell: At Didsbury, Moss 98; at Great Budworth, *C.V.M.* I 70; in Shrewsbury, Burne 301-2.

Money at graveside: At Tarvin, *C.V.M.* II 89; in Wales, Kilvert III 226, and Owen, quoted by Howse 210.

Incidents at funerals: Thunder, Eyre (1) 172; horses sweating, Moss 104-5; shroud ripping, Leather (1) 125; Captain Whittle's Wind, Hole 36, Ingram 173-4.

Month's end: Leather (1) 126, Howse 137, Davies 56.

Virgin's garlands: Burne 310-13.

Disturbing graves: Fletcher (1) 42, quoting Parry; Leather (2) 296-8.

9 THE TURNING YEAR: JANUARY TO MAY, pp. 139-164

Letting the new year in: A.R. Wright, *British Calendar Customs: England*, 1936-40, II 2-3; Burne 314-17, Leather (1) 90, Hole 123-4, Eyre (1) 174, Hayward 231, Fletcher (1) 85, Kilvert I 252-3.

Cream of the well: Leather (1) 91, Howse 211, *South Wales Argus* 10/3/1928.

Burning the bush: Leather (1) 92, Howse 206.

House-to-house begging: Burne 317; Howse 213; Jones 157-8; M.M. Rix, 'More Shropshire Folklore', *Folklore* LXXI, 1960, 184-7; Iona and Peter Opie, *The Lore and Language of Schoolchildren*, 1959, 223-4. Decorated apple or orange, Wright II 30-1, Eyre (1) 174, Baty 27, Wherry (1) 86, Waters 11-13.

Straw fires and cattle wassailing: On New Year's Day, Fletcher (1) 85-6; H.C. Ellis, 'Monmouthshire Notes', *Folklore* XV, 1904, 221; *Folklore* XII, 1901, 350. On Twelfth Night, Wright II 57-9; Leather (1) 93-5, quoting *The Gentleman's Magazine*, 1791 and 1820; Murray-Aynsley 387. Moss 52-3 describes a custom of scaring witches by running through the fields with bundles of blazing straw, at Standon, just over the Staffordshire border.

Apple-tree wassailing: Chris Barltrop, 'Wassail This About, Then?' *Folklore* 113, 2002, 92-3. (*Folklore* website www.tandf.co.uk)

Twelfth Night: Wright II 74-5, 80; Leather (1) 95-6, Kilvert III 354, Fletcher (1) 85, Waters II, *South Wales Argus* 10/3/1928.

Holy thorn: Kilvert III 355, 447; Leather (1) 17-19, 256; Howse 202-3; Bett (2) 139; *The Times*, 14/1/1949; personal communication from Mrs W. Leeds of Ross-on-Wye, 8/3/1975.

Candlemas: Wright II 120, Burne 249, 251.

Valentine's Day: Leather (1) 96, Howse 214.

Shrove Tuesday: Pancakes, Moss, 32-4, Hole 75-7, *C.V.M.* I 24, II 89. Pancake bells in Radnorshire up to the 1880s, Howse 212; at Shrewsbury, Newport and Edgmond in the 1880s, Burne 318. Football, F.P. Magoun, *Shrove Tuesday Football*, 1932, 10-13. Tug-of-war at Ludlow, John Brand, *Popular Antiquities*, 1870, I 92; W. Hone, *The Everyday Book*, 1838, II, cols. 256-7; Burne 319-21. Tug-of-war at Presteigne, Howse 215-216. Cock-fighting and cockshies, Hole 75-7, *C.V.M.* I 120. Magic aids for fighting cocks, Moss 79, Burne 246-7. Water spraying at Kington, Parry 199. Blackamoor Night, Howse 217. Clipping the church, Burne 321-2.

Mothering Sunday: Wright I 43-9, Burne 323-7, Leather (1) 96-7, Waters 15, Eyre (1) 174, Kilvert I 313, I. and P. Opie, 243. The simnel cake legend, R.W. Chambers, *The Book of Days*, 1862-4, I 337.

Palm Sunday: The golden arrow at Pontesford, Burne 330-2, Fraser (2) 108. Pax Cakes, Leather (1) 97-8; Mrs W. Leeds informs me that the custom, which had lapsed at Hentland in Mrs Leather's time, has been revived there and now is well kept up at both Hentland and Sellack (personal communication, 8/3/1975). At King's Caple, Haines 143. Graves decked with flowers. Waters 8, Howse 213-14, Leather (1) 99, Eyre (1) 174.

Good Friday: Rules and taboos, Wright I 80-1, Leather (1) 98, Burne 334, Crossley 314; the washer and the baker, Mrs Murray-Aynsley, *Symbolism of East and West*, 1900, 162. Hot Cross Buns, Leather (1) 78-9; Burne 191, 333-4; Wherry (1) 86; Moss 38; Howse 203; Fletcher (1) 47.

Easter Saturday: Decking graves, Kilvert I 92-4, 98-9, II 116; *The Chepstow Advertiser* 4/4/1885, quoted in Waters 8. Howse 213-4 notes that the custom in Radnorshire was formerly observed on Palm Sunday, and only later transferred to Easter Saturday; Leather (1) 99 reports similar fluctuation in Herefordshire, with preference for the later date. The custom is still widespread, as I am informed in personal communications from the Hon. Secretary of the Kilvert Society, Mr C.T.O. Prosser (20/1/1975), Mrs E. Butcher of Hereford (21/2/1975), and Mrs W. Leeds of Ross-on-Wye (8/3/1975). But nowadays the flowers are usually put in vases or laid as sprays, not set into the turf as Kilvert described.

Pace Egging: T.F. Thistleton-Dyer, *British Popular Customs*, 1876, 169; Hole 77-8; Moss 40-1; Crossley 45; *C.V.M.* I 38. The Pace Eggers' Song given here is from V. Newall, *An Egg at Easter*, 1971, 367, and was collected by her from Arthur Hulme of Marple in 1966; other pace-egging rhymes are in *The Cheshire Sheaf*, 3rd series, 1899, 76. For details concerning the texts of the Pace Eggers' Play at Neston and Stalybridge, see E.C. Cawte, A. Helm, and N. Peacock, *English Ritual Drama*, 1967, 41. For egg games, see Newall 334, Wright I 90, Crossley 45, Hole 78, I. and P. Opie 253. Egg-rolling is occasionally revived; a game was organized by Hereford City Museum on April 1, 1975; see *The Hereford Times* 21/3/1975. For a recent study of the closely related Lancashire play, see Eddie Cass, *The Lancashire Pace-Egg Play: A Social History*, 2001.

The sun dancing: Wright I 97-8, Leather (1) 99, Burne 335-6, Kilvert I 96, 247.

Texts in church: At Aberedw, Howse 135.

Luck at Easter: Hearing cuckoo lucky, lying late unlucky, Kilvert I 96.

Corn-showing: Leather (1) 99-100, Ellis 221.

Lifting or heaving: Wright I 107-8; in Shropshire, J. Brand, *Popular Antiquities*, 1870, I 183, and Burne 336-40; in Herefordshire, Leather (1) 100; in Cheshire, Moss 39-40, Hole 79-81, Crossley 45, *C.V.M.* I 115, II 102-3. In Radnorshire, Howse 216, quoting an indignant eye-witness at Rhayader in 1839.

May Eve: House-to-house singers, Leigh 239-41, 275-7 (with tune). Flowers as compliments or insults, Moss 43, Hole 49, Crossley 46, Wright II 195-6. Birch, rowan or marsh marigolds hung up, Wright II 211-12; Leather (1) 18, 101; Kilvert I 119-20, 135, III 268; Moss 42-3; Burne 356-7; *South Wales Argus* 10/3/1928.

Maypoles and May Queens: Wright II 238; Burne 358-9; Waters 15; Hole 88; at Shrewsbury in 1952, Rix 184-7. Milk women at Hereford,

Leather (1) 101, quoting 'Nonagenarian' in *The Hereford Times* 15/4/1876. At Chepstow, Palmer (1) 263-4.

May dew: Waters 14-15, I. and P. Opie 255.

Puritans and maypoles At Rostherne, Crossley 280-1.

Knutsford May Day: H. Green, *Knutsford, its Tradition and History*; G.A. Payne, *Knutsford*; A. Ballard, *A Rite of Spring*, 1973; M.A. Canney, 'The Magico-Religious Significance of Sand,' *Journal of the Manchester Egyptian and Oriental Society* XIX; information from F.W. Gledhill, Cheshire County Library, 25/10/1974. Joan Leach, *The History of Knutsford Royal May Day*, 1987.

Oak Apple Day Among adults, Leather (1) 102-3, Burne 365-6, Howse 214, M. Baker, *Folklore and Customs of Rural England*, 1973, 123. Among schoolchildren, Moss 45, Boyd 79, *C.V.M.* II 95, 100.

The arbor tree Rix 184-7, Haines 104-5 Information from A.M. Carr, Salop County Library, 27/1/75. John Box, 'Dressing the Arbor Tree', *Folklore* 114 (2003) 13-28; Box further suggests that the tradition of tree-dressing might have originally belonged to May Day, since it was fairly common for May Day celebrations to be transferred to 29 May after the Restoration.

Ascension Day: Well Wakes, Burne 349-50, 433-4; Blessing the Brine, Leigh 62.

St Briavels bread and cheese dole: Rudder 307; *The Gentleman's Magazine* 1816, quoted in Baty 77; Waters 14; Ryder 89-90.

10 THE TURNING YEAR: JUNE TO DECEMBER, pp. 165-188

The Shrewsbury Show: Burne 451-60, Vale 124-7.

The Chester Pageant J. Hemingway, *History of Chester*, 1831, I 199-206; R.H. Morris, *Chester in the Plantagenet and Tudor Reigns*, 1894, 323-330; R.W. Chambers, *The Book of Days*, 1862-4, I 636-7; Crossley 55-65; information from F.W. Gledhill, Cheshire County Library, 25/10/1974.

Barnaby Fair: Wright III 3; information from F.W. Gledhill, Cheshire County Library, 25/10/1974.

Bunbury wake: Wright III 4; J. Coker Egerton, *The Cheshire Sheaf* II 1883, 204, quoting the handbill of 1808.

Barning the thorn: Leigh 164-6, Boyd 76-7, Hole 49-50, Crossley 47-8, Ingram 126, *C.V.M.* I 20; information from the Revd R.A. Alden of Appleton, 12/10/1974.

Rushbearing: Wright III 53, Moss 49, Hole 90-2, *C.V.M.* II 55, 75; A. Helm, 'Rushcarts of the North-West of England,' *Folk Life* VIII, 1970, 20-31. An eyewitness account of the procession at Lymm in 1817 is quoted in Crossley 49-50; information on the present-day custom at Lymm from the Revd A.J. Birch, 8/10/1974.

Wakes: For a general account of wakes, see Leather (1) 156-7, Burne 435-49, Hole 93-9, Crossley 47, Howse 139-40. For Ringing the Chains at Congleton, Hole, Crossley, and Wright III 46.

Bear-baiting and bull-baiting: Hole 95-9; Crossley 71-4; Burne 446, 448, 559, 590; Leather (1) 157. The Congleton rhyme, Leigh 259; Old Nell of Middlewich, Hole 99, Ingram 110; riding on the bear's back, *C.V.M.* I 103 (cf. Burne 203); the bear-master's murder, Waters 35-8.

Harvest suppers: Leather (1) 104-6, 233-5; Hayward 235; Moss 54-6.

Crying the mare and cutting the neck: In Herefordshire, Leather (1) 104; In Monmouthshire, Palmer (1) 221-2; in Shropshire, Wright I 189, Burne 371-4, J. Frazer, *The Golden Bough*, abridged edition 1950, 460; in Cheshire, Hole 30-1, Crossley 42-3, Moss 54; in the Border area generally, I.C. Peate (2), 'Corn Ornaments,' *Folklore* LXXXII, 1971, 177-84. Corn ornaments may be seen at Hereford Museum; at Eye Manor, Leominster; and at the Welsh Folk Museum, St Fagan's, Cardiff.

Michaelmas milk dole: Kilvert I 245-6.

Mobberley wakes: Wright III 99; for apple-throwing at wakes in the Golden Valley, see Leather (1) 157, Fletcher (1) 162.

St Crispin's Day: Leather (1) 106-7, Wright III 103.

Hallowe'en: Divinations, Leather (1) 64-5, 107; Burne 175-7, 381; Kilvert II 77, 334; Hole 115-16. Hallowe'en bonfires, Jones 149. Souling at Frodsham, *C.V.M.* I 64. Party games and turnip lanterns, Howse 213, Hole 116, I. and P. Opie, 269-73, 275. The servant girl and the mistress, Kilvert ed. Hope, 1921.

Souling: Alms for the dead, W. Cox, *A Historical Tour Through Monmouthshire*, 1801 (1904 edition) 23. For a discussion of Cheshire souling in all its aspects, see Hole 110-15. House-to-house singing by adults, Moss 60-1, Leigh 128-9, quoting Ormerod's version of the song; Burne 385-6. Souling by children in Shropshire, Burne 381-8, Wright III 128-9, Hayward 233; in Cheshire, *C.V.M.* I 71-2, 89, II 58, 100, Boyd 76, W.T. Kenyon in *The Cheshire Sheaf* II, 1880, 185-6.

The Soulers' play and the wild horse: Helm 1968; E.C. Cawte, *Ritual Animal Disguise*, 1978, 125-31; Hutton 376-7; Wright III 131-3;

Hole 113-15; *C.V.M.* II 73; for sources of the play and a list of eighteen places where it is known to have been performed, see E.C. Cawte, A. Helm, and N. Peacock, *English Ritual Drama*, 1967, 41. On the making of Hodening Horses, Crossley 67-8. On the play at Comberbach and Great Budworth, Boyd 68-76; A. Helm, 'In Comes I, St George,' *Folklore* LXXVI, 1965, 131-2; information from the Revd L.J. Foster of Great Budworth, 22/10/1974. See also Susan Pattison, 'The Antrobus Soulcaking Play: An Alternative Approach to the Mummers' Play', *Folk Life* 15 (1977), 5-11.

Guy Fawkes: At Newport, Dunhill 109; at Chepstow, Waters 13-14.

St Thomas's Day: Wright III 203-4, Burne 392-3, Leather (1) 108, Eyre (1) 147, Howse 90.

Christmas: Decorations and Yule log, Wright III 245-50, Burne 396-400, Hole 119-22, Leather (1) 109, Fletcher (1) 85, Howse 135-6, 207. First footing, Leather (1) 108-9, Eyre (1) 174. Borrowing fire unlucky, Leather (1) 108, Moss 65-6, Burne 400-2. No work done, Burne 403, Leather (1) 109, Moss 66, Crossley 43.

Holy Innocents' Day: Burne 408-9, Leather (1) 110, Howse 212.

Plygain: Howse 137, Dunhill 102, Fletcher (2) 60-1; D.R. Saer, 'The Christmas Carol Singing Tradition in the Tanad Valley,' *Folk Life* VII, 1969 15-42.

The Mari Lwyd: Palmer (1) 279-85; Palmer (2), 229-32; Kilvert ed. Hope (1921); E.C. Cawte, *Ritual Animal Disguise* (1978), 93-109.

The Mummers' play: At Edgmond and Newport, Burne 410, 482-9; at Ross on Wye, Leather (1) 141-6; in Cheshire at Alderley Edge, Astbury, Barthomley, Bromborough and Frantby, E.C. Cawte, A. Helm, and N. Peacock, *English Ritual Drama* 1967, 41. At Monmouth, Maria and Andrew Hubert, *A Monmouthshire Christmas*, 1995, quoted in Palmer (1) 272-4. For the 'Robin's Hood's Men' at Chepstow, see Waters 8; the boys at Bridgnorth, Rix 184-7.

New Year's Eve: The Monty, Wherry (2) 86; Burning the Bush, Murray-Aynsley 386.

SELECT BIBLIOGRAPHY

The following are the chief works consulted; others, from which only occasional items have been taken, will be found in the Notes under the relevant heading. Identifications such as 'Bett (1)', 'Bett (2)' are those used in the Notes to distinguish between works by the same author. *C.V.M.* in the Notes refers to the volumes of *Cheshire Village Memories* compiled by the Cheshire Federation of Women's Institutes, which were edited by D. Haworth and W.M. Comber.

Axon, W.E.A. (1) *Nixon's Cheshire Prophecies*, 1873
Axon, W.E.A. (2) *Cheshire Gleanings*, 1884
Baty, H. *The Forest of Dean*, 1952
Bett, H. (1) *English Legends*, 1950
Bett, H. (2) *English Myths and Traditions*, 1952
Boyd, A.W. *A Country Parish*, 1951
Briggs, K.M. *A Dictionary of British Folktales in the English Language*, 4 vols, 1970-1
Burne, C.S and Jackson, G.F., *Shropshire Folk-Lore*, 1883-6.
Cawte, E.C., Helm, A. and Peacock, N., *English Ritual Drama*, 1967
Cheshire Federation of Women's Institutes, *Cheshire Village Memories*, 2 vols, 1952 and 1961
Crossley, F.H., *Cheshire*, 1949
Davies, T.A., 'The Folklore of Gwent', *Folklore* XLVIII, 1937, 41-59
Devlin, J.D., *The Mordiford Dragon*, 1848
Dunhill, E. J., 'Welsh Folklore Items: Monmouthshire,' *Folklore* XXIV, 1913, 107-10
Ellis, H.C., 'Monmouthshire Notes', *Folklore* XV, 1904, 221
Eyre, L.M. (1) 'Folklore Notes from St Briavels', *Folklore* XIII, 1902, 170-7
Eyre, L.M. (2) 'Folklore of the Wye Valley', *Folklore* XVI, 1905, 162-79
Fletcher, H.L.V. (1) *Herefordshire*, 1948
Fletcher, H.L.V. (2) *Portrait of the Wye Valley*, 1968
Fraser, M. (1) *West of Offa's Dyke*, 1958
Fraser, M. (2) *Welsh Border Country*, 1972

Haines, G.H., *Shropshire and Herefordshire Villages*, 1974

Hartland, M.E. and Thomas, E.B., 'Breconshire Village Folklore', *Folklore* XXIV, 1913, 505-17

Hayward, L.H., 'Shropshire Folklore of Today and Yesterday', *Folklore* XLIX, 1938, 223-43

Helm, A., *Cheshire Folk Drama*, 1968

Helm, A., 'Rushcarts of the North-West of England', *Folk Life* VIII, 1970, 20-31

Hole, C.M., *Traditions and Customs of Cheshire*, 1937 (reprinted 1970)

Howse, W.H., *Radnorshire*, 1949

Hughes, J. (1) *A Light-Hearted Look at Our Shropshire History*, 1969

Hughes, J. (2) *Shropshire Folklore, Ghosts and Witchcraft*, 1973

Hutton, Ronald, *The Stations of the Sun: A History of the Ritual Year in England*, 1996.

Ingram, J.H., *Companion into Cheshire*, 1947

Jones, T. Gwyn, *Welsh Folklore and Folk Custom*, 1930

Kilvert, F.R., *Kilvert's Diary*, ed. W. Plomer, 3 vols., 2nd ed. 1960

Kilvert, R.F., ed. Mrs E. Hope. 'Radnorshire Legends and Superstitions', *Occult Review* (1921), 152-60.

Leach, Joan, *The History of Knutsford Royal May Day*, 1987.

Leather, E.M. (1) *The Folk-Lore of Herefordshire*, 1912

Leather, E.M. (2) 'Scraps of English Folklore: Monmouthshire and Radnorshire', *Folklore* XXIV, 1913, 110

Leather, E.M. (3) 'Scraps of English Folklore: Shropshire', *Folklore* XXV, 1914, 372

Leather, E.M. (4) 'Scraps of English Folklore: Herefordshire', *Folklore* XXXVII, 1926, 296-8

Leigh, E., *Ballads and Legends of Cheshire*, 1866

Massingham, H.J., *The Southern Marches*, 1952

Matthews, J.H., 'Collecteanea', *Folklore* XV, 1904, 349

Moss, F., *Folklore: Old Customs and Tales of my Neighbours*, 1898

Murray-Aynsley, M., 'Scraps of English Folklore: Herefordshire', *Folklore* XXXIX, 1928, 381-92

Newall, V., *An Egg at Easter*, 1971

Opie, I. and P., *The Lore and Language of Schoolchildren*, 1959

Owen, D.E. 'Pre-Reformation Survivals', *Transactions of the Honorable Society of Cymmrodorion*, 1910-11, 92-114

Palmer, Roy (1) *The Folklore of (Old) Monmouthshire*, 1998

Palmer, Roy (2) *The Folklore of Radnorshire*, 2001.
Parry, R., *The History of Kington*, 1845
Peate, I.C. (1) 'Letter to the Editor', *Folklore* XLVIII, 1937, 218-19
Peate, I.C. (2) 'Corn Ornaments', *Folklore* LXXXII, 1971, 177-84
Peele, J.H., *Portrait of the Severn*, 1968
Phillips, O., *Monmouthshire*, 1951
Raglan, Lord, 'Letter to the Editor', *Folklore* XLVIII, 1937, 334
Rix, M.M., 'More Shropshire Folklore', *Folklore* LXXI, 1960, 184-7
Rhys, W.J., *Celtic Folklore, Welsh and Manx*, 1901
Rudder, S., *A New History of Gloucestershire*, 1779
Ryder, T.A., *Portrait of Gloucestershire*, 1966
Saer, D.R., 'The Christmas Carol Singing Tradition in the Tanad Valley', *Folk Life* VII, 1969, 14-52
Simpson, J., 'Nixon's Prophecies in their Historical Setting', *Folklore* LXXXVI, 1975, 201-7
Smith, A.W., 'Some Folklore Elements in Movements of Social Protest', *Folklore* LXXVII, 1966, 241-52
Thomas, K., *Religion and the Decline of Magic*, 1971
Tongue, R.L., *Forgotten Folktales of the English Counties*, 1970
Vale, E., *Shropshire*, 1949
Waite, V., *Shropshire Hill Country*, 1970
Waters, I., *Folklore and Dialect of the Wye Valley*, 1973
Watkins, W.J.H., 'A Cycle of Stories Current in Radnorshire', *Folklore* XLIII, 1932, 424-7
Wherry, B.A. (1) 'Wizardry on the Welsh border', *Folklore* XV, 1904, 75-86
Wherry, B.A. (2) 'Miscellaneous Notes from Monmouthshire', *Folklore* XVI, 1905, 63-7
Woods, Frederick, *Legends and Traditions of Cheshire*, 1982.
Wright, A.R., *British Calendar Customs: England*, 3 vols, 1936-40

INDEX OF TALE TYPES

Folktales are named and classified on an international system based on their plots, devised by Antti Aarne and Stith Thompson in *The Types of the Folktale*, 1961; numbers in this system are preceded by the letters AT. Local legends were partly classificd by R.Th. Christianson in *The Migratory Legends*, 1958; his system was expanded by K.M. Briggs in *A Dictionary of British Folktales*, 1970-1. These numbers are preceded by ML, and the latter are also given an asterisk. Brackets indicate that the resemblance to the prototype is only partial.

(AT 285	The Child and the Snake)	45
AT 300	The Dragon Slayer	45, 47–49
AT 325★	The Sorcerer's Apprentice	65, 195
AT 766	The Seven Sleepers	34–35
AT 820	The Devil as Farm Labourer	60
AT 960A	The Cranes of Ibycus	55
AT 974	The Homecoming Husband	45
AT 1030	The Crop Division	60
AT 1036	Hogs with Curly Tails	60
AT 1090A	The Mowing Contest	60
AT 1191	The Dog on the Bridge	60
AT 1525M	Mak and the Sheep	51
ML 3020	Inexperienced Use of the Black Book	65, 195
ML 3025	Carried by the Devil	61
ML 3055	The Witch that was Hurt	71
ML 4021★	A Troublesome Ghost Laid	95–101
ML 5006★	The Ride with the Fairies	71–72
ML 5080	Food from the Fairies	76
ML 5085	The Changeling	78–79
ML 5086★	Rescue from Fairyland	77
ML 5090	Married to a Fairy Woman	82–83
ML 7020	Vain Attempt to Escape a House Spirit	79–80
ML 7060	The Disputed Site for a Church	30
ML 7070	Legends about Church Bells	23–25
ML 8000	The Wars of Former Times	21, 31–33, 36–38
ML 8010	Hidden Treasures	27–29, 35–36
ML 8025	Robber Tales	50–52

MOTIF INDEX

A motif is an element recurring within the plot of several folktales (e.g. 'cruel stepmother' in 'Snow White', 'Cinderella' etc.) They have been classified thematically in Stith Thompson's *Motif Index of Folk Literature*, 1966, and in E. Baughman's *Type and Motif Index of the Folktales of England and North America*, 1966, from which the numbering below has been taken.

A 920.1 Origin of lakes   23-24
A 941.5 Spring breaks out by power of saint   103
A 969(b) Hill from spadeful of earth dropped by giant or devil   16, 18-19, 21
A 971.1 Rocks rent at time of Crucifixion   17
A 972(a) Gash in hill is hero's footprint   20
A 972(c) Marks on rock made by hero's fingers or knees   20, 22
A 977 Origin of particular stone or group of stones   19-22, 83-84
A 1455 Origin of cooking   148
A 1535 Origin of secular feast   46, 146, 161, 163, 164
A 1617 Origin of place-names   14, 21, 24, 29, 31-32, 83-84, 161
B 11 Dragon   27, 45, 47-49
B 60 Mythical fish   26-27
B 81 Mermaid   25-26
B 155.1 Building site determined by halting of animal   30
B 184.1.1 Horse with magic speed   52, 61, 183
B 251.1.2.3 Cows kneel on Old Christmas Eve   144
B 251. 3 Animals (bees) sing songs of praise on Old Christmas Eve   144
B 871.1.1(da) Giant cow fills any vessel until milked into sieve   83-84
C 31.11 Tabu: reproaching supernatural wife about her origins   82-83
C 401 Tabu: speaking   24-25, 27, 34, 77, 106, 109, 113, 175
C 493 Tabu: thanking   112
C 494 Tabu: cursing   24-26
C 993 Unborn child affected by mother's broken tabu   117-18
D 950 Magic tree   25, 72, 113-14
D 965 Magic plant   72, 114, 116, 157
D 1031.1.1 Consecrated bread or wine as magic object   109-10, 128-31, 147, 201-02
D 1162.2 Magic candle   63-64, 99-101, 128, 132
D 1254.1 Magic stick   61-64

D 1273.3 Bible text as magic spell   63, 96-97, 99-101, 110-11
D 1323.1 Magic clairvoyant mirror   66
D 1385.7 Magic circle averts evil spirits   87-88, 96
D 1500.1.6.1 Corpse's hand as remedy   112-13
D 1500.1.7.1 Skull as remedy   113
D 1500.1.10.3 Money from offertory as remedy   108
D 1500.1.15 Magic healing ring   108
D 1500.1.18.2 Baptismal water as remedy   109, 121
D 1500.1.18.3 Holy water as remedy   109, 140
D 1500.1.2 3 Magic healing charm (spell)   63-64, 108-15
D 1601 Object labours automatically   60
D 1641.2.3 Stone moves of itself   22
D 1654.1 Stone refuses to be moved   21
D 1654.10 Sunken bell can only be raised under conditions   24-25
D 1782.2 Curing wound by treating weapon   108
D 1791.1 Sunwise circuit for good luck   133-34
D 1810.0.2 Magic knowledge of magician   63-67
D 1812.5.1 Bad omens   119-21, 126-27, 139-40, 175, 185-86
D 1812.5.2 Good omens   119-21, 139-40, 143, 175, 185-86
D 1825.1 Magic view of future lover   175
D 1823.7.1 Phantom funeral seen before real funeral   95, 127
D 1827.1.1 Church door vigil to hear names of those who will die   176
D 1896 Magic ageing of person who returns from fairyland   85-86
D 1960.2 King asleep in mountain will awake to save his people   33-35
D 2063.1.1 Tormenting person by making and ill-treating image   68-69, 73
D 2072.0.2.2.1 Person charged to keep birds from crops confines them in barn by magic   61
D 2122 Journey with magic speed   61
D 2161 Magic healing power   63-64, 102-16, 151, 159-60
D 2161.2.2 Flow of blood magically stopped   63
D 2161.4.1 Cure by transferring disease to animal   114-15
D 2161.4.5 Cure by passing through cleft tree or looped plant   113-14
D 2161.14.3 Cure by washing in dew   159-60
D 2172.1.2 Wizard forces person to run in circles   64
D 2174(b) Wizard forces person to dance till released   64
D 2192.1 Supernatural force moves church foundations by night   30
E 265.1 Meeting ghost causes sickness   92
E 272.2 Ghost rides behind rider on horse   95, 97
E 291.2.1 Ghost guards treasure   52
E 332 Non-malevolent ghost haunts road   38, 88-89
E 334 Non-malevolent ghost haunts scene of crime or tragedy   88

E 334.2 Ghost haunts burial spot   89, 91
E 352(a) Ghost returns to make amends for fraud   92
E 363.2(ac) Ghostly black dog protects traveller   89
E 376(a) Ghost returns to confess to selling watered milk   95–96
E 402.1.1.3 Ghost cries and screams   95–96
E 402.1.3(aa) Ghost of fiddler in cavern heard playing   29
E 411.0.3 Horse unable to draw evil dead man   136
E 413 Murdered person cannot rest in grave   38, 52–53, 90, 98
E 415.3 Ghost of priest cannot rest because he failed to say certain Mass   93
E 416 Man who moved landmarks cannot rest in grave   92
E 419.11(a) Persons who bury iron cannot rest in grave   92–93
E 419.11(b) Persons who bury money cannot rest in grave   92–93
E 422.1.1 Headless ghost   38, 88, 98
E 422.1.11.5 Ineradicable bloodstain   27, 53, 103
E 422.3.1 Revenant as small man   91–92
E 422.4.4(aa) Female ghost in white dress haunts pool or stream   89–90
E 423(b) Ghost in animal form changes shape to various animals   98–100
E 423.1.1.1(b) Ghostly black dog   83, 89, 93–94
E 423.1.5 Revenant as pig   89, 93, 176
E 423.1.8 Revenant as bull or calf   89, 98–100
E 423.2.9 Revenant as man-monkey   95
E 423.3.10 Revenant as duck   89
E 423.7 Revenant as fly   98–99
E 437.2 Ghost laid in body of water   97–100
E 437.4 Ghost laid under stone   96–97, 101
E 437.6(a) Ghost laid in box   98–100
E 437.6(e) Ghost laid in bottle   88, 97–98
E 443.2.4 Ghost laid by clergyman   96–97, 101
E 443.2.4.1 Ghost laid by group of clergymen   97–100
E 491.1 Phantom funeral procession   95, 127
E 492 Midnight service of the dead   95, 176
E 501 The Wild Hunt   33–34, 84–86, 94
E 502 The sleeping army; dead soldiers march as omen of war   33–35
E 530.1.6 Ghostly lights as death omens   127
E 535.1 Phantom coach and horses   95
E 574 Appearance of ghost as death omen   89–90
E 574(ia) Ghost dog appears as death omen   94
E 752.10 Precautions to keep evil spirits from corpse   87–88, 128
E 756.3 Raven and dove fight over man's soul   61–62, 195
F 91 Entrance to Otherworld through door in mountain   34–35
F 92.6 Entrance to Otherworld through cave   29, 34–35, 85

F 218* Entrance to fairyland through fairy ring   76-77
F 233 Colour of fairies   75-76
F 239.4.2 Fairies are the size of small children   75-76, 85
F 246 Fairy tobacco pipes   81
F 261 Fairies dance   75-78
F 262 Fairies make music   75-77
F 302.2 Man marries fairy   82-83
F 320 Fairies carry people off into fairyland   76-77, 84-86
F 321.1 Changeling   76, 78-79, 81
F 342.1 Fairy money   81
F 343.17 Fairies give men food till knife is stolen   76
F 346(a) Brownie helps with housework   79-80
F 365(a) Invisible fairies steal from shop   77
F 369.7 Fairies lead travellers astray   46, 76, 78
F 379.5* Person joins fairy dance   76-78
F 384 Charm to keep fairies away   76, 157
F 388 Fairies depart from district   76
F 420.1.4.8 Water spirit with green teeth or green eyes   82
F 456.1 Knockers (mine spirits)   33-34, 83
F 516.3 Person unusual as to his hands   39
F 517.1 Person unusual as to his feet   39, 85
F 531.3.2. Giant throws a great rock   19-20
F 531.6.6.4 Giant's blow makes cleft in rock   18
F 531.6.8.3 Enmity between giants   18-19
F 531.6.13 Giant's grave   22, 28
F 713.2 Bottomless pool   24, 149
F 721.1 Underground passages   13, 28-29, 36-38
F 757 Extraordinary cave   29, 34-35
F 944.1 Village sinks in lake as punishment   23-24
F 944.1(1) Well overflows and drowns land as punishment   24
F 971.5.2.1 Tree blossoms on Old Christmas Eve   144-45
F 974 Grass will not grow on certain spot   31, 48, 53-54, 99
F 991.1 Stone bleeds when pricked   22
F 993 Sunken bell sounds   23-25
F 1071 Prodigious jump   20, 52
G 211.2.7.1 Witch in form of hare is hunted   71
G 212.1 Witch in form of blade of straw   72
G 224.1(a) Witch is made to say 'May God bless you', not 'My God bless you'   69-70
G 224.3 Witches and wizards get power from books   63-65, 195
G 224.4 Person sells soul to Devil for witch power   59-63, 70

G 225 Witch's (wizard's) familiar   61, 65, 70
G 241.3.3 Wizard leaves object on steeple as he rides through air   61
G 242.1 Witch rides broomstick   71-72
G 242.5 Witch rides other object   71-72, 196
G 242.7 Man flies with witch by imitating her; is caught in cellar   71-72
G 262 Murderous witch   67-68
G 263.5 Witch causes sickness   67-69
G 263.7(a) Witch causes mental defectiveness   68
G 265.3 Witch rides horses at night   72
G 265.4 Witch causes disease or death of animals   67-69
G 265.10.2* Witch kills trees   69
G 269.4 Curse by disappointed or offended witch   69
G 271 Means of breaking witch's spell   70, 73-74, 115
G 272 Protection against witches   72-74, 107, 120, 123, 142, 157-58, 163, 202-3
G 273.6 Witch rendered powerless by drawing blood from her   73
G 273.7.2 Steel driven into witch's tracks immobilizes her   72-73
G 293* Wizard detects thief   63, 66-67
G 295*(a) Wizard causes apparitions   63-64, 66
G 295*(f) Devil aids wizard in building bridge, farming etc.   19-20, 60-62
G 295*(o) Wizard raises Devil to prove his powers   63-64
G 297*(b) Wizard's apprentice raises Devil   65, 195
G 303.3.3.1.1(a) Devil in form of black dog   87-88
G 303.3.3.1.3 Devil in form of horse   52
G 303.3.3.4.4 Devil in form of fly   61
G 303.9.2 Devil performs deeds of unusual strength   19-21, 30, 60-62
G 303.17.1.1 Devil disappears when cock crows   17, 186
G 510.4 Hero overcomes devastating animal   44-49, 104
H 94 Identification by ring   45
H 251.3.2 Thief detected by Bible and key   67
J 1700 Fools   49-50
J 1772.21 Watch mistaken for devil   50
J 1904.2 Pent cuckoo   49-50
K 42.2 Mowing contest won by trickery   60
K 171.1 Deceptive crop division   60
K 171.4 Deceptive division of pigs   60
K 183.8 Land acquired: as much as can be encompassed in a certain time   193
K 219.4 Devil cheated by burial neither inside nor outside church   61-62
K 219.6 Devil gets animal instead of soul   60
K 406.2 Stolen deer dressed as baby in cradle   51
K 534.1 Escape by reversing horse's shoes   51

K 581.1 Drowning the eel (newt) as punishment   49
K 1747 Cobbler tricks giant or Devil with sack of shoes   18-19
K 1817 Disguise as beggar   45-46
K 1836 Disguise of man in woman's dress   56-58
K 2368.1 Enemy deceived into overestimating opponents   38
K 2369.5 Vibrating drum reveals enemy undermining castle   38
M 219.2.2 Devil flays corpse of person contracted to him   87-88
M 235 Woman rides naked through streets to obtain privilege for citizens   46
M 266 Promise: gift to church in exchange for safety   46-47
M 400 Curses   36-37, 53, 68-69, 118, 122, 151
N 271.3.1 Ravens pursue murderer   55
N 511 Treasure in ground   27-29, 35-36
N 513 Treasure hidden in water   26, 36
N 513.2 Sword hidden under water   26
N 564 Storm deters treasure-diggers   36
N 571 Devil as treasure-guardian   27-28, 36
N 571.2* Ghostly animal as treasure guardian   27
N 686 Husband returns home as wife is about to marry another   45
Q 211 Murder punished   23, 45-46, 53-55, 171
Q 223.6 Sabbath-breaking punished   23, 26
Q 386 Dancing punished   21, 77
Q 433.2 Defeated giant imprisoned underground   18
Q 551.3.4 Transformation to stone as punishment   21, 83-84
Q 552.5 Monstrous birth as punishment   118
Q 556.1 Curse for participation at Crucifixion   151
V 111.1 Stones for church miraculously shifted   30
V 115.1 Church bell sunk in lake or river   23-25
V 134 Holy wells   35, 102-07, 140, 163-64
V 134.1 Oracles and auguries from holy wells   106
V 134.2 Offerings to holy wells   35
V 476 Warrior retires to monastery   32-33
W 181.2 Man kills architect after completion of building lest he build another as fine   52-53
Z 71.1 Formulistic number: three   105, 108, 111, 127, 134, 171
Z 71.5 Formulistic number: seven   96, 112, 118, 146
Z 71.6 Formulistic number: nine   22, 23, 72, 73, 94, 100, 105, 113-14, 116, 123, 141, 160, 175
Z 71.8 Formulistic number: twelve   99-100, 108, 140-42
Z 140 Symbolic colours   88, 122

GENERAL INDEX

Bracketed initials after a place-name indicate the Border county in which the place lies; county boundaries and names are those that were in use before 1974. B: Breconshire; C: Cheshire; D: Denbighshire; F: Flintshire; G: Gloucestershire; H: Herefordshire; M: Monmouthshire; Mont: Montgomeryshire; R: Radnorshire; S: Shropshire

Abbey-cwm-hir (R)   32
Aberedw (R)   154
Abergavenney (M)   65
Aconbury (H)   98, 105
Acton (C)   19
Acton Burnell (S)   16, 138
Adam's Rocks (H)   20
Alderley Edge (C)   34-35
All Saints' Day   174
All Souls' Day   174-83
angels   74, 111, 154, 186
animals, supernatural   26-27, 83-84, 87-88, 89, 93-95, 98-101, 176
Antrobus (C)   162, 181-83
Appleton (C)   167-68
Arbor Tree, the   162-63
archaeological features, legends about   19-22, 28
Arden (C)   20
arrow, golden   149
Arthur, King   22, 34-36, 163-64
Ascension Day   107, 109
Astley Abbots (S)   138
Aston-on-Clun (S)   162-63
Aubrey   50, 130-33
Audlem (C)   84, 145
Aymestrey (H)   46, 143

babies   76, 78-79, 81, 109-110, 113, 116-20
Bagbury (S)   99-101

baptism   27, 109, 121
Barber's Bridge (G)   31
barning the thorn   167-68
Barthelmy (C)   94
Bartestree (H)   19
Baschurch (S)   25, 30, 94
battles   31-32, 38-40, 146
Beachley (M)   32
bears   45-46, 118, 170-71
Bebbington (C)   30
bees   56, 133, 144, 150
Beeston (C)   36
begging customs   141-42, 147, 152-53, 155-56, 158-59, 173-74, 177-80, 184-85
Beguildy (R)   65
bell-ringing customs   121, 127, 135-36, 145, 169
bells, legends about   23-25
Berrington (S)   44
Bible, power of   63, 67, 96-101, 110-11
Biddulph (C)   21
Binghill (H)   93
birds   14, 18, 27, 55, 62, 126, 195
Birkenhead (C)   36
Bishop's Castle (S)   19, 22, 93
blackberries   173
black dogs   83, 89, 93-94
Black Hill (C)   53
Blackwood (M)   56
bloody streams   31-32, 40
Blount, Sir George   98

GENERAL INDEX

Bluestone (C)   19
bogies   62, 82
boggart or buggan   79-80, 91-92
Bolitree (H)   81
Bollington (C)   51
Bomere (S)   23-24, 26
bones, human   90, 113, 138; of giant cow   84
bonfires   140-41, 176, 184, 202-03
bottles (boxes) in ghost-laying   88, 97-101
Brampton Bryan (H)   106
Bream (G)   19
Bredwardine (H)   127
Brereton, Sir William   45-46
Bridestones, the (C)   21
Bridgnorth (S)   28-29, 188
Brilley (H)   134
Brinsop (H)   47, 141
Bromborough (C)   103
Bromyard (H)   64, 161
Bronsil Castle (H)   27
Broomfield (S)   94
Brough (C)   62-63
Broughton (S)   30
Brown Clee (S)   20
Broxwood (H)   113
Bryngwyn (R)   173-74
Builth (R)   32
bull-baiting   167, 170
bull-ghosts   99-101
Bunbury (C)   44-45, 69, 94, 167, 170
Burleydam (C)   88, 90
burning the bush   140-41, 144, 188
Buxton (C)   51

Caerleon (M)   34
cairns   134
Calverley, Sir Hugh   44-45
Canon Pyon (H)   18
Canute, King   161
Capel-y-ffin (R)   53, 75
Cardington (S)   52-53
Catholicism   17, 93, 102-03, 108-11, 128-30, 136, 150, 165-66, 177, 186
cattle, supernatural or ghostly   25, 30, 83-84, 99-101; customs concerning   142-43
caul   119
caves   28-29, 34-36, 85
Celtic traditions   27, 32, 78, 83, 90, 103, 106, 134, 174
changelings   76, 78-79, 81
charities   46-47, 136, 150, 164, 184-85
charmers   11, 63-64, 110-12
charms, healing   63, 108-16, 123, 128, 136, 142, 157-58, 163; protective or lucky   72-74, 107, 120
Chepstow (M)   32, 46-47, 60, 131, 142, 148, 150, 151-52, 158, 184, 188
Chester (C)   32, 126, 146, 153, 155-56, 158-59, 165-67
Chetwynd (S)   97
childbirth   117-19
children's customs   106, 141-42, 152-53, 158-59, 162, 177-80, 188
Child's Ercall (S)   14, 25-26
chimney sweeps   159, 169-70
Christ   17, 110-11, 149, 151, 154
Christchurch (M)   108-09
Christmas   185-88
Church Stoke (Mont)   107
churches, legends about   17, 19, 23-25, 30; customs at   137-38, 147, 149-54, 168-69, 176
Civil War   31-32, 36, 38, 161
Cleobury North (S)   69-70
Clodock (H)   30
Clun (S)   28, 139, 184-85
Clyro (R)   12, 67, 140, 151-52, 154, 157, 173-74, 176
coats-of-arms   45-46
cobblers   15, 18-19, 56, 166, 174
cock-fighting   146-47, 170
Colemere (S)   23, 25
Colwall (H)   22
Comberbach (C)   90-91, 179, 181-83
Combermere (C)   25, 37, 88
Condover Hall (S)   53
Congleton (C)   145, 169-70
corn dollies   172-73

Corpus Christi   109, 165
Courtfield (H)   45
counter-spells   72-74
Crasswall (H)   129-30
Croesmere (S)   23
Cromwell, Oliver   24, 36, 38, 161
Cross Keys (S)   174
Crucifixion   17, 110-11, 150-51
curfew   46-47
curses   36-37, 67-69, 118, 122
Cusop (H)   72, 122
Cutberry Hollow (S)   93

Danes (Vikings)   21, 146
Dawnton Castle (S)   21
Deerhurst (G)   47
Devauden (M)   63, 69, 142
Devil   15, 18-21, 26, 28, 30, 52, 59-65, 70-71, 87-88, 123, 128, 134, 147, 173, 187
Devil's Chair (S)   19
Devil's Pulpit (G)   19
Devil's Rocks (S)   21
Devil's Shovelful (H)   19
Didsbury (C)   107, 135
divinations   106-07, 175-76
Dolfach (R)   144
Dorstone (H)   21-23, 27, 31, 109
dragon   28, 45, 47-9, 166-67
Duddon (C)   37-38, 88
Dymock (G)   68

eagles' flesh   112
Easter   25, 151-54
Easthope (H)   36
Edgmond (S)   49-50, 97, 134-36, 157, 160, 178, 185
effigies   12, 44-45, 123-24
eggs   120, 152-54
Ellesmere (S)   24, 26, 52, 82, 147
Ercall Hill (S)   18
evil spirits   30, 36, 65, 74, 87-88, 120, 128, 140, 177
exorcism of ghosts   88, 90, 95-101

fairs   146, 166-67, 169-70, 173
fairies   11, 28, 30, 51, 72, 75-86, 149, 157
fairy cow   83-84
fairy dog   85-86
fairyland   29, 77, 85-86
farming customs   73, 115, 140-41, 144, 154-55, 157-58, 171-73, 186
Farndon (C)   168-69
Fawnhope (H)   162
first-footing   139-40, 185-88
fish   26-27, 37
Flaxley (G)   105
foods, seasonal   107, 145-46, 148-53, 164, 169, 171, 173-74, 177-80, 184
fools   49-50
football   146
Ford (S)   127
Forest of Dean   19, 22, 46, 104-05, 144
Frandley (C)   91-92
Frodsham (C)   181
funerals   17, 128-38

games and sports   65, 145-48, 153-54, 166-67, 169-70
Garnstone (H)   98
Garway Hill (H)   21
Gawsworth (C)   88-89
Gayton (C)   106
ghosts   11, 14, 30, 37-38, 53, 87-101, 127, 138
giants   16, 18-20, 27, 52, 166
Giant's Chair (S)   19
Giant's Grave (S)   28
Giant's Shaft (S)   20
Glasbury (R)   54
Godley Green (C)   94
Good Friday   109, 150-51
Gorsey Bank   79-80
graves   12-13, 22, 28-29, 32, 36, 53-54, 61-62, 89, 96, 122, 134-36, 138
Great Budworth (C)   135, 162, 181-83
Grimesditch (C)   47
Grosmont (M)   21, 59-62, 64, 138
Guilden Sutton (C)   36
Guy Fawkes Night   184

Hale Barns (C)   74
Hallowe'en   174-83
hares   71, 117
Harold Godwinson, King   21, 32-33
harvesting   171-73
Hay (H)   20, 31, 95, 127
healing powers   14, 63-64, 102-16, 121, 151, 157, 171
Hentland (H)   150
Hereford (H)   18-20, 38, 48, 65, 68-69, 86, 103, 125-26, 130, 159
Hereford, Countess of   46, 164
Hergest (H)   22
Hergest Court (H)   45, 94, 98-99
Herla, King,   84-86
Hewelsfield (G)   32
Higher Whitley (C)   181
highwaymen   50-52
Hocktide   155-56
Hodening horses   56, 152, 180-83, 187
Holm Lacy (H)   37, 50
Holy Thorn   144-45, 167-68
Holywell (Flint)   103
holy wells *see* wells
Hoo Green (C)   51
horses, extraordinary   52, 61, 91, 180-83
horse-skull   56, 152, 180-83, 187
Hyssinton (Mont)   99-101

Ince (C)   30, 37
Ippikin   52

Jack of France   176
Jack o' Kent   20-21, 59-62
Jacobites   38, 40-41
Jenny Greenteeth   82
John, King   46
Johnson, 'Maggotty'   88-89
Jones, William   46

Kenchester (H)   81
Kentchurch (H)   59-61, 64
Ketley (S)   156
Kilgwrrwg (M)   30
King's Caple (H)   150

King's Pyon (H)   18
Kingsland (H)   30, 161
Kingstone (H)   114
Kington (H)   57, 77, 94, 98-99, 127, 138, 147, 170
Kinlet (S)   98
Knevet, Lord   53
Knighton (R)   125, 177
Knockin (S)   54-55
Knutsford (C)   51, 123, 160-61
Kynaston, Humphrey   52

lakes   23-26
Leighton, Judge William   52-53
Leominster (H)   123, 143
lifting   155-56
Lindow (C)   51
Llanbedr (R)   76
Llanbadarn Fynedd (R)   65
Llandeilo Graban (R)   47-48
Llandridod Wells (R)   104
Llanfair Caereinion (Mont)   98
Llanfair Waterdine (R)   62
Llanfyllin (Mont)   98
Llangollen (D)   57
Llangorse (B)   23, 131
Llanigon (B)   98
Llanishen (M)   87-88, 140
Llanofer (M)   187
Llan Pica (R)   76
Llanshifr (R)   92-93
Llansilin (D)   38
Llanthony   71
Llanveyno (H)   157
Llanymynech (S)   28
Llewellyn ap Gruffydd   32
Llowes (R)   20, 94
Llynclys Lake (S)   23
Longtown (H)   27, 55, 66
Lostock Gralam (C)   51, 89
Lower Bebbington (C)   42
luck, bad   36-37, 119-23, 137, 139-41, 145, 150-51, 154, 185
luck, good   17, 106-07, 119-23, 139-42, 144, 150-51, 154, 160, 163-64, 172, 185

Ludlow (S)   21, 103, 106, 114, 146
Luddites   56-57
Lymm (C)   169

Macclesfield (C)   34-35, 51, 126, 167
Madeley-on-Severn (S)   49
Map, Walter,   82-86
Marbury Hall (C)   90-91, 182
Marden (H)   25, 103
Mari Lwyd   187
Marple (C)   153
May Day   156-61
May Eve   156
Maypoles   158, 160
megaliths *see* stones
Meldonra Castle   62-63
Meol Stocks (C)   14
Merlin   35
mermaids   14, 25-26
Merton Sands (C)   62
Michaelchurch (H)   157
Michaelmas   173-74
Middlewich (C)   107, 170
midnight   22, 23, 90, 105, 113, 140, 144-45, 176
Midsummer Day   166-67
milkmaids   159
Minsterley (S)   33, 138
Mitchell's Fold (S)   83-84
Mobberley (C)   51, 174
Moll Walbee   20
Mollington (C)   51
Monmouth (M)   46, 76, 188
monsters   44-45, 47-49, 104
Monty   141-42
Mordiford (H)   48-49
Morris dancers   160, 168
Morville (S)   135-36
Moston (C)   45
Mothering Sunday   146-48
Mottram (C)   45, 125, 137
Mountford (S)   94
Much Cowarne (H)   30, 45
mumming   56, 152-53, 180-83, 187-88
murders   22-23, 38, 45-46, 52-55, 171

Nantgwillt (R)   11
Nantmel (R)   37
Nantwich (C)   56, 107, 164
Nantyglo (M)   56
Nass (M)   53
Neston (C)   93
Newland (G)   46
Newport (M)   184
Newport (S)   161
New Year's Day   139-43
Nicky Nicky Nye   82
Nixon, Robert   38-43
noon   140-41, 163
Norley (C)   89
Northen (C)   96
Northenden (C)   124
Northwich (C)   107, 180

Oak Apple Day   161-63
omens of war   33-34; of death   89, 94, 126-27; agricultural   140-44
Orcop (H)   29
origins, legends about   13, 17-24, 103-04, 146, 148, 161 *see also* place names
Oswestry (S)   23, 30, 103, 106
outlaws   51-52
Over (C)   30
'Owd Scriven'   44

pace-egging   152-53
Painscastle (R)   20, 81
Palm Sunday   149-50, 152
patterns   72, 123, 160-61
Pax Cakes   150
Pembridge (H)   133-34
Pencombe (H)   30
Penlascarn (M)   35
Peterchurch (H)   26-27
Peynard Castle (H)   27
Pigott, Madam   95, 97
place-names, origins of   13, 21, 24, 29-30, 32, 83-84, 161
placenta   119
Plaish Hall (S)   52-53
plants, magic or symbolical   21, 69, 113-

16, 122, 134-5, 144-45, 154, 156-58, 175, 185
Plemstall (C)   103
plygain   186-87
poachers   51, 55
Pontesford Hill (S)   149-50
Pontypool (M)   56, 153, 177
pools, bottomless   24, 149; haunted   75-76, 81-82, 89-90, 94
Prees Heath (S)   66, 81
Prestbury (C)   170-71
Presteigne (R)   73, 118, 141, 185
prophecies   25, 35, 38-45, 53
punishments for impiety or crime   21, 23-26, 33, 36-37, 45-46, 53-54, 83-84, 118, 136-37

Quakers   55-56

Ratlinghope (S)   95
ravens   14, 18, 27, 55, 61-62, 103
Rebeccas   56-58
Reformation   24, 36-37, 42, 136, 160, 165-66
Rhayader (R)   57-58, 73, 134
Rhos Goch (R)   76
Rhosgoch (S)   106
Richard II, King   36
Richard III, King   119
riding the stang   123-24
ringing the chains   169-70
rings, curative   108
roads, haunted   38, 89, 93-95, 97, 99
robbers   50-52
Robin Hood   18-21, 55, 160, 188
Robin Hood's Butts (H)   18-19, 21
Rorrington (S)   33, 107, 163
Ross (H)   30, 130, 133, 174, 188
Rostherne (C)   25, 160
Royal Oak Day   161-63
rush-bearing   168-69

sacraments   108-10, 120-21, 128-30, 150
Saviour's Letter   110
St Briavels (G)   46, 71-72, 115, 123, 142, 150, 164
St Clydawg   30
St Crispin   56, 174
St Ethelbert   32, 103
St George   47, 187-88
St Milburga   103
St Oswald   103, 106
St Peter   27, 40, 169
St Weonard's Tump (H)   28
St Winifred   103
sale of wives   125-26
salt   120, 128, 132
'Scotch Cattle', secret society,   56
Sellack (H)   150
Severn, the   29
Shobdon (H)   19, 23
Shocklach (C)   95
Shomere (S)   25
Shrewsbury (S)   18, 46, 112, 123, 130, 135, 137, 157-58, 161, 166-66
Shrove Tuesday   146-47
silver display   121, 159, 166, 168
simnel cakes   148-49
sin-eating   150-53
Skenfrith (M)   27-28, 61
Skirrid, the (R)   17, 20
sleeping warriors   29, 33-35
smugglers   51
Soul-Caking Play   180-83
souling   177-83
spas   104
spells, harmful   67-70, 115 see also witches
Stanney (C)   89
Staunton (G)   22
Staveley, Sir Ralph de   45
Stiperstones, the (S)   19, 34
Stoak (C)   89
Stock (C)   30
Stockport (C)   19, 56-57, 158
Stoke St Milborough (S)   103
Stoke-upon-Tern (S)   30, 121
Stokesay (S)   27
stones   19-23, 97, 99
Stretton Hills (S)   83, 94
Stroat (M)   21

Sunday letter   110
sunken villages or churches   23-24
Swettenham (C)   90
Symond's Yat (H/G)   32, 35-36

Talgarth (R)   69
Tanad Valley (R)   187
Tarporley (C)   104
Tarvin (C)   38, 136, 145
Tattenhall (C)   92
theft detected   65-67
Thornbury (M)   21
Thurstaston (C)   21
Thruxton (H)   114
Tintern Abbey (M)   19, 29
Titterstone Clee (S)   19
Tomassing   184-85
Tong (S)   46, 173
Trade Unions   56
Trafford (C)   49
treasures   13, 26-29, 35-36, 38, 52
trees, customs concerning   162-3, 167-8; legends about   32, 76; magic powers of   25, 72, 106-07, 113-114
Trelleck (M)   20-21, 23, 29, 31, 63-64, 71-72, 76, 94, 104, 106, 113, 133, 188
Trinity Sunday   107, 165
tunnels   13, 28, 34-36, 38
Turpin, Dick   51
Twelfth Night   105, 142-45
Twemlose (S)   66
Twm o'r Nant   98

Upton (C)   123

Vale Royal (C)   39-40, 42, 155
Valentines   145
Vaughan, Sir Thomas (Black Vaughan)   98-99
Venables, Sir Thomas   45
Vikings (Danes)   21, 146
Virgins' Garlands   137-38

wakes (festivals)   107, 163, 167, 169-70, 181
wakes (funerals)   128
Walton (R)   22
Warburton (C)   162
warts   11, 114-15
wassailing   142-44
water spirits   81-82 see also mermaids
Waverton (C)   162
Webb, Mary   97-98, 117, 132, 149
weddings   121-23, 163
well-dressing   107, 140, 163-64
Wellington   147
wells   15, 24, 27, 32, 35, 47, 102-07, 140, 163-64
Wem (S)   38
Weobley (H)   60-61, 64-65, 111, 114, 123
Werneth Low (C)   20
Westwood Common (S)   73
Whitchurch (S)   24, 66, 81
Whitsun   164
whooping cough   112, 114, 171
Wigmore (H)   77
Willaston (C)   21
Wildboarclough (C)   14
Wild Edric   26, 33-34, 82-84, 94
Wild Hunt, the   34, 85-86, 94
Wirral, the (C)   14, 152
wishing wells   35, 106
witches   11, 14, 67-73, 83-84, 107, 140-41, 157, 163
Withington (C)   89
wizards   14, 34-35, 59-67
Wolvesnewton (M)   114
Woodsheaves (S)   95
Woofferton (H)   29
Woolhope (H)   69
Woolston (S)   105-06
Woonton (H)   64-65
Worfield (S)   30
Wormelow Barrow (S)   28
Wormesley (H)   18, 145
Wrekin, the (S)   15, 18, 166
Wulvarn Brook (C)   14
Wye, the   21, 68, 86, 154

Yule log   185